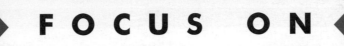

FOCUS ON

IELTS

Longman

SUE O'CONNELL

Map of the book

Lead-in	Reading	Writing	Listening	Speaking	Vocabulary
16 ▶ Falling forward *page 128*					
Predictions		1 *Explaining how something works* (Task 1) 2 *Summarising sentences* (Task 2)	1 *Reality or science fiction?* (Section 3) Note completion 2 *The techno-house* (Section 4) Multiple choice; labelling a diagram; table completion	1 *Predicting the future* (Part 3) 2 *Personal goals* (Part 2)	Spot the error Error Hit List
17 ▶ Avoiding gridlock *page 136*					
Driver types	1 *Smashing stereotypes* Short answers; classification; T/F/DNS 2 *Avoiding Gridlock* Matching; sentence and diagram completion			*On four wheels* (Part 3)	*More or less?*
18 ▶ Wish you were here *page 144*					
Tourist destinations; pronunciation: diphthongs		1 *Presenting the solution to a problem* (Task 2) 2 *Dealing with different data* (Task 1)	1 *Worldwide Student Projects* (Section 2) Short answers; table and flow-chart completion 2 *The end of oil* (Section 3) Table and sentence completion; labelling a diagram; multiple choice	1 *Tourism* 2 *Time off* (Parts 1, 2, 3) Exam practice	Error Hit List
19 ▶ Face value *page 152*					
Facial expressions	1 *Face the facts 2* Skimming/scanning; reading for detail; cohesive features 2 *Face* Short answers; table completion; multiple choice			1 *Face the facts 1* (Part 3) 2 *Exam practice* (Parts 2, 3)	Word families; dependent prepositions
20 ▶ Through the lens *page 160*					
Uses of photography; pronunciation: word stress		*Describing an object* (Task 1)	1 *Photography courses* (Section 1) Table completion; multiple choice 2 *History of cinema* (Section 4) Table and flow-chart completion; short answers	*Practice interview* (Parts 1, 2, 3)	Error Hit List

► The IELTS Test: overview

Introduction

IELTS stands for *International English Language Testing System*. The test consists of four modules – Listening, Speaking, Reading and Writing – and takes two hours and 45 minutes to complete.

This book provides preparation for the Listening and Speaking modules, which all candidates take, and also for the Academic Reading and Writing modules, which are normally taken by candidates intending to use English for study purposes. General Training versions of these modules are also available and, while much of the material in the book would provide useful practice, there is no specific exam preparation for these modules.

The test result is published in the form of a report, which places candidates on a scale of one to nine according to language ability (see page 7). There is a score for each of the four modules and also an overall score. Most universities and colleges require an IELTS score of 6.0 or more, but it's important to check the specific requirement for your intended course of study.

IELTS can be taken at test centres in over 100 countries. Test dates are not fixed, and tests are normally available throughout the year in most areas. Further information and a list of local centres is available on the IELTS website – www.ielts.org

IELTS modules in brief

Listening	Time: 30 minutes

There are four sections and a total of 40 questions, testing different listening skills. You will hear a variety of recorded texts, including monologues and dialogues. Texts and tasks become more difficult as the test progresses. The tape is played **only once**, but you are allowed time to read the questions beforehand. There is an **extra ten minutes** at the end for you to transfer your answers to the answer sheet.

Academic Reading	Time: 60 minutes

There are three reading passages and a total of 40 questions, which test a range of reading skills. Passages come from magazines, journals, books and newspapers, and the topics are of general interest. Texts and tasks become more difficult as the test progresses. There is **no extra time** for transferring your answers to the answer sheet.

Academic Writing	Time: 60 minutes

There are two tasks, one of at least 150 words and the other of at least 250 words. In **Task 1**, you have to look at a diagram or table and present the information in your own words. In **Task 2**, you have to present and justify an opinion or present the solution to a problem.

Speaking	Time: 11–14 minutes

This interview between the candidate and an examiner has three main parts. In **Part 1**, you are asked general questions about yourself, your home or family, your job or studies, etc. In **Part 2**, you are given a topic and allowed one minute to prepare. You then have to talk on the topic for between one and two minutes. **Part 3** is a discussion of more abstract issues related to the topic in Part 2.

IELTS modules: details

Listening

The first two sections are concerned with social needs. In **Section 1**, you will hear a conversation in a social situation, for example, two friends discussing holiday plans or an interview at an accommodation agency. In **Section 2**, you will hear a monologue on a general subject, for example, a short talk on healthy eating or tourist information.

The last two sections are concerned with educational or training contexts. In **Section 3**, you will hear a conversation between up to four people, for example, a tutorial discussion between tutor and student, or several students discussing an assignment. In **Section 4**, you will hear a monologue, for example, a lecture or talk of general academic interest.

The recordings may include a range of accents including British, American or Australian English. For this reason, different accents are used on the tapes accompanying this course, and you can also help yourself further by listening to as wide a variety of English as possible, on the radio or television, for example.

QUESTIONS

Questions include multiple choice, short-answer questions, completion and matching tasks, and diagram labelling. Each one requires a specific approach and specific skills, and these are outlined in the **Exam briefing** boxes and **Task approach** sections in the book.

You are allowed an extra ten minutes at the end of the test to transfer your answers onto the answer sheet.

NB Take care when transferring your answers – you will lose marks if you make spelling or grammar mistakes.

MARKING

One mark is awarded for each of the 40 questions, and the result is translated into a score on the IELTS nine-band scale (see page 7).

Reading

The three reading passages contain up to 2,700 words, which means that you will need to read efficiently, using appropriate reading skills for each task, in order to complete the paper in the time allowed. The course includes a varied selection of reading texts, and you can help yourself further by reading from as wide a range of sources as possible, such as newspapers, magazines and journals.

QUESTIONS

Questions include multiple choice, short-answer questions, completion and matching tasks, and Yes/No/Not Given or True/False/Does Not Say. Each one requires a specific approach and specific skills, and these are outlined in the **Exam briefing** boxes and **Task approach** sections in this book.

You must write your answers on an answer sheet, but there is no extra time for this.

NB Take care when transferring your answers – you will lose marks if you make spelling or grammar mistakes.

MARKING

One mark is awarded for each of the 40 questions, and the result is translated into a score on the IELTS nine-band scale (see page 7).

Writing

There are two tasks. The instructions specify the minimum number of words for each task and also recommend the amount of time you should spend on each one. It's important to follow these guidelines, because Task 2 carries more weight in marking than Task 1, and you will need to give the appropriate time to each part in order to get good marks. Answers must be written on the answer sheet. They must be written in full, not in note form.

Task 1: You are given a diagram or table of some kind and you have to present the information in your own words. For example, you may have to consider a set of statistics and then write a report outlining the key features; you may have to study a diagram of a machine and explain how it works; or you may have to look at a flow chart and describe the main stages in a process.

You have to write at least **150 words** for Task 1 and you are recommended to spend **20 minutes** on it.

Task 2: You are given brief details of an opinion, an argument or a problem, and you have to write an essay in response. For example, you may have to consider an opinion in relation to evidence, or weigh up the pros and cons of an argument before presenting your own view on the matter. You may also have to discuss various aspects of a problem and then outline your ideas for solving it.

You have to write at least **250 words** for Task 2 and you are recommended to spend **40 minutes** on it.

NB You will lose marks if you write less than the required number of words.

MARKING

Task 1 scripts are assessed on the following criteria:

- **Task Fulfilment:** Have you followed the instructions exactly? Have you given a clear, accurate and relevant description of the information?
- **Coherence and Cohesion:** Is your writing well organised? Are sentences logically linked?
- **Vocabulary and Sentence Structure:** Have you used a variety of appropriate vocabulary, and are your sentences well constructed?

Task 2 scripts are assessed on performance in the following areas:

- **Arguments, Ideas and Evidence**: Have you evaluated arguments and ideas? Have you compared and contrasted evidence and opinions?
- **Communicative Quality**: Have you presented your ideas clearly and coherently and organised your writing logically?
- **Sentence Structure**: Have you used a variety of vocabulary and sentence structures? Is your writing reasonably accurate?

The overall result is translated into a score on the IELTS nine-band scale (see right).

Speaking

The interview is in three parts.

Part 1 Introduction and interview (4–5 minutes)
In the first part, the examiner will ask a number of general questions. Be prepared to introduce yourself, to say where you come from and to talk about such topics as your family or home, your country or city, your job or studies, your interests or hobbies.

Part 2 Individual long turn (3–4 minutes)
In this part, you are given a card outlining a particular topic and asked to talk about the topic for one to two minutes. You have one minute to prepare and make notes if you wish. Be prepared to describe people, places or events and to explain their significance to you.

Part 3 Two-way discussion (4–5 minutes)
In the last part, the examiner asks questions linked to the topic in Part 2 and develops a discussion of more abstract issues. Be prepared to listen carefully and respond appropriately, to express opinions and preferences and give reasons.

MARKING
Performance is assessed on the following criteria:

- **Fluency and Coherence**: Do you express ideas and opinions clearly and coherently, without long hesitations?
- **Lexical Resource**: Do you use a wide range of vocabulary?
- **Grammatical Range and Accuracy**: Do you use a wide range of structures and make only a few minor mistakes?
- **Pronunciation**: Are you easy to understand? Do you use English pronunciation features naturally?

The overall result is translated into a score on the IELTS nine-band scale (see right).

THE IELTS NINE-BAND SCALE

Band 9 – Expert User
Has fully operational command of the language: appropriate, accurate and fluent with complete understanding.

Band 8 – Very Good User
Has fully operational command of the language with only occasional unsystematic inaccuracies and inappropriacies. Misunderstandings may occur in unfamiliar situations. Handles complex detailed argumentation well.

Band 7 – Good User
Has operational command of the language, though with occasional inaccuracies, inappropriacies and misunderstandings in some situations. Generally handles complex language well and understands detailed reasoning.

Band 6 – Competent User
Has generally effective command of the language despite some inaccuracies, inappropriacies and misunderstandings. Can use and understand fairly complex language, particularly in familiar situations.

Band 5 – Modest User
Has partial command of the language, coping with overall meaning in most situations, though is likely to make many mistakes. Should be able to handle basic communication in own field.

Band 4 – Limited User
Basic competence is limited to familiar situations. Has frequent problems in understanding and expression. Is not able to use complex language.

Band 3 – Extremely Limited User
Conveys and understands only general meaning in very familiar situations. Frequent breakdowns in communication occur.

Band 2 – Intermittent User
No real communication is possible except for the most basic information using isolated words or short formulae in familiar situations and to meet immediate needs. Has great difficulty in understanding spoken and written English.

Band 1 – Non User
Essentially has no ability to use the language beyond possibly a few isolated words.

Band 0 – Did not attempt the test
No assessable information provided.

1 ▶ Workout

In this unit you will practise:
- Talking about exercise and sporting activities
- Forming a general picture; reading for detail; dealing with unknown vocabulary
- Summary completion; True/False/Does Not Say
- Comparing and contrasting; vocabulary: word partners

Exam Focus
Speaking: Parts 1, 2
Reading skills
Reading: Exam tasks
Speaking: Part 3

Lead-in

Look at the activities below. Which do you think uses the *most* energy? Put them in order 1–6 (1 = most energy).

Check your answers on page 216. What conclusion can you draw from the result?

Focus on speaking 1 *Talking about personal interests*

▶ EXAM BRIEFING

Speaking module, Parts 1 and 2
In Part 1 of the Speaking module the examiner will ask you questions about familiar topics such as your home or your family. In Part 2, he/she will ask you to speak for one to two minutes on a particular topic. You will have one minute to prepare.

▶ Parts 1 and 2: Interview and Individual long turn

Work with a partner.

1 Take turns asking and answering the questions on page 9. Before you begin, look at the *Useful language* box below them.

What kind of exercise …

- do you do regularly? (Where and when?)
- do you enjoy least? (Say why.)
- should you do more often? (Say why.)

Useful language	

(*Well*) I jog / I go jogging
       I swim at the local pool
	on a regular basis / most days / three
	       times a week, etc.

The thing I (*really*) hate / loathe is … (*I'm afraid*) I (*just*) can't stand …	because I find it so *boring / monotonous*, etc.

(*Actually*) I ought to walk more
       I should play tennis more
       often
	but I always take the bus because …
	but I'm always making excuses not
	       to play.

2   Now discuss the following questions.

1 Why is exercise good for you? Think of as many reasons as you can.
2 What form of exercise would you suggest to someone who was very unfit?

Focus on reading *Working out*

► **EXAM BRIEFING**

Reading module

In the IELTS Reading module, your reading skills will be tested through a variety of tasks. It is important to remember, however, that there is only a limited set of task-types:

- Completion
- Matching
- True/False/Does Not Say or Yes/No/Not Given
- Multiple choice
- Labelling

Each of these task-types will be introduced in detail, and you will be shown ways of dealing with each task effectively. The general strategies set out in the section below, however, apply to all texts and task-types.

GENERAL READING STRATEGIES

1   In order to complete the reading module within the time limit, you need to tackle each task in the most effective way. Read the following advice.

- Don't read the whole text in detail. This is unnecessary and wastes time.
- Do look at the heading and read through the text quickly. This will help you to form a general picture of the content.
- Do study the questions and identify the sections of text you need to read in detail.
- Don't waste time trying to understand every word. When necessary, try to rough guess the meaning of unknown words.

FORMING A
GENERAL PICTURE

2 Before you read a text for detail, it's essential to get a general idea of what kind of writing it is and what it's about. Read the headline and look through the text on page 11 quickly to answer these questions.

1 What kind of writing is it?
   a) an article from a scientific journal, presenting detailed scientific facts
   b) a humorous piece from a popular magazine – not to be taken too seriously
   c) an article from a magazine which is of interest to the general reader
   d) part of a leaflet advertising a new sports centre

2 What is it about?
   a) the benefits of joining an organised fitness programme
   b) ways of preventing people from getting serious diseases
   c) advice on efficient methods of housekeeping
   d) the most effective forms of exercise for improving health

TARGETED READING
FOR DETAIL

3 To answer an exam question, you need to read certain parts of the text in detail. This saves reading the whole text several times. Find the paragraph which deals with these topics as quickly as possible. They are not in the correct order.

1	The health benefits of some everyday activities	Paragraph ....
2	Exercise and the prevention of specific diseases	Paragraph ....
3	The general health benefits of doing housework	Paragraph ...1...
4	The effect of exercise on digestion	Paragraph ....
5	Official advice about exercise	Paragraph ....
6	A popular reason for not taking exercise	Paragraph ....

DEALING WITH
UNKNOWN VOCABULARY

4 Recognising whether an expression is important to your understanding or whether it can safely be ignored is a key reading skill. Read the following advice.

- Study the questions and identify the relevant sections of text. Unknown expressions outside those sections can generally be ignored.
- With unknown expressions which are important to understanding, try to rough guess the meaning by identifying the **part of speech**, and looking for **clues in the context**.
- Specialised technical terms which you aren't expected to know are usually explained in a footnote at the end of the text.

5 In paragraph 7 of the text, underline the term *hypertension*. What is the general meaning? How do you know?

Why ironing shirts is better than working out

1. Those people who find the idea of joining an exercise class unappealing can sit back on their sofas and relax. New research shows that doing a few household chores can be just as effective at lowering your heart rate and reducing your weight as working out vigorously in the gym.

2. "You don't need to follow a structured programme someone else has devised, and wear a fancy outfit to get healthy," says Dr Adrianne Hardman, a lecturer in sports science at Loughborough University.

3. In many studies, walking, stair-climbing, gardening and even ironing have been more closely linked with reductions in heart disease and other serious illnesses than jogging, cycling and playing tennis.

4. Furthermore, you can no longer plead lack of time as an excuse for not taking exercise. The myth that you have to work out for at least 30 minutes a day has been exploded by American researchers. Three ten-minute bouts of brisk walking spread over the day are as effective as one lasting half an hour.

5. Dr Adrianne Hardman says that official recommendations from the Health Education Authority and the Sports Council, which advise us to exercise at least three times a week and for a minimum of 20 minutes a time, are more geared to improving fitness than health.

6. "We need to inject a bit of realism into the whole exercise debate," she says. "If doctors really want to improve the population's health, then there is no point talking about high-intensity, frequent exercise. All that does is put off the most inactive people, who are the ones who would gain the most by increasing their activity.

7. "It is more effective just to encourage everyone to do a little. Let's concentrate on what is the minimum amount of exercise that is useful."

She also claims that those who think the more intense the exercise the better are wrong. Many benefits of exercise – reducing the risk of hypertension, heart disease, diabetes and cancers – can be achieved from any level of activity.

8. "Some long-term benefits don't just depend on how fit you are, but rather on regular activity," says Dr Hardman. "If you want to get healthier, then just use more energy. It doesn't matter how you do it."

9. Even the smallest level of activity, like a brisk walk, can reduce heart disease by altering the way the body deals with fat and carbohydrate. In tests, Dr Hardman found that the blood fat levels in those people who had done some low-intensity exercise before eating were 30 per cent less than those who had done nothing. "Fat and carbohydrate from the meal are handled more quickly after the activity than they would otherwise have been," she says. "This means that the level of fat in the blood does not rise so much and the artery walls are less likely to fur up."

10. The greatest benefits occur when people who are least active do a little. But you can overdo it. As you increase the amount of exercise, you also increase the risk of injury.

Adapted from 'Why Ironing Shirts is Better Than Pumping Iron'
by Helen Reilly in the *Sunday Mirror*

▶ EXAM BRIEFING

Reading module, completion tasks

Your reading skills may be tested through a variety
of completion tasks, including:

- summary completion
- sentence completion
- note completion
- diagram, flow-chart, table completion

You will receive specific advice for each of these
tasks in this book.

General strategies

- Read the instructions very carefully and study the
  example (if given). There are many different completion
  tasks so it's important to be very clear about what you
  have to do.
- Read the question(s) and think about the information
  that is missing **before** you look back at the text.
- Make sure your answer fits both **logically** and
  grammatically.

INTRODUCING EXAM TASKS
▶ Summary completion

6 In this task you have to complete a short summary of the text. There are two
versions: in one you choose words or phrases from a list (as in the example
below); in the other you use words from the text.

TASK APPROACH

- Study the example and read through the summary quickly for general
  understanding.
- Read it again carefully, studying the words before and after each gap.
  Consider the general meaning and also the kind of word needed to fill the
  gap. For example, Question 1 needs a verb in the infinitive (after *can*). Note
  that there are just two to choose from in the list of words.
- To decide between them, find the relevant section of text and re-read it
  carefully to check meaning.

Questions 1–7
*Complete the summary below. Choose the answers from the box and
write them in the spaces provided.*

Dr Adrianne Hardman explains that it is ..*Example*.. to follow a
special programme at a gym in order to improve your health.
Answer unnecessary

Research has shown that doing everyday household tasks can
1 .... the risk of serious disease. It has also been found that,
2 .... to popular opinion, several short periods of exercise
are as beneficial as longer ones. This is especially good news for
those who **3** .... take exercise, because they are likely to
experience the greatest benefits. Dr Hardman takes issue with
traditional advice, which emphasises the need for **4** ....
activity, believing that this **5** .... many people. Her overall
message is that it isn't essential to be **6** .... in order to be
healthy, we simply need to be more **7** ....

List of Words

prevents	unnecessary
regular	careful
discourages	contrary
rarely	frequently
according	vigorous
important	increase
helps	gentle
fit	active
lessen	suits

KEY LANGUAGE
Verb formation: the suffix *-en*
▶ ex. 1, p. 186
e.g. *less* (adj) ➔ *lessen* (verb)

INTRODUCING EXAM TASKS
▶ True/False/Does Not Say
and Yes/No/Not Given

7 This is a very common task in the exam. The only difference between the two versions is that True/False/Does Not Say concentrates on facts, while Yes/No/Not Given concentrates on opinions.

TASK APPROACH

- Read each statement and locate the section of text which deals with the topic.
- Study the relevant section carefully to see if the statement matches the information.
- Look for expressions which mean the same as the words in the question.
- Answer **True** or **Yes** only if the statement exactly matches information in the text.
- Answer **No** or **False** if the statement says the opposite to information in the text.
- Answer **Does Not Say** or **Not Given** if the information isn't mentioned in the text, even if you think it's likely to be true (or false).

This task is based on paragraphs 7–10 of the text. There are three False answers, two True answers, and just one Does Not Say. Be prepared to justify your answers by referring to information in the text.

Questions 8–13
Do the following statements agree with the information given in the reading passage?

Write

TRUE	*if the statement is true according to the passage*
FALSE	*if the statement is false according to the passage*
DOES NOT SAY	*if the information is not given in the passage*

8 Dr Hardman believes that more health benefits are gained from exercising vigorously than exercising gently. ....

9 One effect of exercise is to help prevent cancer. ....

10 Taking exercise before a meal prevents blood fat levels from rising. ....

11 The body processes food more rapidly after exercise. ....

12 You should consult a doctor before you take up any new form of exercise. ....

13 The more exercise you do, the better it is for you. ....

TASK ANALYSIS

8 Compare your answers with another student and discuss any differences of opinion.

DEALING WITH UNKNOWN VOCABULARY

9 Was it necessary to know the precise medical meaning of the word *hypertension* in order to answer the exam questions (see Question 1 in Task 1 and Question 2 in Task 2)?

In order to complete Tasks 1 and 2 successfully, you probably needed to guess the meanings of the following expressions. Study how each is used in the text and then:

- circle the correct part of speech. (The first one has been done for you.)
- say what the general meaning is. If you need help, choose answers from the box below.

1 chores (para. 1)	(noun (pl.))	verb	adjective	adverb
2 vigorously (1)	noun	verb	adjective	adverb
3 devised (2)	noun	verb	adjective	adverb
4 myth (4)	noun	verb	adjective	adverb
5 exploded (4)	noun	verb	adjective	adverb
6 bouts (4)	noun (pl.)	verb	adjective	adverb
7 brisk (4)	noun	verb	adjective	adverb
8 geared to (5)	noun	verb	adjective	adverb
9 put off (6)	noun	verb	adjective	adverb

a) something many people believe which is actually false
b) short periods (of activity)
c) ~~regular or boring tasks~~
d) discouraged (from doing something)
e) shown to be untrue
f) very actively or energetically
g) quick or fairly energetic
h) concerned with / designed to be useful for
i) made up or invented

KEY LANGUAGE
Grammatical terms
▶ ex. 2, p. 186

Focus on vocabulary *Word partners*

1 Which eight of the following words describe types of sports?

Example: target sports (e.g. golf, archery, darts)

amateur	blood	car	combat	competitive	fighting	horse	ice
private	prize	snow	spectator	~~target~~	team	water	winter

2 Which six of these words can be combined with *sports*?

Example: sports page, sportsperson

car	centre	commentator	equipment	house	player	reader
stadium	suit	teacher	vehicle	wear		

Focus on speaking 2 *Comparing and contrasting*

▶ Part 3: Discussion

▶ **EXAM BRIEFING**

Speaking module, Part 3

In Part 3 of the Speaking module, you will take part in a discussion with the examiner. You may need to discuss with the examiner the similarities and differences between things.

1   Read the following practice conversation between two students who are comparing rowing a boat and using a rowing machine. Note how the words in bold are used.

A: Well, they're **both** a good way of exercising, especially if you want to strengthen your arms and legs.

B: And they're **both** very hard work!

A: That's right! But there are quite a few **differences between them** as well. **For example**, it's much more convenient to use a rowing machine.

B: Yes, you can go to the gym or you could have one in your home.

A: **Also**, with a rowing machine you don't need to get wet! That's important.

B: **But on the other hand**, it's pretty boring using a machine. At least you can go somewhere in a real boat!

COMPARING ACTIVITIES   **2**   Work with another student to compare the following activities. Try to use the prompt words in bold in the example above to guide you.

1   swimming in a pool / swimming in the sea
2   playing tennis / playing golf
3   housework / gardening
4   exercising at an aerobics class / dancing at a club or party

DISCUSSION TOPICS   **3**   Work in pairs to discuss the following questions.

1   Which is more exciting to watch: athletics or gymnastics?
2   If you were a professional sportsperson, would you rather be a footballer or a golfer? Why?
3   Is it better to attend a sporting event or watch it on television?
4   Some people say children shouldn't be encouraged to play competitive games. What do you think?

2 ▶ Food for thought

In this unit you will practise:

- Talking about diet and eating habits
- Answering multiple-choice questions; completing notes
- Interpreting and presenting data from graphs
- Paragraphing: cohesion; logical and grammatical links

Exam Focus

Speaking: Part 1
Listening: Sections 1, 2
Writing: Task 1
Writing: Task 2

Lead-in

Who eats more healthily: men or women? Look at the following table which compares eating habits for men and women in England, and then discuss these questions with another student.

1 Which of the eating habits are healthy? Which ones are unhealthy? Why?
2 Which group has a healthier diet, men or women? Why?

Check your answers to Question 1 on page 216.

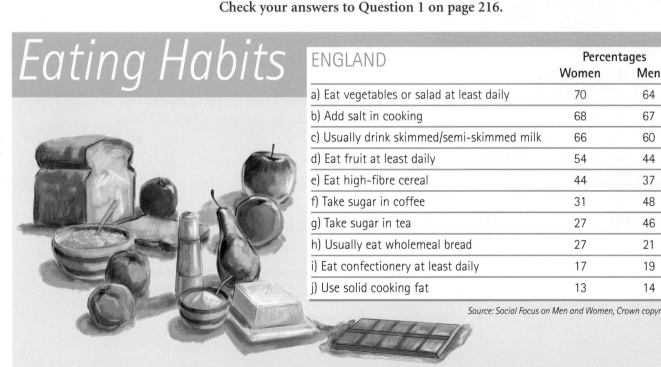

Eating Habits

ENGLAND	Percentages	
	Women	Men
a) Eat vegetables or salad at least daily	70	64
b) Add salt in cooking	68	67
c) Usually drink skimmed/semi-skimmed milk	66	60
d) Eat fruit at least daily	54	44
e) Eat high-fibre cereal	44	37
f) Take sugar in coffee	31	48
g) Take sugar in tea	27	46
h) Usually eat wholemeal bread	27	21
i) Eat confectionery at least daily	17	19
j) Use solid cooking fat	13	14

Source: Social Focus on Men and Women, Crown copyright

Focus on speaking *Eating habits*

▶ Part 1: Interview

Work in pairs to discuss the following questions.

1 What are your favourite and least favourite foods?
2 If you invite a friend round for a meal, what are you likely to offer them?
3 Do you prefer eating at home or in a restaurant? Why?
4 What special dish from your country would you recommend to a visitor?

Focus on writing 1 *Interpreting information from diagrams*

GRAPHS
▶ Task 1

KEY LANGUAGE
Names of tenses
▶ ex. 3, p. 187

▶ **EXAM BRIEFING**

Academic writing module
Task 1 is a description task. You have to look at a diagram or table and then present the information in your own words. You need to write at least 150 words and you are advised to spend about 20 minutes on the task. Task 2 is a discussion task. This task will be introduced in more detail in Unit 4.

Graphs A and B below show trends in two activities in Britain.

meat consumption (red meat vs poultry)
cigarette smoking (male vs female)

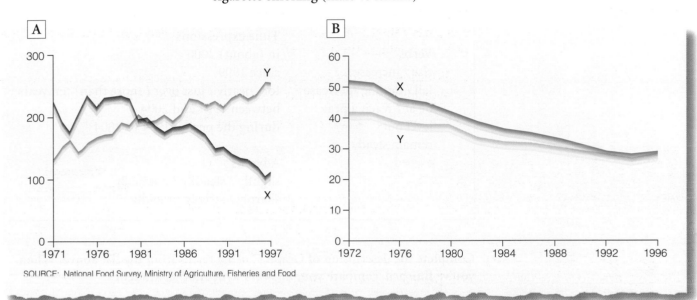

SOURCE: National Food Survey, Ministry of Agriculture, Fisheries and Food

1 Fill in the chart by matching Graphs A and B to the following short paragraphs. Then say which activities you think each graph represents.

1 This graph shows that there was **a steady downward trend** in the activity for both X and Y. This **trend**, which **lasted for over 20 years**, has since begun to **level out**.

2 Activity X was **at a peak** from about 1975 until 1980, but there was **a steep decline** over the next 16 years, and **a** corresponding **increase in** Activity Y.

Graph	Paragraph	Activity
A		
B		

Make sure you can match each expression in bold to features on the graphs.

2 **a** Read through the language in the *Useful language* box and check any expressions you don't know.

b Find another way of saying the following.

1 a very small increase
2 from 2000 until 2003
3 a steep decline

4 to rise quickly
5 to reach a maximum
6 to stop falling

Useful language

a

Adjectives	Nouns
slight / marginal	increase / rise (in)
steady / gradual	decrease / decline / fall / downward trend (in)
sharp / steep / rapid	
marked / significant	

Time expressions
in (about) 2000
since 1999
for (nearly / just over / more than) ten years
between 1994 and 2004
during the period 1994 to 2004

to

Verbs
rise / increase
fall / decline /decrease
be at / reach a peak
level out
remain steady
exceed

Adverbs
slightly / steadily / gradually
sharply / steeply / rapidly

---

3 Complete the description of Graph C using terms from the list above. When you've finished, compare your answers with another student.

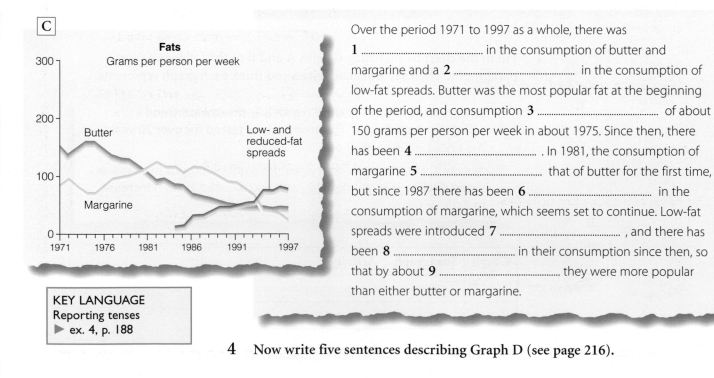

C

Fats
Grams per person per week

300

200

Butter

Low- and
reduced-fat
spreads

100

Margarine

0

1971   1976   1981   1986   1991   1997

KEY LANGUAGE
Reporting tenses
► ex. 4, p. 188

Over the period 1971 to 1997 as a whole, there was **1** .... in the consumption of butter and margarine and a **2** .... in the consumption of low-fat spreads. Butter was the most popular fat at the beginning of the period, and consumption **3** .... of about 150 grams per person per week in about 1975. Since then, there has been **4** .... In 1981, the consumption of margarine **5** .... that of butter for the first time, but since 1987 there has been **6** .... in the consumption of margarine, which seems set to continue. Low-fat spreads were introduced **7** .... , and there has been **8** .... in their consumption since then, so that by about **9** .... they were more popular than either butter or margarine.

4 Now write five sentences describing Graph D (see page 216).

Focus on listening 1 *Students' Union survey*

► Section 1

You are going to hear a student being interviewed as part of a survey.
Before you listen, look through the questions carefully. Study the drawings and think of words to describe them.
After you listen, compare your answers with another student.

Listen to the interview and answer Questions 1–10.

Questions 1–7
Circle the appropriate letters A–C.

> *Example*   What is the survey about?
> A   study methods
> B   leisure activities
> **(C)**   eating habits

1   What is the Students' Union planning to produce?
   A   a report
   B   a leaflet
   C   a newsletter

2   What is the student's favourite food?
   A   B   C

3   What is his least favourite food?
   A   B   C

4   Which meals does he eat in a day?
   A   just breakfast
   B   just lunch
   C   just dinner

5   How many eggs does he eat a week?
   A   none   B   one   C   two

6   How often does he eat fresh fruit?
   A   never   B   very rarely   C   regularly

7   What's his opinion of organic food?
   A   He thinks it's a waste of money.
   B   He thinks it's poor quality.
   C   He would eat it if he could afford it.

Questions 8–10
*Complete the form. Write **NO MORE THAN THREE WORDS** for each answer.*

Name (Optional):	*Jamie* **8** _____
Course:	**9** _____
Faculty:	*Business Studies*
Year:	**10** _____

Focus on listening 2 *Healthy eating*

▶ Section 2

In this section, you will hear a short talk about healthy eating and you are asked to complete a set of notes. Before you start, read the *Exam briefing* and advice.

> ## ▶ EXAM BRIEFING
>
> ### Listening module, completion tasks
>
> In a completion task, you have to fill in missing information in notes, sentences or a summary. This is one of the most common tasks in the IELTS Listening module.
> - Read the **instructions** carefully. Notice how many words you can write.
> - Look at the **heading** and glance through the questions to find out what the topic is.
> - Look at a few questions and think about **possible answers**. This will help you 'tune in' to the topic and vocabulary and enable you to listen more effectively.
> - Remember, **correct spelling** is essential.

Before you listen, work with another student to guess the answer to each question. Fill in your guesses in pencil.

While you listen, check your answers. If your guess was correct, put a tick (✓) next to it. If not, write in the correct answer.

After you listen, discuss your answers with another student.

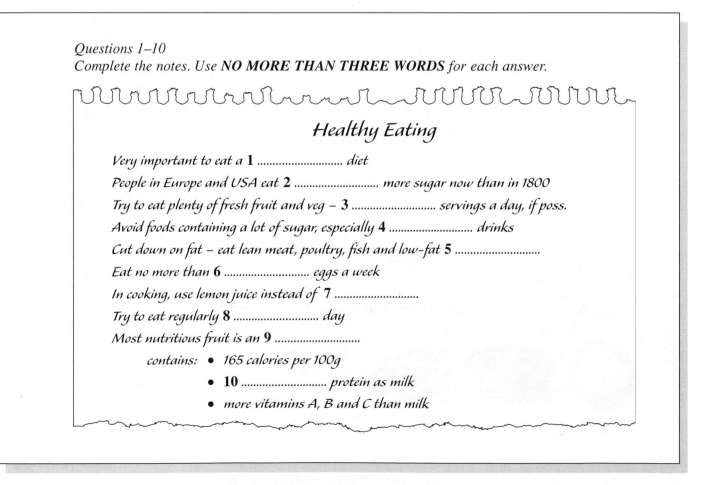

Questions 1–10
Complete the notes. Use **NO MORE THAN THREE WORDS** *for each answer.*

Healthy Eating

Very important to eat a **1** .... *diet*

People in Europe and USA eat **2** .... *more sugar now than in 1800*

Try to eat plenty of fresh fruit and veg – **3** .... *servings a day, if poss.*

Avoid foods containing a lot of sugar, especially **4** .... *drinks*

Cut down on fat – eat lean meat, poultry, fish and low-fat **5** ....

Eat no more than **6** .... *eggs a week*

In cooking, use lemon juice instead of **7** ....

Try to eat regularly **8** .... *day*

Most nutritious fruit is an **9** ....

  contains: • *165 calories per 100g*

    • **10** .... *protein as milk*

    • *more vitamins A, B and C than milk*

Focus on writing 2 *Paragraphing*

▶ Task 2

WHAT IS A PARAGRAPH?

1 a Divide the following text into three paragraphs.

> Almost all food, with the exception of water and salt, provides some energy, and this is measured in calories. About half the calories we consume are used for physical activity and half for growth, breathing, digestion and other bodily processes. The reason people put on weight is simple — they consume more energy than they use up in daily activities. Any excess energy is stored as body fat for later use. Too much body fat puts a strain on the heart and can cause pain in the back and joints. Surveys show that although our energy intake has decreased by about a third over the past 40 years, we're still getting heavier. That's because our energy expenditure is lower than ever; we drive to the shops, use lifts and escalators, and have increasingly sedentary jobs.

  b Compare your answer with another student and discuss these questions.

   1 What kind of text should be divided into paragraphs, and why?
   2 How do you decide when to begin a new paragraph?

COHESION

2 Which of the two following paragraphs is preferable? Why?

A
> Pizza is made with flour, yeast, salt and water. Pizza can be compared with Greek and Middle Eastern flat breads. Pizza is most firmly associated with Naples in Italy.

B
> Pizza, which is made with flour, yeast, salt and water, can be compared with Greek and Middle Eastern flat breads, but it is most firmly associated with Naples in Italy.

Cohesive sentences and paragraphs link ideas together logically and grammatically.

LOGICAL LINKS

3 Logical links include:

Addition	*and, in addition, as well as*
Cause/Result	*because, since, due to, therefore*
Contrast	*while, whereas, on the other hand*
Concession	*but, despite, however*
Purpose	*so, so as to, to, in order to*
Time	*when, before, while, during*

Underline five logical links in Texts A and B.

A
The diet of the earliest humans, although simple, contained all the things that nutritionists say are best to eat. Moreover, according to scientists, emulating primitive diets would improve modern health.

B
Because hunter-gatherer societies do not grow and store crops, there are bound to be times of short supply. To survive such occasions, humans can build up a cushion of fat. When there are no shortages, fat continues to build, creating its own health problems.

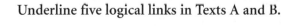

21

GRAMMATICAL LINKS

KEY LANGUAGE
For a longer list of reference links
▶ ex. 10, p. 193

4 Grammatical links include:

Personal pronouns	e.g. *it, they, this, that, these, her, him, us*
Relative pronouns	e.g. *who, which, that, where*
Other substitutions	e.g. *so, such, thus, there, then*
Articles	e.g. *Evidence was found … <u>The</u> evidence suggested …*

Underline eight grammatical links in Texts C and D.

C Plants have only been cultivated for food in the last 30,000 years. Before that, hunter-gatherer societies dominated the earth. A few such societies, including the Kalahari bushmen of southern Africa, still exist. These communities live primarily in warm inland climates, similar to those prevailing when man first evolved. They rely for food on wild nuts and berries, and meat from wild animals.

D Although meat accounts for between 30% and 80% of primitive diets, the meat eaten is different from that found in today's butchers' shops. Wild animals have five times less fat than domestic livestock, which are specially bred to satisfy the modern taste for tender meat.

5 Rewrite the following paragraphs using logical links and grammatical links to connect the idea

A We know that pizzas were eaten in ancient Pompeii. Brick pizza ovens have been uncovered in Pompeii by archaeologists. Early pizzas would have lacked one of their main modern ingredients. The first tomato seeds were not brought to Europe from Peru until 1,500 years later.

B Tomatoes were held in low esteem by most Europeans. The poor people of Naples added tomatoes to their yeast dough. The people of Naples created the first modern pizza. By the 17th century, pizza was popular with visitors. Visitors would go to poor neighbourhoods to taste pizza. Pizza was a peasant dish. Pizzas were made by men called *pizzaioli*.

Spot the error

The following phrases and sentences contain common errors. Identify and correct the errors.

Errors

Corrected version

1 In 1990 there was a slightly decrease …   e.g. *there was a <u>slight</u> decrease*

2 Smoking had a gradual increase …   ....

3 The graph shows an increase of expenditure …   ....

4 Butter has fallen sharply in the last few years.   ....

5 The sale of margarine also has fallen since 1971.   ....

6 The popularity of CDs has raised in recent years.   ....

7 There was a fall of the rate of inflation last year.   ....

8 The standard of living in the USA has increased.   ....

Check your answers by referring to the *Error Hit List* on page 23.

ERROR HIT LIST

do/play/go

✘	✔
He makes several sports.	He <u>does</u> several sports.
You should make more exercise.	You should <u>do/take</u> more exercise.
I play a lot of sport.	I <u>do</u> a lot of sport.
We often do swimming.	We often <u>go</u> swimming.

- Use the verb **do** with the general word *sport*.
- **Play** can be used when the actual sport is named, e.g. *I play a lot of tennis*.
- Use the verb **go** before sports ending in *-ing*.
- Use the verbs **do** or **take** with *exercise*.

which

✘	✔
Pizza, which it was invented in Italy,	Pizza, which ~~it~~ was invented in Italy,

- When **which** is a relative pronoun, don't use another pronoun after it.

increase/decrease

✘	✔
A decrease of the consumption of fish …	A decrease <u>in</u> the consumption …
Standards of living have increased.	Standards of living have <u>risen</u>.
The number of accidents has been increased.	The number of accidents has ~~been~~ increased.

- As nouns, **increase** and **decrease** normally take the preposition *in*. For specific figures we can say: *an increase of 10%*.
- As verbs, they may take various prepositions, e.g. *Houses increased in value; Prices increased from $2 to $3 / by 20%*, etc.
- Don't use the verbs **increase** or **decrease** to refer to the level or standard of something. Use *go up/rise* or *fall*, e.g. *The level of crime has gone up*.
- The verbs **increase** and **decrease** don't normally occur in the passive form.

rise/raise/fall

✘	✔
There has been a fall of spending on books.	… a fall <u>in</u> spending …
The cost of living raised by 5% last year.	The cost of living <u>rose</u> …

- The nouns **rise** and **fall**, when referring to amount, rate, standard, etc., normally take the preposition *in*. For specific figures we can say: *a rise of 10%*.
- As verbs, **rise** and **fall** may take various prepositions, e.g. *Houses have fallen in value; Prices rose from $2 to $3 / by 20%*, etc.
- Don't confuse the verbs **rise** (become more) with **raise** (make something rise), e.g. *Interest rates are set to rise. The Bank of England has raised the interest rate.*

3 ▶ Location is everything

In this unit you will practise:

- Discussing the development of cities / population concerns
- Describing a place
- Identifying topic and text structure; using parallel expressions and grammar clues
- Matching; sentence completion.

Exam Focus

Speaking: Part 3
Speaking: Parts 1, 2
Reading skills
Reading: Exam tasks

Lead-in

1 **Work in pairs to discuss which of the following cities:**

1 is the most highly populated now, in the 21ˢᵗ century.
2 was the most highly populated in the first century.
3 is the fastest growing.
4 is the highest above sea level.
5 had the first underground railway network.
6 has the busiest airport.

| *London* | *New York* | *Mexico City* | *Rome* | *Chicago* | *Bombay* |
| *Tokyo* | *Amsterdam* | *Los Angeles* | *Sydney* | *Hong Kong* | |

KEY LANGUAGE
The passive
▶ ex. 5, p. 188
e.g. *The city is situated on an island; it was founded in the 18ᵗʰ century.*

2 **Can you identify these cities? Look at the plans and read the clues below.**

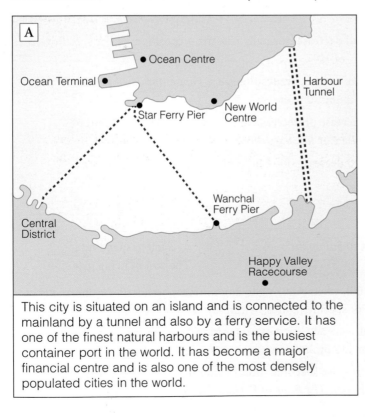

A

Ocean Centre

Ocean Terminal

Star Ferry Pier
New World Centre

Harbour Tunnel

Central District

Wanchal Ferry Pier

Happy Valley Racecourse

This city is situated on an island and is connected to the mainland by a tunnel and also by a ferry service. It has one of the finest natural harbours and is the busiest container port in the world. It has become a major financial centre and is also one of the most densely populated cities in the world.

This is not a capital city, as people sometimes mistakenly think, but it is the largest city in its country, with a population of 3.7 million. It was founded in the 18ᵗʰ century and is situated on a magnificent harbour. One of its most famous landmarks is the harbour bridge.

B

Harbour Bridge

Opera House

Observatory Park

THE ROCKS

Circular Quay Station

BOTANICAL GARDENS

POTTS POINT

ELIZABETH BAY

St James Station

HYDE PARK

KINGS CROSS

Museum Station

DARLINGHURST

This city has roughly the same population as London but covers an area almost three times as large. It has the highest level of car ownership in the world, and two-thirds of its land area are devoted to roads and parking. Not surprisingly, it suffers from serious environmental pollution.

C

N

National Forest

Santa Monica

Venice

Airport

Santa Monica Bay

Anaheim

Pacific Ocean

Long Beach

D

CENTRAL STATION ■

DAMRAK

DAM SQUARE

REMBRANDT'S ■ HOUSE

REMBRANDTPLEIN

AMSTEL

RIJKS MUSEUM

VAN GOGH MUSEUM

Although this is the official capital of the country, the seat of government is, in fact, elsewhere. It is linked to the sea and to a major river by canals which have been cut through the city. It has a number of important art galleries, and its stock exchange is the oldest in the world.

You can check your answers to Questions 1 and 2 on page 216.

Focus on speaking 1 *Urban problems*

▶ Part 3: Discussion

1 What is the problem described in Text C above? In pairs, discuss the following questions.

1 What are the reasons for this problem?
2 Why should citizens be concerned about this problem?
3 What can be done about it?

2 The sentences below describe some of the most pressing problems facing world cities. With your partner, select the most likely answer to complete each sentence.

1 Twenty million people move to cities every *month / year / decade.*
2 One-third of the world's population are under the age of *15 / 20 / 30.*
3 Three people are born every *second / minute / hour.*
4 There are currently *five / twelve / twenty* megacities (cities with over ten million people) in the world.

You can check your answers on page 216.

MINDMAP

3 *Mindmaps* are a useful way of organising your thoughts in an easily accessible form. See the partially completed example below.

    a In pairs, make a list of major problems facing the world's cities now and in the coming years. Organise your ideas in the form of a mindmap. This will enable you to identify the main problem areas clearly and then add further details. Look at the partially filled-in example below. How many ideas can you add?

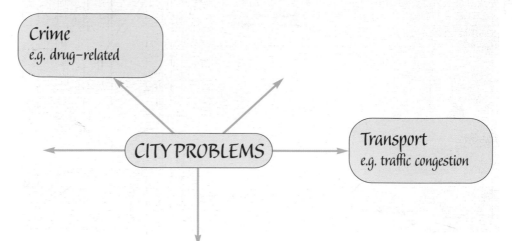

Crime
e.g. drug-related

CITY PROBLEMS

Transport
e.g. traffic congestion

    b Tell your partner about the effect of one or two of these problems in your country.

    c When you have finished, compare results with another pair.

Focus on reading *Location is everything*

IDENTIFYING THE TOPIC

1 Most IELTS reading passages have a title and some also have a subheading introducing the text. Titles and subheadings can give useful information about the text topic.

    a Read the title and subheading on page 27. What do you think the passage will be about?

    b Look through the first few paragraphs quickly to confirm or correct your guess.

TEXT STRUCTURE

2 An important part of gaining a general picture is to understand how a text is organised. Look through the passage and say whether the information is presented:

    1 by geographic region
    2 in chronological order
    3 by type of city layout

Location is everything

The estate agent's advice dates back to 3500BC when the first city of trade took off

Our distant ancestors led pretty simple lives. Until around 10,000BC, all humans were hunter-gatherers and lived a
5 nomadic life, searching endlessly for food. It was the development of agriculture that enabled humans to settle down and live, first as farmers and then as villagers. Around 3500BC,
10 small towns began appearing in Mesopotamia, surrounded by defensive high walls and irrigated fields that fed the town's population.

In the thousand years that followed,
15 when agriculture had become more of a science and crop yields had risen, fewer people were needed to produce food. People took other jobs, became wealthier and more and more chose to
20 live in towns close to shops and markets. This worked well for centuries. Towns flourished and eventually one of the grandest, Rome, became the world's first city of more than one million
25 people around 100AD.

Although the fertile lands surrounding Rome could have adequately fed the city, the Roman people began importing food and
30 became reliant on long supply chains. When Gaiseric the Vandal began withholding vital North African grain supplies from Rome in 455AD, the city's power went into steep decline. The Dark
35 Ages that ensued saw people deserting cities across Europe and returning to the countryside.

Make it accessible

It was not until 1200AD that people
40 began flocking back to the cities, a trend encouraged by the growth of iron technology and further improvements in agriculture. Cities and towns began to spring up across Europe and Asia.

45 The main factor which determined where a city was founded, according to Derek Keene, Director of the Centre for Metropolitan History at the University of London's Institute of Historical
50 Research, was simple geography. "Was it accessible to people who wished to trade there or bring in supplies?"

However, there were other important considerations. "A city might be
55 successfully founded in a desert if there was a need for a staging post or an interchange on a trade route," he says. Then there were the simple demands of a ruler's ego, or a need to defend people
60 against invaders. Finally, there was one other major motivating force: religion. "A sacred site attracts many visitors who require service," Keene says.

In medieval times, cities grew to
65 exploit trade routes. Bruges in Belgium became rich by weaving wool from Britain. Florence, too, prospered from its wool industry until banking came to dominate its economy.

70 Constantinople became by far Europe's largest city and premiere trading centre, the true heir to the Roman legacy during the Middle Ages. The gateway between the Eastern
75 Mediterranean, India and Africa on one side and Europe on the other, Constantinople played a crucial role in the trade of Eastern riches for Western wool and heavy iron products.

80 At the same time, Venice was prospering thanks to trade, its proximity to the sea, Africa and the treasures of Persia. The city-state traded luxury goods such as precious stones, spices,
85 silks and ivory.

Cities that broke the rules

The lure of trading riches has encouraged the growth of cities in unlikely locations. When the East India Trading Company needed a base with
90 good access to the Ganges Valley, it founded Calcutta on swamp land. The site was the furthest inland point that could be reached by ocean-going ships, and the city has grown to a population
95 of 15.5 million today.

The most ludicrously located city has to be St Petersburg, built as the capital of a vast empire by Peter the Great. Thousands of slave labourers died
100 during its construction, and he had to force people to live there.

Other major world capitals had no such problems. London, founded in 50AD, grew steadily and is the least
105 planned world city, with snobbery playing a large part in determining its layout. Mainline stations are dotted around the periphery of inner London, as wealthy 19th-century residents
110 refused construction of a giant central London rail terminal.

By the 1930s, US architect, Frank Lloyd Wright, was arguing that city size should be limited. But as Wright's
115 treatise was published, New York was becoming the world's first city with a population of ten million, and cities have since grown at an astonishing rate – Mexico City is home to 16.5 million
120 people and 26.9 million now live in Tokyo.

► EXAM BRIEFING

Reading module, matching tasks

Matching tasks take many forms. For example, you may be required to match:

- Sentence halves
- Opinions to sources
- Headings to paragraphs
- Causes and effects, etc.

You will receive specific advice for each of the tasks in this book.

General strategies

- Always read the instructions and study the example so you know exactly what you have to do.
- Always check the information in the relevant section of text. Don't rely on guesswork.
- Underline key words and phrases in the question.

INTRODUCING EXAM TASKS 1
► Matching
TASK APPROACH

3 In this particular task, you have to match cities to their descriptions.

- In the text, underline, circle or highlight the cities listed so they are easy to find.
- Read the information about each city in the text and then check the notes to see if any of them apply.
- Look for words and phrases in the notes which mean the same as expressions in the text.

Questions 1–8
*Look at the following descriptions (**1–8**) and the list of cities below. Match each description to one of the cities in the text on page 27.*

NOTES

Example	*Answer*
grew into a successful trading city because of its location close to the sea.	**I**

1	became an important centre for banking	....
2	was the largest city in the world in the 1930s	....
3	had one main industry, weaving, in the Middle Ages	....
4	was built on unsuitable land but has developed into a major world city	....
5	was Europe's most powerful city in the Middle Ages	....
6	has inconvenient rail connections	....
7	lost its power and influence rapidly when it suffered food shortages	....
8	cost many lives to build	....

List of Cities

A Bruges	**D** Florence	**G** Rome
B Calcutta	**E** London	**H** St Petersburg
C Constantinople	**F** New York	**I** Venice

INTRODUCING EXAM TASKS 2
▶ Sentence completion

4 In this sort of task, you have to complete sentences by choosing the best ending from a list. Read the following advice.

TASK APPROACH

- The questions appear in the same order as the information in the text. If you answer them in sequence, it should be fairly easy to find the information you need.
- Study each question and underline the key words or phrases. (These are in italics in the questions on page 30.)
- Locate the relevant section of text and look for **parallel expressions**.
- Choose the best answer from the list of endings, making sure your answer fits both **logically** and **grammatically**.

PARALLEL EXPRESSIONS

5 Instead of using exactly the same words as the text, questions often substitute expressions with the same meaning.

The following words and phrases come from the text on page 27. Find two parallel expressions for each in the box below.

1 population (line 13)
2 became reliant on (line 30)
3 ensued (line 35)
4 deserting (line 35)
5 flocking back (line 40)

6 began to spring up (line 43)
7 accessible (line 51)
8 ludicrously (line 96)
9 vast (line 98)

leaving	*started developing*	*enormous*
depended on	*citizens*	*convenient to get to*
ridiculously	*came afterwards*	*returning*
huge	*easy to reach*	*appeared*
followed	*foolishly*	*couldn't manage without*
migrating back	*inhabitants*	*abandoning*

NB In the sentence completion task which follows, some of the words and phrases in the questions are in italics. Look for parallel expressions from the text to help you identify the correct answer.

GRAMMATICAL CLUES

6 When deciding which phrase best completes a sentence, you may be able to eliminate any answers which are grammatically impossible.

Read the incomplete sentences 9–14 on page 30 and answer these questions.

1 Which three must be followed by phrases beginning with **verbs**?
2 Which three must be followed by phrases beginning with **nouns or -*ing* forms**?

7 Now complete the task on page 30.

Questions 9–14

Complete each of the following statements with the best ending **A–I** from the box below.

Example	Answer
As *farming* became more scientific, *not so many* people	**F**

9 As a result of the development of *farming*, people ....

10 The design of the earliest towns was for ....

11 Towns first *began to grow and prosper* when people ....

12 Rome finally *lost its power* because of ....

13 Cities were usually *established* in places which ....

14 One reason for people to visit a city was ....

A were *convenient* for trade.

B the growth of the population.

C the *protection* of the inhabitants.

D *its dependence on* imported supplies.

E the presence of a *religious* site.

F *were required* to work on the land.

G *made money* and left the countryside.

H were unable to grow their own food.

I were able to *live permanently in one place.*

Focus on speaking 2 *Describing places*

▶ Parts 1 and 2: Interview and Individual long turn

In Part 1 of the interview, the examiner may ask you general questions about your home, your town/city or your country. In Part 2, you may be asked to describe one of these places in more detail.

1 Work in pairs to ask and answer the following questions.

1 Which town or city do you come from?
2 What's the best thing about living there?
3 Is there anything you don't like?
4 Which places would you recommend a tourist to visit?

2 Use information from the maps to help you complete the description of a city on page 31.

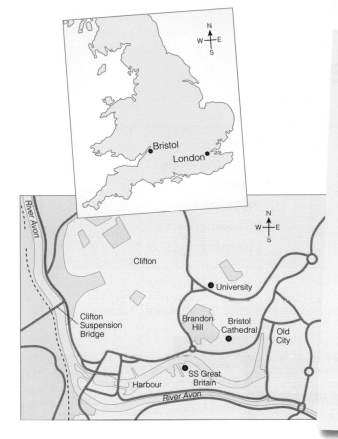

I live in the city of Bristol, which is 1 .... of my country, about 200 kilometres from the capital, London. It has a 2 .... of about half a million.

Bristol 3 .... the River Avon, and in the past it was an important port. Nowadays, that's all finished, and the harbour is mainly used by pleasure boats. The main industries are financial services, which 4 .... things like banks and insurance companies, and also engineering and micro-electronics.

There's an open space 5 .... Brandon Hill 6 .... centre of town and 7 .... of that is a district called Clifton, which has beautiful 18th-century houses. It's a nice place to visit, but unfortunately it's too expensive for me to live there!

There are quite a lot of things to see in Bristol. For example, there's a beautiful 16th-century cathedral and several other 8 .... like the Clifton Suspension Bridge and the SS Great Britain, which is one of the earliest iron ships.

We've got two universities and also several colleges, so there are lots of students and plenty of 9 .... like bookshops and cinemas and restaurants. It's a good place to live!

3 Use the following headings to make notes about your own home town or city in the form of a mindmap. Include any relevant information.

> Location   Size/Population   History   Business/Industry
> Layout   Attractions   Amenities

4 When you've finished, work in groups and describe your city to one or two other students. Try to include one or two personal impressions, as in the example.

Spot the error

Most of these sentences contain common errors. Identify and correct the errors.

1 The city has spent a big amount of money on crime prevention.
2 A number of cities has more than ten million inhabitants.
3 A large proportion of people commute to work by car.
4 The major cities have a large level of unemployment.
5 A number of surveys has been carried out.
6 Only a small percentage of the houses has electricity.
7 The number of private cars is increasing rapidly.
8 People are now enjoying a higher level of living.
9 The food supply is not proportion about the size of the country.
10 Comparing with other countries, Libya spends a high percentage of income on education.

Check your answers by referring to the *Error Hit List* on page 39.

4 ▶ Haves and have-nots

In this unit you will practise:
- Comparing living standards in different countries
- Interpreting and comparing data from diagrams and tables
- Paragraph structure; presenting the solution to a problem
- Labelling a diagram, completing a table, short answers
- Completing notes and a diagram

Exam Focus
Speaking skills
Writing: Task 1
Writing: Task 2
Listening: Section 3
Listening: Section 4

Lead-in

1 Read the following information and then discuss the questions below.

World Population Milestones
- 1 billion in 1804
- 2 billion in 1927 (123 years later)
- 3 billion in 1960 (33 years later)
- 4 billion in 1974 (14 years later)
- 5 billion in 1987 (13 years later)
- 6 billion in 1999 (12 years later)

life expectancy *n* [C] **1** the length of time that a person or animal is expected to live **2** the length of time that something is expected to continue to work, be useful, etc.

the poverty line/level the income below which a person or a family is officially considered to be very poor and in need of help: *More than 20% of American families now live below the poverty line.*

standard of living *n* [C usually singular] the amount of wealth, comfort and things that can be bought that a particular person, group, country, etc. has: *a nation with a high standard of living.*

Source: LDOCE

1 What is most significant about the figures for world population growth?
2 What factors affect life expectancy?
3 What criteria might be used in measuring a country's wealth and 'comfort'?

2 The United Nations monitors the standard of living of countries around the world. The following quiz is based on information published in a recent report. Work with a partner to answer the questions.

Check your answers on page 216.

World Quiz

For questions 1–5, choose the best answer A, B or C.

1 How many countries are there in the world?
   A 112   **B** 194   **C** 224

2 What is the average life expectancy world-wide?
   A 54   **B** 64   **C** 74

3 Which figure is closest to the percentage of the world population living in developing countries?
   A 50%   **B** 65%   **C** 80%

4 Which figure is closest to the percentage of people living below the poverty line?
   A 10%   **B** 18%   **C** 25%

5 How many wealthy people own half of all the property in the world?
   A 358   **B** 1,204   **C** 10,389

For questions 6–9, choose from the list of countries in the box below.

6 Which country enjoys the highest standard of living in the world?

7 In which country do the highest percentage of children complete secondary education?

8 The citizens of which three countries have the longest life expectancy in the world?

9 Which country has the lowest birth rate in the world?

Australia	Brazil	Canada	China	Egypt	France
Germany	Greece	Iceland	India	Italy	Japan
Norway	Spain	Sweden	Thailand	UK	USA

Focus on writing 1 *Interpreting and comparing data*

BAR CHARTS, PIE CHARTS

▶ Task 1

A

The chart shows the average age to which men and women are expected to live.

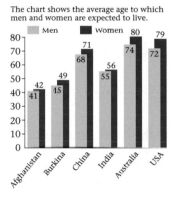

B

The chart shows how many people there are per doctor in each country.

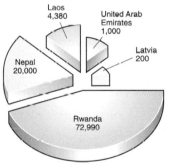

1 Before you look at the diagrams, discuss these questions with another student.

1 Who can expect to live longer: an American or an Australian?
2 Which continent has the highest percentage of people who can read and write: Europe or America?
3 In which country should you be able to see a doctor most quickly: UAE or Latvia?
4 Where did most of the world's population live in 1990: city or country?
5 Where will most of the world's population live by 2025: city or country?

2 Use the information from the diagrams to answer these questions. Choose the correct heading for each diagram as quickly as possible.

1 Healthcare ....   3 City vs Country ....

2 Adult Literacy Rates ....   4 Life Expectancy ....

3 Study the diagrams more carefully to answer these questions.

A 1 What do the figures at the top of the chart (41, 42, etc.) represent?
  2 Who lives the longest of all, men or women, and where?

B 3 How many 'slices' of the pie chart are there? What do they represent?
  4 What do the figures (20,000, etc.) represent?
  5 In which country is a doctor responsible for the fewest patients?

C 6 What does the bar chart compare?
  7 What do the letters F and M represent?
  8 What do the figures at the top of the chart (38.5, 61.7, etc.) represent?

D 9 What proportion of the world is described as 'developing' in 1990?
  10 What proportion of the world is predicted to be 'developing' in 2025?

4 Now use the information in the diagrams to check your answers to Exercise 1.

C

The chart shows the percentage of each region's male and female population aged over fifteen who can read and write.

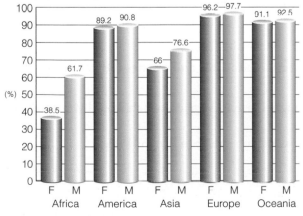

D

These diagrams show the proportion of the world's population living in urban and rural areas in 1990 and the forecast for 2025.

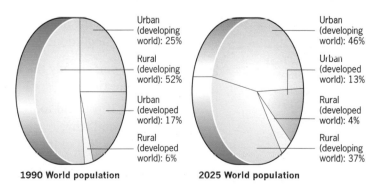

5 Complete the following descriptions using information from the diagrams on page 33. If you need help, there is a list of useful expressions below.

A 1 Life expectancy for men and women in India is almost

....

2 An Australian woman can be expected to live almost .... as long as an Afghan woman.

3 The country with .... difference in life expectancy between men and women is the USA.

B 4 Doctors in Nepal have .... as many patients as doctors in the UAE.

C 5 There is a .... literacy rate for women in Asia than in Oceania.

6 In America, Europe and Oceania, there is .... difference in literacy rates for men and women.

D 7 In 1990, ... of the population of the developing world lived in urban areas.

8 By 2025, ... the population of the developing world will live in cities.

> *almost exactly   a quarter/25%   half/50%   much lower/higher*
> *twice   X times   (very) little   identical   the greatest/smallest*

KEY LANGUAGE
Numerical and other comparative expressions
▶ ex. 7, p. 190
e.g. *twice/ten times as many/much as*, etc.

6 Write three more sentences comparing the following.

1 male/female literacy rates in Africa
2 patients per doctor in Nepal/Latvia
3 the proportion of the world's population living in rural areas in 1990/2025

TABLES

7 In the table on page 35, five of the world's largest cities are compared according to a number of criteria, including population, air and noise pollution and traffic congestion.

a According to the figures, which city:

1 is the noisiest?
2 has the worst air pollution?
3 has the heaviest traffic congestion?
4 is the safest to live in?
5 has the fewest inhabitants?
6 is best supplied with basic services?

b In pairs, study the information in the table and discuss the following questions.

1 If you had to live in Shanghai or Los Angeles, which would you choose, and why?
2 Which of the five cities would you prefer to live in? Why?

KEY LANGUAGE
Forming comparatives and superlatives
▶ ex. 8, p. 191
e.g. *more/fewer, the most/least*, etc.

	Los Angeles	London	Shanghai	Mexico City	Tokyo
Population (millions)	12.5	13	13.6	16.9	27.2
% Homes with water/electricity	94	100	95	94	100
Murders per 100,000 people	12.4	2.5	2.5	27.6	1.4
% Children in secondary school	90	58	94	62	97
Levels of ambient noise (1–10)	6	8	5	6	4
Traffic/km per hour in rush hour	30.4	16.6	24.5	12.8	44.8
Clean air (score out of ten)	3	7	7	2	7

Shanghai

c **Write two paragraphs.**

Paragraph 1: Compare Shanghai and Los Angeles.
- Don't try to describe every detail. Identify the most significant information.

Paragraph 2: Say which of the five cities provides the best environment overall, and why.
- Present the various factors in order of priority and try to describe them in your own words, rather than using the descriptions in the table.

Focus on listening 1 *Wasting energy*

▶ EXAM BRIEFING

Listening module, Sections 3 and 4
In the last two sections, you will hear about situations relating to education or training contexts. Section 3 is a conversation between up to four people, while Section 4 is always a monologue, usually a talk or lecture about a subject of general interest.

1 IELTS listening tasks often include graphs, charts and tables. Read the general advice below before attempting the exam tasks.

TASK APPROACH

- Study the diagram so that you understand how the information is organised. Look carefully at – the **heading(s)** and **layout.**
  – the **main features**, e.g. the unit of measurement, the scale, any Key.
- Try to describe the diagram in your mind – this will help you listen more effectively.
- Many tasks with tables and diagrams involve note completion, so follow the advice in the *Exam briefing* box on page 20 (**Unit 2**).

► Section 3

2 There are three question-types in the following task: labelling a diagram, completing a table and short-answer questions.

WASTING ENERGY

Listen to two students giving a presentation and answer Questions 1–10.

Questions 1 and 2
Label the two bars identified on the graph below.
Choose your answers from the box.

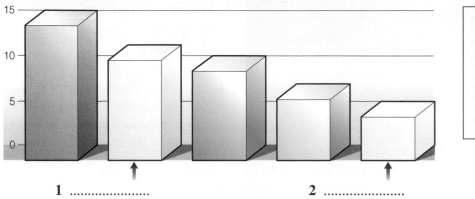

List of Cities
Calcutta
Los Angeles
Mexico City
New York
Tokyo

1 .... 2 ....

Questions 3–7
Complete the table.
*Write **NO MORE THAN TWO WORDS** or **A NUMBER** for each answer.*

Material	Time to biodegrade	Notes
Food (bread)	**3**	
Paper	3–12 months	Needs **4** .... conditions
Metal	1–10 years	Excluding aluminium (used in **5** ....% of soft-drink cans)
6	100 years (estimated)	
Glass	**7** .... (minimum)	

Questions 8–10
List three factors which affect the speed of decay.
*Write **NO MORE THAN ONE WORD** for each answer.*

8 ....

9 ....

10 ....

Focus on writing 2 *Paragraphing*

PARAGRAPH STRUCTURE

1   A typical paragraph contains a main or topic statement, with supporting points. The topic statement is usually, but not always, in the first sentence of the paragraph.

a   Read the paragraph on the right. What topic is discussed?

b   Underline the topic statement. What supporting points are made?

> Since the invention of the internal combustion engine, cities have been shaped by the car and by their inhabitants' reliance on it. The assumption that everybody will own their own car and lead a highly mobile existence is reflected in the low-density layout of modern cities. Such cities were also planned with freeway systems, enabling people to drive great distances every day. However, this attitude takes no account of the elderly, the young, the poor and non-drivers.

2   A paragraph may also contain a qualifying statement which introduces a different perspective, and this may also be followed by supporting points. Qualifying statements are often introduced by concession links such as *but, despite* or *however.* Which is the qualifying statement in the paragraph above?

3   Read the following sentences and complete the table on the left.

1   Much rubbish was simply dumped in a convenient place.
2   There is a shortage of space for depositing waste.
3   In the past, waste disposal was cheap and easy.
4   Increased transport costs make waste disposal expensive.
5   Today there are numerous problems with waste disposal.

Topic statement	....
Supporting point(s)	....
Qualifying statement	....
Supporting point(s)	....

4   Write the sentences above as a paragraph, with appropriate links.

PRESENTING SOLUTIONS TO PROBLEMS
▶ Task 2

> ## ▶ EXAM BRIEFING
>
> **Academic writing module**
> Task 2 of the IELTS Writing module is a discussion topic. You may have to present and justify an opinion, present the solution to a problem, or compare and contrast evidence. You need to write about 250 words and you are advised to spend about 40 minutes on the task. This task carries more weight in marking than Task 1.

5   Individually, write three paragraphs on the following topic.

> *What are the key problems facing the world's cities in the 21st century, and what can be done about them?*

Look back at the mindmap on page 26 to help you plan your ideas.

Follow this plan:
Paragraph 1   Introduce topic; outline two key problems
Paragraph 2   Propose possible solutions to first problem
Paragraph 3   Propose possible solutions to second problem

Begin:
Almost half the world's population now live in urban areas and, as cities grow even larger, conditions for city dwellers are likely to get worse. Two of the most critical problems are …

Focus on listening 2 *Case study: São Paulo*

▶ Section 4   There are two question-types in this task. In one, you have to check information and make changes if necessary; in the other, you have to complete a diagram. Refer to the *Task approach* on page 35 before you begin.

Listen to a short lecture about the city of São Paulo in Brazil and answer Questions 1–10.

Questions 1–4
Look at the fact sheet. Tick (✓) if the information is correct or write in the changes.

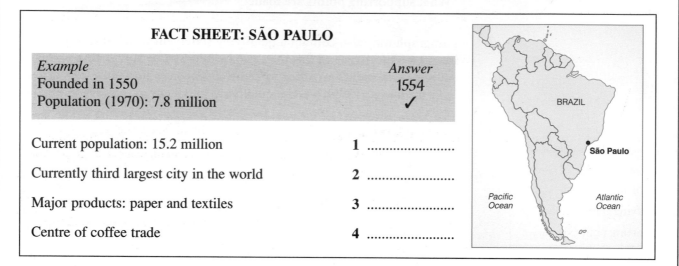

FACT SHEET: SÃO PAULO

Example	*Answer*
Founded in 1550	1554
Population (1970): 7.8 million	✓

Current population: 15.2 million   1 ....

Currently third largest city in the world   2 ....

Major products: paper and textiles   3 ....

Centre of coffee trade   4 ....

Questions 5–10
*Complete the table. Write **NO MORE THAN THREE WORDS** for each answer.*

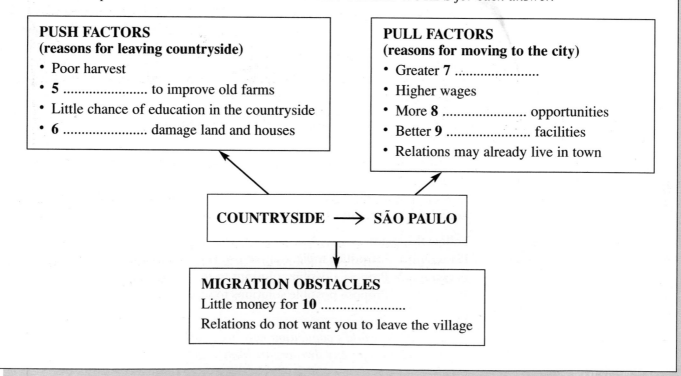

PUSH FACTORS
(reasons for leaving countryside)
• Poor harvest
• **5** .... to improve old farms
• Little chance of education in the countryside
• **6** .... damage land and houses

PULL FACTORS
(reasons for moving to the city)
• Greater **7** ....
• Higher wages
• More **8** .... opportunities
• Better **9** .... facilities
• Relations may already live in town

COUNTRYSIDE ⟶ SÃO PAULO

MIGRATION OBSTACLES
Little money for **10** ....
Relations do not want you to leave the village

ERROR HIT LIST

number/amount

✗	✔
A number of questions was raised.	A number of questions <u>were</u> raised
The number of burglaries have risen.	The number of burglaries <u>has</u> risen
There is a big amount of discussion.	There is a <u>considerable</u> amount of …

- The phrase **a number of** is followed by a **plural** verb.
- The phrase **the number of** is followed by a **singular** verb.
- Don't say **a big number** or **a big amount**. Use *large/considerable/substantial*.

percentage/proportion

✗	✔
A small percentage of students drops out of the course.	A small percentage of students <u>drops</u> out …
There is a big proportion of people over 60.	There is a <u>large</u> proportion …
London is large with proportion to Oxford.	London is large <u>in</u> proportion <u>to</u> Oxford.

- If the noun after **percentage** is plural, the verb is usually plural.
- Don't say **a big percentage** or **a big proportion**. Use *high/large* and *small/low*.
- Something is small/large, etc. **in proportion to** something else.

level/standard

✗	✔
There is a big level of air pollution.	There is a <u>high</u> level of air pollution.
The level of living in the inner city …	The <u>standard</u> of living in the inner city …

- Don't say **a big/large level** or **a small level**. Use *high/low*.
- When you are talking about the quality of something, the usual word is **standard**.

compared with / compared to / in comparison

✗	✔
Comparing with other countries, the UK …	<u>Compared</u> with other countries, the UK …
By comparison to the USA, Canada has …	By comparison <u>with</u> the USA, Canada has …

- Use **compared with** or **compared to** when comparing two or more things. **In comparison (with)** or **by comparison (with)** can also be used to compare things but these are fairly formal and are most often used in written English.

5 ▶ Hurry sickness

<table>
<tr>
<td>
In this unit you will practise:

• Talking about time management and work patterns

• Forming a general picture; scanning; fact v opinion

• Matching headings; multiple choice; summary completion; dealing with unknown vocabulary
</td>
<td>
Exam Focus

Speaking: Parts 1, 3

Reading skills

Reading: Exam tasks
</td>
</tr>
</table>

Lead-in

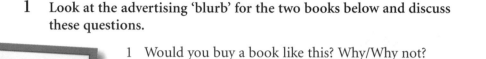

1 Look at the advertising 'blurb' for the two books below and discuss these questions.

1 Would you buy a book like this? Why/Why not?

2 Look at the topics listed on the covers (three for Book A and seven for Book B). Which would you personally find most useful? Why?

3 If you had an extra hour a day, what is the most useful thing you could do with it?

A

alpha books

"Jeff abandons the antiquated maxims about time management and offers real-world, hands-on, this-will-work-for-you suggestions that you'll . . . feel are right . . . ."
—Bob Losure, former CNN headline news anchor and author of *Five Seconds to Air.*

THE COMPLETE **IDIOT'S** GUIDE® TO

Brand-new edition! Completely revised and updated.

Managing Your Time

SECOND EDITION

♦ **Quick and easy guidance** for getting the most out of every minute at home and at work

♦ **Idiot-proof steps** for prioritizing and organizing

♦ **Down-to-earth advice** on handling work overload

Jeff Davidson, MBA, CMC

B

Who Doesn't Need a 25 Hour Day?

This is the book that can give you the extra hour you wish you had. 2.5 million readers worldwide have acclaimed it as the bible of effective time-management. Ray Josephs' classic guide to ultimate efficiency is now completely revised and updated for the 1990s.

Whenever you work, whatever you do, you can do it better in less time:

• **Turn your desk into a time-saving work station**

• **Keep household clutter from cluttering your schedule**

• **Put fax, electronic mail, and the computer to work for you**

• **Turn travelling time into useable time**

• **Delegate as much as you can to whoever you can (including your kids!)**

• **Determine your peak hours and use them to get things done**

• **Set aside a fixed time each day to improve yourself, your opportunities and your life!**

HOW TO GAIN AN EXTRA HOUR EVERY DAY   RAY JOSEPHS

HOW TO GAIN AN EXTRA HOUR EVERY DAY

New Time Strategies That Work

RAY JOSEPHS

Thorsons

UK £7.99
AUS $19.95*

ISBN 0-7225-2995-3   00799>

*recommended price   9 780722 529959

2 a Find words or phrases from the two 'blurbs' which mean:

Book A 1 (verb) to arrange things in order of importance
          2 (adj) practical

Book B 3 (noun) an untidy collection of things
          4 (verb) to give someone else a job to do on your behalf
          5 (adj) at the best or most efficient point

b **Work in pairs to discuss these questions.**
1 What are your peak hours for working?
2 Do you suffer from clutter at home or at work? What's the best way to prevent it?
3 Is there anyone you can delegate jobs to when you're short of time?
4 Who can you rely on for down-to-earth advice about your life or problems?

Focus on speaking *Personal priorities*

▶ Part 3: Discussion

Prioritise the following, according to how important they are in your life. Then discuss your decisions in pairs.

Health	*Wealth*	*Family*	*Society*	*Career growth*	*Intellectual growth*

Focus on reading 1 *Hurry sickness*

FORMING A GENERAL
PICTURE

1 a **Look at the title of the article on page 43.**

Have you heard of 'hurry sickness'? What do you think it could be?

b **Read through the article quickly and decide which of the following best describe its overall topic.**

A Ways to improve your efficiency at work.
B Illnesses caused by working too hard.
C Problems arising from the increased pace of life.
D The importance of relaxation.

SCANNING FOR SPECIFIC
INFORMATION

2 **Complete these sentences in your own words.**

1 Barton Sparagon is a doctor who researches …
2 The term 'hurry sickness' has been in use for …
3 Jill Stein's area of expertise is …

INTRODUCING EXAM TASKS
► Matching

3 This task requires you to match headings to sections of a text. There are two versions, each requiring a different approach. In one, the headings summarise information, so you need to look for the main idea in each section. In the other, the headings pick out key information, so you need to scan for specific detail in each section.

TASK APPROACH

- Always study the example, if there is one, to help guide your approach, either looking for the main idea in each section or scanning for specific detail.
- With summarising headlines, read the first section carefully and try to say what it's about in a few words in your mind, **before** looking at the headings.
- Choose the best answer from the list of headings. Make sure the one you choose sums up the section as a whole.

Questions 1–6
*The reading passage has eight sections **A–H**.*
From the list of headings below, choose the most suitable headings for each section.

List of Headings

i   The effects of social change
ii   How do we begin to tackle the problem?
iii What are the effects on our health and why are we so susceptible?
iv   Who is responsible for the problem?
v   Danger signs
vi   A disease with no age limits
vii What is 'hurry sickness'?
viii A treatment for heart disease
ix   What is the cause?
x   Is there a cure?

Example	Section A	Answer	v
1	Section B	....	
2	Section C	....	
Example	Section D	Answer	i
3	Section E	....	
4	Section F	....	
5	Section G	....	
6	Section H	....	

There is more to life than increasing its speed.
MAHATMA GANDHI

hurry sickness

by Alyson Geller, MPH

A According to statistics, it is becoming increasingly rare in many Western countries for families to eat together. It seems that people no longer have time to enjoy a meal, let alone buy and prepare the ingredients. Meanwhile, fast food outlets are proliferating. Further evidence of the effects of the increasing pace of life can be seen on all sides. Motorists drum their fingers impatiently at stop lights. Tempers flare in supermarket queues. Saddest of all is the success of an American series of books called "One Minute Bedtime Stories". What, one has to ask, do parents do with the time thus saved?

B According to Barton Sparagon, M.D., medical director of the Meyer Friedman Institute in San Francisco, and an expert on stress-related illness, the above are all symptoms of a modern epidemic called "hurry sickness". The term was coined nearly 40 years ago by a prominent cardiologist, who noticed that all of his heart disease patients had common behavioural characteristics, the most obvious being that they were in a chronic rush. Hurry sickness has been an issue in our culture ever since, but the problem is escalating in degree and intensity, leading to rudeness, short-tempered behaviour and even violence, alongside a range of physical ills.

C The primary culprit, according to Sparagon, is the increasing prevalence of technology – like e-mail, cell phones, pagers and laptop computers. We can bring work home, into our bedrooms and on our vacations. Time has sped up for so many people, and there is increased pressure to do more in the same number of hours, says Sparagon.

Jill Stein, a sociologist at the University of California at Los Angeles, agrees that time is being more compressed than ever. "In the past, an overnight letter used to be a big deal. Now if you can't send an e-mail attachment, there's something wrong. Because the technology is available to us, there is an irresistible urge to use it."

D What about those annoying people who shout into their cell phones, oblivious to those around them? Stein says that self-centred behaviour is related to larger social trends as well as technology.

"There is a breakdown of the nuclear family, of community, of belonging; and an increased alienation and sense that we're all disconnected from one another. This breakdown came before the technology, but the technology has exacerbated it." Now we connect through this technology, says Stein, and we don't have face-to-face interaction.

Ironically, as people pull their cell phones out in the most unlikely venues, our personal lives are available on a public level as never before. People are having work meetings and conversations about their spouses and their therapy sessions with complete impunity. Ordinarily we'd never be exposed to this information, says Stein.

E Sparagon claims that there is more a sense of entitlement now than ever ("Why should anyone slow me down?"). But he warns that there is more than civility at stake. "This chronic impatience is damaging not only to our social environment, but to our physical health. It builds, and then it doesn't take much to explode. And for those who repress it, it's equally damaging."

The high-tech revolution and the lifestyle it has spawned have brought with them a rash of serious health problems, including heart attacks, palpitations,

depression, anxiety, immune disorders, digestive ills, insomnia and migraines. Sparagon says that human beings are not designed for prolonged, high-speed activity. "When you look at our heart rates, brain-wave patterns – our basic physiology has not evolved to keep pace with the technology – we are hard-wired to be able to handle a 'fight-flight' response where the stress ends within five to ten minutes. In our current culture, though, we struggle for hours on end."

F Even children are not spared the ills of modern-day overload. There's a hidden epidemic of symptoms like hypertension, migraines and digestive problems among children as young as ten – disorders never before seen in children, says Sparagon. Whether these problems result from being swept into the maelstrom of their parents' lives, or from full loads of extracurricular activities and unprecedented homework requirements – up to five hours a night for some – children are experiencing the same sense of overload, time pressure and demands that their parents experience, says Sparagon, "and they don't have coping mechanisms to deal with it."

G Recovery is possible, but Sparagon emphasises that there is no quick fix. Many of these stress-related behaviours have become deeply ingrained to the point where people are hardly aware of them. The greatest paradox, he says, is that even when people are ready to change their behaviour, they are in a hurry to do so.

H Sparagon works with people to become aware of their stress and the impact it's having on their lives. They examine their belief systems (What is really important? What can they let go of?) and they learn to challenge their behaviours. One popular exercise is to assign a chronically impatient person to stand in the longest line in the grocery store.

The only answer is to take it one day at a time. The irony is that all the techniques and technology designed to streamline our lives may ultimately be counterproductive. As Sparagon says, "People are finding that all of this multi-tasking, rushing and worrying is not only making life intolerable, but actually making them less efficient than they could otherwise be."

from 'Oxygen' website

INTRODUCING EXAM TASKS

▶ Multiple choice

4 There are several types of multiple-choice question. You may have to choose one answer from four options (e.g. Question 7 in the task below), or more than one answer from a longer list of options (e.g. Questions 8–11 below). The approach, however, is the same.

TASK APPROACH

- Study the options first and ask yourself which seem(s) likely to be correct.
- Find the relevant section of text and read it very carefully.
- For each option, ask yourself these key questions:
  1 **Is it mentioned in the article?**
    It may look true or logical but make sure the idea actually comes from the text.
  2 **Is it true?**
    The article may contain words like this, but check to see if this is the real meaning.
  3 **Is it relevant?**
    It may be mentioned in the article, and true, but not answer the question.

Question 7
Choose the appropriate letter A–D.

7 One result of technology and the increased pace of life is that people

    A frequently meet work colleagues in public places.

    B have personal telephone conversations in public.

    C need to visit therapists on a regular basis.

    D no longer have offices to work from.

Questions 8–11
The article mentions a number of factors that contribute to 'hurry sickness'.
*Which **FOUR** of the following (**A–H**) are mentioned?*

List of Factors

A Jobs are less secure and people must work harder to keep them.

B Our bodies are not designed to cope with stress for long periods.

C People are becoming more short-tempered and violent.

D People are expected to try and achieve more in the time available.

E Communications have become faster.

F Too much stress can lead to physical disease.

G Globalisation has led to 24-hour trading.

H People want to use the new technology which is available.

The four factors which contribute to 'hurry sickness' are:

8 ....   **9** ....   **10** ....   **11** ....

EXTRA PRACTICE

5 In addition to the four correct answers, find:

- two which are **results** rather than causes of 'hurry sickness'.
- two possible factors which are **not** mentioned in the passage.

► Summary completion

6 This task was introduced in Unit 1 (page 12). In this second example, your answers must be words or phrases taken from the text.

TASK APPROACH

- First, read through the whole summary for general understanding.
- Read it again carefully, studying the words before and after each gap and thinking about the general meaning.
- Find the relevant section of text and re-read carefully to find the answer.
- Make sure your answers fit logically **and** grammatically.

Questions 12–16
Complete the summary below.
*Choose **NO MORE THAN THREE WORDS** from the passage for each answer.*

> Hurry sickness is not a new condition but it has increased both in
> **12** .... in recent years, mainly as a result of the rapid
> development of **13** .... Typical symptoms include chronic
> impatience, which experts believe can have potentially serious effects not only
> on those around us but also on our **14** .... The fact that
> children are also beginning to suffer from a variety of **15** ....
> suggests that they are as vulnerable to the pressures of modern life as their
> parents. Curing the condition is a slow process, which requires the sufferer to
> **16** .... the stress in their lives, and try to change their
> behaviour patterns.

VOCABULARY

7 The following words occur in the text on pages 43–44. Study the context and choose the correct meaning from the list on page 47. This will be easier if you first identify what part of speech each one is.

1 … fast food outlets are *proliferating* (Section A)
2 … a modern *epidemic* called 'hurry sickness' (B)
3 The term was *coined* nearly 40 years … (B)
4/5 The primary *culprit* … is the increasing *prevalence* of technology … (C)
6 This breakdown came before technology, but the technology has *exacerbated* it. (D)
7 … conversations about their *spouses* … (D)
8 … full loads of *extracurricular* activities … (F)
9 The greatest *paradox* … is that even when people are ready to change their behaviour, they are in a hurry to do so. (G)
10 … all the techniques and technology … may … be *counterproductive* (H)

A	*n*	widespread existence
B	*n*	statement which seems to be impossible because it says two opposite things
C	*v*	made worse
D	*adj*	having the opposite effect to that intended
E	*n*	something which develops and spreads quickly (e.g. an infectious disease)
F	*n*	husbands or wives
G	*adj*	outside the regular course of work in a school or college
H	*v*	invented
I	*v*	rapidly increase in numbers
J	*n*	person or thing guilty of a crime or offence

KEY LANGUAGE
Prefixes and suffixes
▶ ex. 9, p. 192–193
e.g. *idiot-proof; overload, extracurricular, counterproductive*

Focus on reading 2 *Distinguishing fact from opinion*

1 When you read a detailed argument, it's important to distinguish between facts (statements which are known to be true or based on generally accepted evidence) and opinions (personal beliefs which may or may not be true).

Which of the statements (or parts of the statements) should be read as Fact (F) and which should be read as Opinion (O)?

1
On my way to work once, I saw a man walking down the street while shaving with an electric razor, which seemed to me extraordinary.

2
James Gleick is a science writer and the author of several fascinating books including *Faster: The Acceleration of Just About Everything.*

3
We are subject to certain biological constraints. For example, diseases can't be cured more quickly because we're in a hurry.

4
Despite the undoubted speed of the Internet, there's a sense in which it has made us even more impatient.

2 Which of the following phrases are more likely to be associated with facts (F) and which with opinions (O)?

1 Professor Brown argues that …
2 According to the latest statistics, …
3 Several experts claim that …
4 Scientists have discovered …
5 Some people say …
6 Research findings confirm that …
7 It is a commonly held belief that …
8 In his view, …
9 Many scientists suspect that …
10 As has been frequently demonstrated, …

6 ▶ Time out

In this unit you will practise:

- Discussing leisure activities; vocabulary: describing people
- Describing a leisure activity; discussing topic issues
- Completing notes
- Structuring an argument: analysing the question; providing evidence; giving supporting reasons; argument-led approach

Exam Focus
Speaking skills
Speaking: Parts 2, 3
Listening: Sections 1, 2
Writing: Task 2

Lead-in

1 a Which of the following leisure activities have you taken part in during the last four weeks? Tick as many boxes as necessary in Column 1.

	1	2
Listening to tapes/CDs		
Reading books		
Visiting/entertaining friends or relations		
Watching TV/video		
DIY		
Gardening		
Listening to the radio		
Dressmaking/needlework/knitting		

b Compare your list with another student's. Find out more about the way they spend their leisure time. For example, find out the kind of TV programmes they never miss and the ones they turn off immediately!

2 Work with a partner.

a Think in general about young people (of both sexes) aged 16 to 19. Rank the activities 1–8 in order of their popularity for that age group (1 = most popular). Write your answers in Column 2. Afterwards, have a quick look at other pairs' results.

b Now consider two other age groups: 25–29 and 60–69. Which activities (if any) would you expect to change position in your table? Give reasons for your answers.
e.g. *I'd expect DIY to be more popular with 25–29-year-olds, because at that age people often get married and settle down, and DIY can be a cheap way of improving your home.*

You can compare your answers with the results of an official UK survey on page 207.

WRITING PRACTICE
Presenting and comparing data
▶ ex. 1, p. 207

Focus on vocabulary *Describing people*

Work in pairs to do these exercises.

1   Sociological studies have shown that people commonly associate a number of distinct attributes with particular leisure activities. What adjectives would you use to describe the people below? Try to think of two or three for each.

> *Weight trainer   Guitarist   Kayaker   Volleyball player   Chess player*

2   Match each person with one of the following lists of attributes. Check any vocabulary you're not sure of.

A ....

Athletic
Competitive
Concerned with physical
   appearance
Energetic
Health conscious
Physically fit
Sports minded
Team player

B ....

Able to concentrate
Analytical
Cerebral
Competitive
Good problem-solver
Logical
Maths-minded
Quiet
Strategic

C ....

Athletic
Competitive
Concerned with physical
   appearance
Health conscious
Physically fit
Sports-minded

D ....

At peace with themselves
Creative
Determined
Introspective
Intelligent
Patient
Quiet

E ....

Adventurous
Fun
Fun loving
Likes scenic beauty
Loves fresh air
Outdoor type
Sociable

3   Which adjectives would you use to describe a backpacker?
When you've finished, compare your ideas with the list on page 216.

4   Work in pairs to describe someone you know or admire. Spend a few moments making notes before you begin.

Focus on listening 1 *Student interviews*

▶ Section I

EXAM PRACTICE

▶ Note completion

You are going to hear interviews between a Student Counsellor and two students. You will have to complete the Counsellor's notes.

Before you listen, look through the headings and the example answers. Think about the kind of questions the Counsellor might ask, and the answers the students might give.

Questions 1–10
Complete the notes. Use **NO MORE THAN THREE WORDS** *for each answer.*

Interview One

Name:	Linda Richmond
Course:	1 ....
Where living:	2 ....
Membership of student societies/clubs:	3 ....
Comments on facilities:	Quite good
Suggestions for improvements:	4 ....
Other leisure activities:	5 ....

Interview Two

Name:	6 ....
Course:	Marine Biology
Where living:	5 kilometres away
Membership of student societies/clubs:	7 ....
Comments on facilities:	8 ....
Suggestions for improvements:	9 ....
Other leisure activities:	10 ....

Focus on speaking *Leisure activities*

▶ EXAM BRIEFING

Speaking module, Part 2

In the second part of the Interview, the examiner will hand you a topic card and also a pencil and some paper. You will then have one minute to make notes. You will need to talk about your topic for one to two minutes without interruption. When this time is over, the examiner will ask one or two 'closing questions', which you can answer briefly.

General strategies

- Study the topic card very carefully. Each topic has two elements: describe and explain. You will lose marks if you don't cover both.
- Use the one-minute preparation time to jot down as many ideas as possible. **Mindmaps** enable you to identify the main points clearly and then add further details.
- Keep your notes in front of you, so you can refer to them for ideas.

▶ Part 2: Individual long turn

1 Look at this topic card for a typical Part 2 task. How many points need to be discussed?

> **Describe a leisure activity that you enjoy.**
>
> > **You should say:**
> >
> > > **what the activity is**
> > > **where and when you take part in it**
> > > **what it involves**
> >
> > **and explain why you enjoy it so much.**

MINDMAPS

2 In pairs, think of a heading for each set of notes on this mindmap.

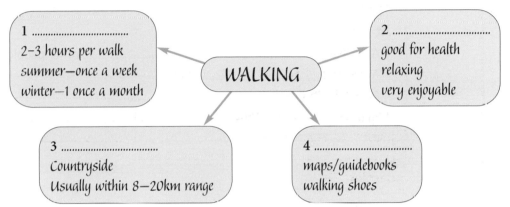

1 ....
2–3 hours per walk
summer—once a week
winter—1 once a month

2 ....
good for health
relaxing
very enjoyable

WALKING

3 ....
Countryside
Usually within 8–20km range

4 ....
maps/guidebooks
walking shoes

3 Prepare to discuss your own leisure activity. Make notes using a mindmap.

4 Work in pairs. Take it in turns to describe your chosen leisure activity in as much detail as possible. Try to keep talking for one to two minutes. Remember the main aim is for you to demonstrate your *fluency*.

Afterwards, tell the class two things about your partner's activity.

▶ Part 3: Discussion

5 Work in pairs to discuss the following questions.

- Why is it a good idea for a child to have a hobby?
- Do young people get enough physical exercise these days?
- Is watching television a good way of relaxing?
- What leisure activities would you recommend as a way of combating stress?

Focus on listening 2 *Ten ways to slow down your life*

▶ Section 2
EXAM PRACTICE
▶ Note completion

You are going to hear a speaker giving advice on how to deal with stress in everyday life. This task is slightly more challenging than Task 1 because, apart from giving the right information, your answers must also fit into the sentence grammatically.

Before you listen, read through the task and, with another student, discuss possible answers. It may not always be possible to make a guess, but the thinking process will help you to listen more effectively.

TEN WAYS TO SLOW DOWN YOUR LIFE

Questions 1–10
Complete the sentences. In this practice task, each answer is **TWO WORDS**.

At work

• Decide on a **1** .... and stick to it.

• Make sure that you take a **2** .... of at least 30 minutes.

• Prioritise your e-mails, faxes and **3** ....

• Make good use of the **4** ....

• Accept that there will still be things in **5** .... at the end of the day.

• Talk to someone about something **6** ....

At home

• After work, concentrate on **7** .... other people.

• Avoid **8** ....

• Play a part in your **9** ....

• Take up an activity like painting, learning a **10** .... or a new sport.

Focus on writing *Structuring an argument*

▶ Task 2

TASK APPROACH

1 Read the following advice on structuring.

- Analyse the question carefully. Underline or circle the key points and consider what you understand by them.
- Decide on your overall response, and think about the evidence you need to provide, including any personal experience you have.
- Make a paragraph plan. This will help you cover all the key points and organise your writing as clearly and logically as possible.
- Remember to link ideas within and between sentences and paragraphs.

ANALYSING THE QUESTION

2 Read the following Task 2 question. The key points in this task have been underlined for you. Consider carefully what you understand by them and discuss the questions on page 53 with a partner.

> Discuss the following:
>
> > ***Do young people today make <u>good use</u> of their leisure time? Or do they spend <u>too much time</u> watching television and playing video games, instead of taking part in <u>more productive activities</u>?***
>
> Use your own ideas and experience and support your arguments with examples.
>
> Write at least 250 words.

- *good use* Is there a right and wrong way to use leisure time?
- *too much time* How much is too much?
  Is there an acceptable level?
- *more productive activities* What makes an activity 'productive'?
  What kind of activities are 'more productive' than watching TV?

PROVIDING EVIDENCE

3 **Discuss these questions, mentioning any relevant personal experience you've had. Make notes of the main points using a mindmap (see page 51).**

1 What **problems** (if any) do you see in children spending a lot of time watching TV or playing video games?
2 What **benefits** (if any) might children gain from these activities?
3 List a few **alternative activities** and suggest how these can be more 'productive'.

4 **When providing evidence, you may need to discuss the reasons for something. Read the following *Useful language* box and answer Questions 1 and 2.**

Useful language: expressing reasons	
Because	**Because** children spend so much time indoors, they … Children may have health problems **because** they ….
because of / as a result of	Their schoolwork can suffer **because of / as a result of** …
so / such	Some games are **so** realistic that children may … Some games have **such** realistic effects that …

1 What is the difference in usage between *because* and *because of*?
2 What is the difference between *so* and *such*?

PRESENTING SUPPORTING POINTS

5 **When presenting a written argument, it's important to make it clear whether you are stating a reliable fact or expressing an opinion – your own or someone else's.**

Stress is arguably one of the most serious modern diseases. According to a survey carried out by the Institute of Management, approximately 270,000 UK workers take time off work every year because of work-related stress, at a cost to the nation in sick pay, lost production and medical bills of about £7 billion.

Experts have often suggested that stress is less of a problem for bosses than for their subordinates, and this view is confirmed by the survey, which found that only 9 per cent of junior managers looked forward to going to work. Furthermore, only 7 per cent felt they were in control of their jobs.

KEY LANGUAGE
Reference links
▶ ex. 10, p. 193–194
e.g. *a survey / the survey*
the UK / the nation

a Circle words or phrases in the text used to introduce or indicate an opinion.

b In order to present a convincing argument, opinions need to be supported by facts. Which facts are used to support the opinions you identified in the text above?

c When you have more than one supporting reason, you can use linking expressions like the following.

> *In the first place,   One reason for this is …   Another (reason) is …*
> *In addition,   Furthermore,   Moreover,*

Think of two facts to support the following opinions. Then make statements linking the points suitably.

- It's a bad idea to give children too much pocket money.
- Mobile phones are an extremely useful means of communication.

ARGUMENT-LED APPROACH   **6** Here is a basic model for a Task 2 answer. In this approach, you consider all the evidence and work towards an overall conclusion. This is known as an *argument-led approach*. An alternative approach will be discussed in Unit 12.

Study the paragraph plan below and then complete the sentences in the first two sections with your own ideas.

PARAGRAPH PLAN   SAMPLE LANGUAGE

Opening paragraph
- Introduce topic   Since television became widely available in the 1950s, it has grown steadily
- Provide background information   in popularity. Nowadays, many families …

Middle paragraphs
- Analyse evidence   Some experts believe that young people are becoming more and more …
- Start a new paragraph for each point   In evidence of this, they …
- Give reasons/examples to illustrate your views   On the other hand, it can be argued that watching TV can actually …

Closing paragraph
- Summarise main points   We have seen that …
- State your overall conclusion   To sum up, …

EXAM PRACTICE   **7** Now write your answer to the task.

Spot the error

Most of these sentences contain common errors. Identify and correct the errors.

1 There never seems to be anything worth watching on the television.
2 Young people tend to hear the radio more than older age groups.
3 According to statistics, Americans spend 2.9 hours a day seeing television.
4 She finds playing piano the best way to relax.
5 Why don't you move the television so that you can see it better?
6 Ninety per cent of people in Britain listen the radio at some time during the day.
7 Do stop talking and concentrate in your driving.
8 You have to take a two-year training course in order to qualify as a teacher.

Check your answers by referring to the *Error Hit List* on page 55.

ERROR HIT LIST

television/TV/radio

✘	✔
Is there anything on the television tonight?	… anything <u>on television</u> tonight?
I'd rather stay at home and see television.	… <u>watch</u> television.
Did you hear the radio last night?	… <u>listen to</u> the radio …

- Use **television** and **TV** (without an article) to talk about the system of broadcasting programmes, e.g. *Television can be educational. What's on TV?* Only use **the television** and **the TV** to talk about the piece of furniture, e.g. *Put that chair in front of the television.*

- Say **watch television**, not 'see television'. When you are talking about a particular programme, you can say **see** or **watch**, e.g. *Did you see the weather forecast?*

- Say **listen to the radio**, not 'hear the radio'. When you are talking about a particular programme, you can say **hear** or **listen to**, e.g. *Did you hear the news yesterday?*

concentrate/listen/play

✘	✔
You must be concentrated in your work.	You must <u>concentrate on</u> …
Be quiet. I need to concentrate myself.	I need to <u>concentrate</u> ~~myself~~.
I enjoy listening jazz.	I enjoy listening <u>to</u> jazz.
I wanted to learn to play guitar.	… to play <u>the</u> guitar

- **concentrate** takes the preposition *on*. It is never used with reflexive pronouns.

- **listen** takes the preposition *to*.

- In British English, we say 'play **the** guitar/piano/flute', etc. In American English, the definite article is sometimes omitted.

game/match

✘	✔
We had a match of football.	… a <u>football match</u>/a <u>game of</u> football.

- Although **match** and **game** have the same meaning, they are used slightly differently. **Match** is only used after the name of the sport, while **game** is usually used in the phrase **a game of**.

plural expressions with numbers

✘	✔
We have a ten years old daughter.	… a <u>ten-year-old</u> daughter.

- When qualifying expressions with numbers are used before nouns, singular forms are used. Use a hyphen between the number and the noun it refers to, e.g. *a three-week holiday; a two-litre bottle, a four-hour journey.*

7 ▶ The sound of music

In this unit you will practise:

- Discussing tastes in music/the cultural role of music
- Tackling long texts: sampling a text, scanning
- False/Does Not Say questions; sentence completion; matching
- Vocabulary: linking expressions; compound words
- Describing an object

Exam Focus

Speaking: Parts 1–3
Reading skills
Reading: Exam tasks
Speaking/Writing
Speaking skills

Lead-in

Work with another student to answer these questions.

1 In your opinion, which of the instruments below …
- has the most beautiful sound?
- is the best one for a child to learn?
- is the most versatile?
- would be the worst to hear your neighbour practising?

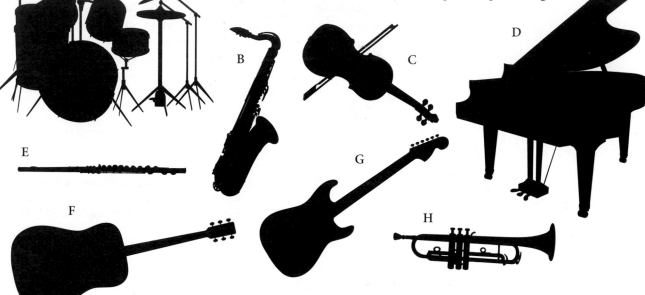

2 What is the national music of your country? What instruments are used?
3 How important is music in your culture and traditions?
4 On what occasions does music play an important role in your country?

Focus on speaking 1 *Your tastes in music*

▶ Part 1: Interview

The list on page 57 shows the main categories of music included in a recent international survey.

Individually: On the list below, put a tick (✓) by the two types of music which you **most** enjoy listening to and a cross (✗) by the two types you **least** enjoy.

In pairs/groups: Find out as much as you can about your partner's choices.

- classical music
- opera
- musicals (e.g. *Les Miserables*)
- jazz
- easy-listening music
- country and western music
- modern folk music
- contemporary rock/pop

- rhythm and blues
- rap/hip hop
- dance music
- Caribbean music (e.g. reggae)
- Latin music (e.g. mariachi, salsa)
- your national music
- oldies/classic rock
- heavy metal

Useful language

(*So*) **what kind of music do you like / enjoy listening to (most)?**
The music / thing I enjoy (listening to) most is …   I love …

(*And*) **is there any kind of music you don't (*particularly*) like?**
I'm not (*very / all that*) keen on …   I don't (*really*) like … (*all that much*)
(*I'm afraid*) I (*just*) can't stand …

(*And*) **how do you feel about … ?**
I find …   (*very / extremely / fantastically*) relaxing / exciting / beautiful, etc.
          (*rather / awfully*) monotonous / boring / unpleasant, etc.
… makes me feel relaxed / calm / happy,   bored / irritable / on edge,
… puts me in a good mood   … gives me a headache

You can compare your musical tastes with the results of the survey on page 216.

Focus on reading *The sound of music*

▶ EXAM BRIEFING

Academic reading: tackling long texts
A major challenge of the Reading module is dealing with a large amount of text in a short time. A single passage may be up to 900 words long, and the three passages together contain 2,250–2,700 words. In addition, at least one passage will put forward a detailed, logical argument, which needs careful analysis, and one may include diagrams or graphs.

General strategies
- **Form a general picture** of the content and how it is organised.
- **Study the questions** in order to identify the information which is needed.
- **Locate the relevant section(s)** of text and then read closely for detail.

SAMPLING A TEXT

1   This is one way of forming a general picture of the text. The main topic of an article is usually set out in the first paragraph, and sub-topics are often made clear in the first sentence of each paragraph, so these are good places to begin.

Read the first paragraph of the article on pages 58–59, and the first sentence of each of the following paragraphs. Then decide which answer (A–D) best describes the overall topic.

A The history of music
B The function of music in human society
C The importance of music in popular culture
D The development of musical instruments

Why we are touched by the sound of music

ANJANA AHUJA reports

1 From simple folksongs to the complex sound of a symphony orchestra, music has been created by every known society. Almost every pivotal event in life can be signposted with music, whether it's a joyful occasion like a wedding or a sad one such as a funeral. Music, which consistently emerges in surveys as the most popular form of art, can be used not only to tap into an emotion a person is already feeling, but to manipulate it in a powerful way. Yet the existence of music mystifies scientists. It is not a primary means of communication, unlike language. While human beings are the only species to make musical instruments, music does not seem to help us to live longer or pass on our genes more efficiently. So what purpose does it serve?

2 Participants at the American Association for the Advancement of Science recently attended a performance of the kind of music Neanderthal man might have heard. Working from fragments of musical instruments found alongside Neanderthal relics in Slovenia in 1995, Dr Jelle Atema from Boston University crafted a flute from the 50,000-year-old leg-bone of a bear. His replica showed the flute was not a sophisticated instrument – in fact, it had a range of less than one octave – but it was an instrument nonetheless. Dr Atema's guess is that cavemen used the instrument to attract prospective mates. Although some psychologists feel this is somewhat feeble

and doesn't really explain why a cavewoman should find a caveman flautist more appealing than a tone-deaf rival, the question remains. After all, something must explain why our ancestors were creating music 200,000 years ago.

3 Psychologists are united in one belief – that music speaks to the heart. What is more, the evidence that music elicits emotion is startlingly direct. A Cornell University study showed recently that certain pieces of music induce physiological changes in the body that correspond to certain emotions. "Sad" pieces caused the pulse to slacken, the blood pressure to rise and the temperature to drop, which is exactly what happens when a sense of sadness sets in. "Happy" songs did the opposite, inducing a cheery feeling. Somehow, music can tap into sensitive emotional circuits.

4 Geoffrey Miller, a scientist at University College, London, thinks it is clear that music has all the hallmarks of an adaptive behaviour, meaning it was a factor in selecting a mate. "It is universal across cultures, and kids are motivated spontaneously to learn how to play music around the age of puberty," says Dr Miller. He recently conducted an intriguing study of 3,000 jazz albums. The peak age of the performers was 30, and there were ten male performers for every one female. "That's the same age at which other cultural displays peak, such as painting, poetry and philosophy," Dr Miller points out.

5 Musical talent, he says, can indicate many desirable qualities in a mate: the mental competence to learn notes and lyrics; the social intelligence required to be part of an orchestra and co-operate, literally harmoniously, with other people; creativity and energy. But just because musical competence may have once signalled a good mate doesn't necessarily mean that every modern woman is searching for that quality – human beings have come to differ in their preferences.

6 Dr Adrian North, a music psychologist at Leicester University, surveyed Staffordshire teenagers last year about what kind of music they listen to and why. "The findings were almost too stereotypical to be true," says Dr North. "While the girls listened to influence their mood, boys used music as a way of impressing their friends. Boys seem to like rock and rap because it shows how cool, trendy and macho they are. Boys use music as a badge of identity; it's a way of telling people about who you are." He also adds that an individual's choice of music directly influences attractiveness. However, Dr North shies away from saying that music has evolved as a mechanism for mate selection.

7 Stephen Pinker, the American psychologist, does not subscribe to the view that music has evolved as a way of showing off to prospective mates. "Compared with language, vision, social reasoning and physical know-how, music could vanish from our species and the rest of our lifestyle would be virtually unchanged," he writes in *How the Mind Works*. Directly contradicting Dr Miller, he concludes: "Music shows the clearest signs of not being an adaptation."

8 So if music confers no survival advantage, why does it exist? Pinker calls it "auditory cheesecake", a confection of sounds put together to tickle faculties that our brain already possesses. In his view, songs with lyrics appeal to a brain already attuned to language; the ear is sensitive to

harmonies, and sounds in the natural world, such as birdsong and even thunder, echo such harmonies; we derive pleasure from patterns and rhythm, and repetitive sounds appeal to the ear in the same way that a repeated doodle appeals to the eye.

9 But how does music "move" us? Last week scientists from the University of Manchester revealed that loud music stimulates a part of the inner ear called the sacculus, which is connected to the hypothalamus, the brain's "pleasure centre".

This could explain why music is so evocative. Interestingly, the sacculus exists only in fish and human beings (it came from a common ancestor). That might shed light on why human beings alone attach such importance to making music. The sacculus responds only to music, which suggests one reason why music, rather than any other form of sound, inspires such delight.

SCANNING FOR SPECIFIC INFORMATION

2   Questions 14–19 on page 61 ask you to match scientists with their opinions. Find and clearly underline the names of the four scientists mentioned in the article.

EXAM PRACTICE
▶ True/False/Does Not Say

TASK APPROACH

3   It can sometimes be tricky to choose between No/False and Not Given/Does Not Say answers, and this exercise concentrates on that distinction.

- The main difference between the two answers is that **if you make a No/False statement negative, it should be true according to the text**. If you make a Not Given/Does Not Say statement negative, it will not necessarily be true.

In this specially adapted task, there are four False and four Does Not Say answers. Note that the questions are in the same order as the information in the text.

Questions 1–8
Do the following statements agree with the views of the writer?
Write

| **FALSE** | *if the statement contradicts the views of the writer* |
| **DOES NOT SAY** | *if it is impossible to say what the writer thinks about this* |

| *Example* | *Answer* |
| Music is twice as popular as painting as a form of art. (Paragraph 1) | **DNS** |

1	Scientists have a clear explanation for the existence of music.	....
2	Dr Atema recently played an ancient instrument in public.	....
3	Research shows that listening to certain types of music can reduce pain.	....
4	Scientists have found that listening to 'sad' music can make one feel warmer.	....
5	The majority of jazz artists in Dr Miller's study were women.	....
6	According to the survey carried out by Dr North, girls don't like rock or rap music.	....
7	Stephen Pinker's book, *How the Mind Works*, is a best-seller.	....
8	Scientists have discovered that the sacculus is unique to human beings.	....

TASK ANALYSIS

4   Compare your answers and discuss your reasons with another student.

▶ Sentence completion

5 In this example of a sentence completion task, all the possible answers fit grammatically, so concentrate on meaning and look for parallel expressions in the text.

NB The questions appear in the same order as the information in the text.

Questions 9–13
Complete each of the following statements with the best ending A–H from the box below.

9 The fact that music is not a primary means of communication makes it … *H* ......

10 The fact that human beings make musical instruments means they are … ....

11 The flute produced by Dr Atema was … ....

12 One point on which psychologists agree is that music is … ....

13 Dr Miller says that 30 is the age when artists produce works which are … ....

List of Endings

A different from other species.	**E** limited in range.
B of the highest quality.	**F** sensitive to emotions.
C extremely direct.	**G** able to affect the emotions.
D of little or no importance.	**H** different from language.

TASK ANALYSIS

6 Compare your answers with another student and discuss any differences.

▶ Matching

7 In this task, you are given a list of opinions and you have to match them to sources which are mentioned in the text. Tasks like this are often set with texts which discuss slightly controversial topics, where a number of expert opinions are quoted. Note that the questions may not be in the same order as the information in the text.

TASK APPROACH

- Find the names of the experts or sources in the questions and underline or highlight them in the text.
- Carefully study what is said about the first expert's views.
- Look for a match in the list of opinions. Remember that the question is unlikely to use the same words. Look for synonyms and parallel expressions.
- Continue in this way. Be careful, some experts may be quoted more than once in a text, and you may need to spot a 'he said' or 'In her opinion'.

Questions 14–19
Look at the following statements and the list of people below (A–D).
Match the statements with the people who made them.

14   Musical skills may suggest a number of positive qualities in a person.   ....

15   If music disappeared, it would have almost no effect on our lives.   ....

16/17 Music first developed as a way of attracting a mate. (2 answers)   ....

18   Young people's tastes in music differ according to their sex.   ....

19   We find repeated sounds pleasurable to listen to.   ....

> **A** Dr Jelle Atema
> **B** Dr Geoffrey Miller
> **C** Dr Adrian North
> **D** Stephen Pinker

TASK ANALYSIS

8   Compare your answers with another student and discuss any differences. Make sure you can refer to a particular phrase or sentence from the text for each answer.

Focus on vocabulary

DEALING WITH
UNKNOWN VOCABULARY

1   Remember these points:
- you don't need to, and are not expected to, understand every word in a text.
- if you don't need to understand a word to answer a question, ignore it!
- if a word is important to understanding, try to guess the general meaning.

2   Look at the word *pivotal* in paragraph 1 of the text on pages 58–59.

1   Was it necessary to understand it in order to answer the questions?
2   If you had needed to understand it, the text gives two examples of *pivotal* events in life. What are they?
3   What do you think is the general meaning?

3   The words and expressions in bold below may not have been familiar to you. Look at each one in context and try to guess the general meaning.

1   … some psychologists feel this (idea) is somewhat **feeble** and doesn't really explain … (para. 2)
2   'Sad' pieces caused the pulse to **slacken** … (para. 3)
3   … Dr North **shies away from** saying that music has evolved … (para. 6)
4   Stephen Pinker … does not **subscribe to the view** that music has evolved … (para. 7)
5   So if music **confers** no survival advantage … (para. 8)
6   That might **shed light on** why human beings alone … (para. 9)

LINKING EXPRESSIONS

4 Find and underline these linking expressions in the text. Study the way each one is used and then complete the table below.

Yet (para. 1) **After all,** (para. 2) **However,** (para. 6)
In fact, (para. 2) **What is more,** (para. 3)

- Saying what the real truth of a situation is
  1 .... = really, actually (used to add emphasis)
  2 .... = it must be remembered that (to remind the reader of an important fact)
- Saying something is true in spite of information that makes it seem unlikely
  3 .... = despite this (especially used in written English)
  4 .... = despite this (used to introduce an idea or fact that seems surprising or difficult to believe in relation to what's been said before)
- Adding something new to what you have said
  5 .... = also and more importantly

KEY LANGUAGE
Talking about research
▶ ex. 11, p. 195

COMPOUND WORDS

5 The article contains a number of compounds – combinations of two words. Use words from the box to make compound words which match the definitions below. The first one is done for you.

~~cave~~	break	sign	deaf
know	post	bird	life
song	tone	how	~~man~~
style	store	in	up

1 *n* Another term for one of our Neanderthal ancestors: *caveman*

2 *adj* Unable to tell the difference between musical notes: ....-............

3 *n* The sound made by flying creatures: ....

4 *v* To indicate the way / to show clearly: ....

5 *n* Practical ability or skill: ....-............

6 *n* Way of living: ....

6 New compound words are constantly entering the language, particularly in the context of business. Explain the following common expressions.

1 The new financial advice website is the brainchild of a young accountancy graduate.
2 The computer course I took was excellent, with plenty of hands-on experience.
3 The job is great, but the downside is that I have to spend a lot of time away from home.
4 We may be seeing the beginning of a long-awaited upturn in the economy.
5 Many companies are downsizing to reduce costs.

Focus on speaking 2 *Describing objects*

► Part 2: Individual long turn

1 When describing the appearance of an object, think about its key aspects: size, shape, colour, what it's made of and how it's used.

Complete the following descriptions and say what the objects are.

A These are long thin sticks about 25 centimetres long, and they come in pairs. They're made of wood, plastic or ivory and they sometimes have beautiful decorations on them. You hold them both in one hand and they're used for ... *eating* *chopstcks*

B This is an extremely thin piece of metal about four centimetres long. It's got a hole in one end and the other end is pointed and sharp. It's used for ... *sewing*

C This is a flattish object which is usually square or rectangular in shape and made of plastic. There are buttons with numbers and mathematical symbols on them on top, and also a small clear window. You use it for ...

2 Practise describing these objects.

A

B

C

D

E

> **Useful language**
>
> It's (*roughly/sort of*) square, rectangular, round/circular, etc. (in shape)
>
> It's ... (colour/texture)   It's made of ... (material)   You use it for ... + *-ing*
>
> It's flatt*ish*, squar*ish*, etc.; silvery, silky, etc.

3 Work in pairs to describe a number of objects and see if your partner can identify them.
Student A: Turn to page 216. Student B: Turn to page 218.

EXAM PRACTICE

4 Work in pairs.

1 Read the topic card below and think of a suitable possession to describe. Notice that describing appearance is only one part of the task, so you don't need to go into a lot of detail.
2 Spend a few moments making brief notes in the form of a mindmap.
3 Take it in turns to describe your chosen possession. You should try to keep talking for one to two minutes, without interruption. Keep an eye on the time while your partner is speaking and let them know when their time is up.

> **Describe a personal possession which means a lot to you.**
>
>   **You should say:**
>
>   **what the item is**
>   **what it looks like**
>   **where you keep it**
>
>   **and explain why it's important to you.**

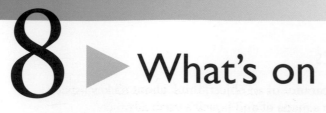

8 ▶ What's on

In this unit you will practise:

- Discussing cultural attractions; describing an event
- Topic vocabulary and word stress
- Multiple choice; sentence and table completion; short answers; labelling a diagram
- Describing tables: organising and presenting data; presenting and justifying an opinion: disagreeing; discussing implications

Exam Focus

Speaking: Parts 1, 2
Speaking/Writing
Listening: Sections 1, 2
Writing: Tasks 1, 2

Lead-in

1 Organise the words or phrases in the box into one of these categories:

Cinema   Theatre / Concert / Opera   Museum / Gallery

sculpture	stage	subtitles	exhibit	screen	collection	stunt
conductor	still life	scenery	on location	act	programme	
dress rehearsal	special effects	landscape	soundtrack	catalogue		

PRONUNCIATION:
WORD STRESS

2 Examples A and B show two different word stress patterns. Each word has three syllables, represented by the number of circles. The large circle shows which syllable is stressed in each case. Find four more examples for each pattern from the categories and words above.

A museum   o O o   *conductor, collection, location, exhibit*

B gallery   O o o   *subtitle, scenery, landscape, catalogue*

Focus on speaking 1 *Discussing cultural attractions*

▶ Part 2: Individual long turn

Work with one or two other students to talk about the following topic. You can make a few notes before you begin. Try to speak for one to two minutes without interruption. Refer to the language in the *Useful language* box.

Describe a visit you can remember to one of the following places and explain what you remember especially about it.

museum   cinema   historic building   art gallery   theatre   concert hall

> **Useful language**
>
> **The thing I remember most** (about it / the film, etc.) **was** …
> **What I liked** (most) (about it / the day, etc.) **was** …
> The (best / most interesting, etc.) **thing** (about it) **was** …
> **It was the** (best / worst / most beautiful, etc.) …   I've ever … (seen / been to / heard, etc.).

Focus on listening 1 *Music festival*

▶ Section I
▶ Multiple choice; table completion; short answers

TASK APPROACH

The following task contains various question-types. Remember to read through the different instructions and the questions in advance.

Question 1 below introduces a new type of multiple-choice question where you have to choose **two** answers from a list of seven or eight options.

- Look through the list and say each item silently. Thinking about the pronunciation will make it easier to identify the answers when you hear them.
- Listen carefully – the information may come quickly, and the words you need may be combined in longer phrases.

---

*Listen to the conversation between two students about a music festival and answer Questions **1–10**.*

Question 1
*Circle **TWO** letters **A–G**.*

1 Which **TWO** of the following types of music will be performed at the festival?

   A heavy metal   **C** *(circled)* jazz   **E** *(circled)* folk music   **G** dance music
   B rock music   **D** opera   **F** country and western

Questions 2 and 3
*Circle the correct letters **A–D**.*

2 When does the festival begin?
   A 1st May   **B** *(circled)* 9th May   **C** 12th May   **D** 16th May

3 How long does the festival last?
   A a weekend   **B** a week   **C** ten days   **D** *(circled)* two weeks

Questions 4–8
Complete the booking form below.
*Write **NO MORE THAN THREE WORDS** for each answer.*

Event	Code	Time	Ticket price
Cuban music: talk	A5	**4** *10.30*	£6
The sounds of Scotland	A12	2 p.m.	**5** *£8*
6 *africa Relive*	B17	7 p.m.	£15
Canal boat cruise (with **7** *lunch* and talk)	B9	2–5 p.m.	**8** *£14.50*

Questions 9–10
*Write **NO MORE THAN THREE WORDS** for your answer.*

9 What art exhibition do the friends intend to visit?
   The *Bus Stop* Gallery.

10 What should Maria take with her?
   Student Card

Focus on listening 2 *The Museum of Anthropology*

▶ Section 2
▶ Short answers; labelling; sentence completion; table completion

The tasks below are based on radio feature about a museum. In one of the tasks, you have to label the plan of a building. Read the following advice before you begin.

▶ **EXAM BRIEFING**

Listening module, transcoding tasks

In the Listening module, you may be required to label or complete diagrams (e.g. plans, maps, charts) using information on the recording. These are called **transcoding tasks**.

General strategies
- Study the diagram and try to 'read' it, by asking yourself some basic questions. e.g. if it's **a building**: *Is it a floor plan or a cross-section? Which is the way in?*

a map: *Which way is north? What are the main features (rivers, towns, etc.)?*
an object: *Which is the top/bottom, back/front, etc.? What are the key features?*
a process: *Where does the process start and end? What are the stages?*

- Look at any labels given – thinking about them will help you recognise the words when you hear them.

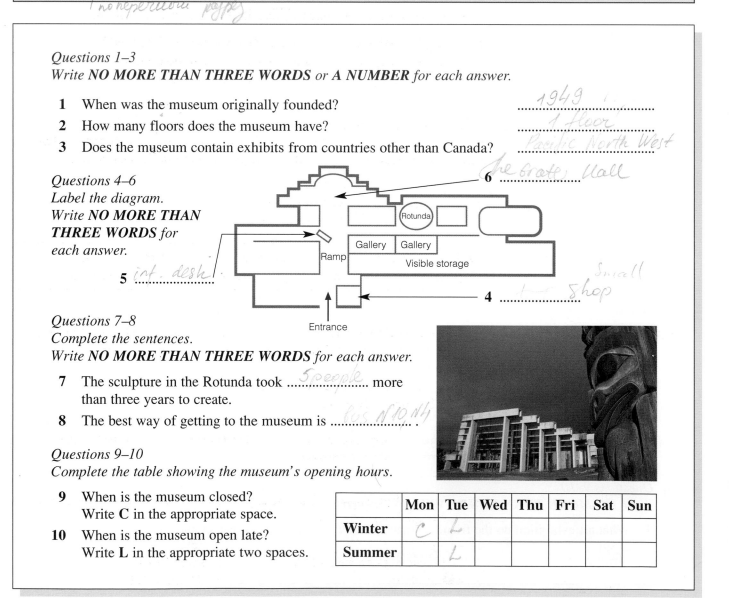

Questions 1–3
Write NO MORE THAN THREE WORDS or A NUMBER for each answer.

1   When was the museum originally founded? *........1949........*

2   How many floors does the museum have? *........1 floor........*

3   Does the museum contain exhibits from countries other than Canada? *Pacific North West*

Questions 4–6
Label the diagram.
Write NO MORE THAN THREE WORDS for each answer.

6 *...the Great, Hall...*

5 *...int. desk...*

4 *...Small Shop...*

(diagram labels: Rotunda, Gallery, Gallery, Visible storage, Ramp, Entrance)

Questions 7–8
Complete the sentences.
Write NO MORE THAN THREE WORDS for each answer.

7   The sculpture in the Rotunda took *...5 people...* more than three years to create.

8   The best way of getting to the museum is *...bus N10 N4...*

Questions 9–10
Complete the table showing the museum's opening hours.

9   When is the museum closed?
    Write **C** in the appropriate space.

10 When is the museum open late?
    Write **L** in the appropriate two spaces.

	Mon	Tue	Wed	Thu	Fri	Sat	Sun
Winter	C	L					
Summer		L					

Focus on writing 1 *Describing tables*

▶ Task I

INTERPRETING STATISTICS

1 Read the following findings from a museum survey into visitor satisfaction, then answer Questions 1–3.

Visitors surveyed:	10,000
'Very satisfied':	2,000
'Satisfied':	5,080
'Quite satisfied':	2,320
'Not satisfied':	500
'Don't know':	100

- **Twenty per cent / a fifth** of the people surveyed said they were 'Very satisfied'.
- **Approximately / just over 50 per cent of / half** the visitors said they were 'Satisfied'.
- Only **one per cent of / one in a hundred** visitors had no opinion.

1 What proportion of visitors were 'Very satisfied' or 'Satisfied'?
2 What percentage of visitors to the museum had no opinion?
3 What percentage of visitors expressed dissatisfaction?

2 Statistics can be expressed in a number of ways, as fractions (half, a quarter, etc.), percentages (20%) or in expressions like 'one in ten'. Match each of the percentages 1–6 with two expressions from the box below.

1 10 per cent   4 33 per cent
2 20 per cent   5 75 per cent
3 25 per cent   6 90 per cent

| *a third   three out of four   one in three   three-quarters   one in ten* |
| *a quarter   nine out of ten   a fifth   a tenth   one in five   one in four* |

QUALIFIERS

3 It's often helpful to describe statistics in terms of the nearest 'round figure', e.g. 47% = approximately/almost 50%; 25.5% = just over a quarter / one in four.

Useful language: Qualifiers			
exactly	about	more than	less / fewer than
	approximately	(just) over	(just) under
	almost / nearly		

Rewrite the following statistics. Use expressions from the box in Exercise 2 and a suitable qualifier.

1 48.5%   4 65%
2 30 people out of a total of 90   5 seven in 100
3 4□ out of 80   6 74 out of 100

ORGANISING AND
PRESENTING DATA

4 Use information from the table to complete the text below.

Attendance at cultural events in Great Britain Percentages			
	1987–88	1991–92	1997–98
Cinema	34	44	54
Plays	24	23	23
Art galleries/exhibitions	21	21	22
Classical music	12	12	12
Ballet	6	6	6
Opera	5	6	6
Contemporary Dance	4	3	4

Source: *Social Trends 30* The Stationery Office

KEY LANGUAGE
Cohesion: avoiding repetition
▶ ex 12, p. 195
e.g. *did so, the former ... the latter ... respectively,* etc.

WRITING PRACTICE
Describing information from a table (guided practice)
▶ ex. 2, p. 208
Describing information from a table (exam task)
▶ ex. 3, p. 209

When asked in 1997–98 whether they attended particular types of cultural events 'these days', **1** .... adults said that they attended ballet or opera, while **2** .... said that they attended plays. The proportion of adults who attend most types of cultural events has **3** .... over the last decade or so. The exception to this is cinema attendance. Whereas in 1987–88, **4** .... of adults said they went to the cinema, **5** .... said that they did so in 1997–98.

5 For a detailed *Task approach* to this kind of task, turn to *Writing practice* Exercise 3, page 209.

Focus on writing 2 *Presenting and justifying an opinion*

▶ Task 2

In exam topics which require you to present and justify an opinion, you may need to express disagreement or discuss the implications of an assertion.

EXPRESSING DISAGREEMENT **1** As part of your answer to a Task 2 question, you may wish to challenge a fact or claim.
e.g. *Insurance fraud is a crime without a victim.*

It's not (completely) true to say that ...
Many people would disagree with the assertion/idea that ...
It's hard to believe that ...

You may also need to point out a false conclusion.
A lot of people exceed the speed limit so it must be acceptable.

The fact that ... doesn't mean ...
(Just) Because ... it doesn't necessarily follow that ...
It may be true that ... but ...

2 Read the following statements. Decide which three you disagree with most and write sentences giving reasons and/or pointing out false conclusions.

1 Teaching children is easier than teaching adults.
2 Everyone would benefit from taking more exercise.
3 The prison population has increased, so more crimes must have been committed.
4 Motor cycles should be banned – they're the most dangerous form of road transport.
5 Only a fifth of hospital consultants are female. Women doctors can't be very ambitious.
6 It's not worth trying to give up smoking, because a lot of people try and fail.

DISCUSSING IMPLICATIONS

3 It's often important to consider the implications of an assertion. One way to do this is to use a conditional tense. Another is to ask a rhetorical question.

Argument: Increasing the price of petrol would encourage people to use public transport.
But if petrol costs rose, the cost of many goods would also be affected.
And what about people who live in the countryside, who have no regular bus service?

With a partner, take it in turns to suggest some of the implications of the following arguments.

> **KEY LANGUAGE**
> Conditionals
> ▶ ex. 13, p. 196–197
> e.g. *If more people travelled by public transport, there would be less traffic congestion.*

1 The sale of cigarettes should be banned.
2 Cars should not be allowed to enter city centres.
3 Income tax is too high. We should vote for the party which would lower taxes.
4 Tertiary education should be free for all students.

EXAM PRACTICE

4 Refer to the *Task approach* on page 52 before attempting this task.

You should spend about 40 minutes on this task.

Present a written argument or case to an educated reader with no specialist knowledge of the following topic.

> *The government spends about £220 million a year supporting museums and galleries in the UK, and a similar amount subsidising the visual and performing arts.*
>
> *This is a huge sum to spend on minority interests, and the money would be better spent on more important things. It should be up to the people who enjoy cultural attractions to pay for them.*
>
> *What are your views?*

You should use your own ideas, knowledge and experience and support your argument with examples and relevant evidence.

You should write at least 250 words.

Focus on speaking 2 *Describing an event*

▶ Part 2: Individual long turn

One of the things you may be asked to do in Part 2 of the Speaking module is to describe an event, either public or private. Look at the example task in the box on the right before doing the exercises.

> **Describe a big public event that you have attended.**
>
> **You should say:**
>
> what it was
> when was it held, and why
> what happened
>
> **and describe how you felt about being there.**

1 Work in pairs and discuss the following questions.

 1 Make a list of as many public events as you can you think of, big or small.
 2 What kind of public events do you enjoy attending? Why?
 3 Is there anything you dislike about such events?

GUIDED EXAM PRACTICE

2 • Think of a public event you have attended. Before you tell your partner about it, spend a moment or two preparing.
 • Choose a particular event you remember well.
 • Use a mindmap to note down the key points. Main headings could include *When, Why, What* and *How*, and subheadings could include *music, fireworks*, etc.
 • Refer to the *Useful language* box on page 64.

EXAM PRACTICE

3 With a partner, take it in turns to do this exam task.

> **Describe a party you particularly remember.**
>
> **You should say:**
>
> why the party was held
> who attended
> what happened
>
> **and explain what made it memorable.**

Spot the error

Most of the sentences contain common errors. Identify and correct the errors.

 1 It is worth to point out that this is not the only possible cause of the problem.
 2 There has been an increase of interest in classical music in recent years.
 3 One of the most important things in life is a good health.
 4 Only half the people who responded to the survey were satisfied.
 5 In the end of the period in question, imports had increased by ten per cent.
 6 It can be true that people are living longer, but what about their quality of life?
 7 Four out of five tourists who visit the country arrive by air.
 8 The new airport will be only two and quarter kilometres away from the school.
 9 Although you can encourage people to stop smoking, you can't force them to.
 10 The training scheme was unpopular, and at the end the government had to abandon it.

Check your answers by referring to the *Error Hit List* on page 71.

ERROR HIT LIST

at the end/in the end

✘	✔
They fought the case for years, but at the end they lost.	... <u>in the end</u> they lost.
In the end of the course there is a test.	<u>At</u> the end of the course ...

- **At the end** refers to the point where something finishes, and it is usually followed by the preposition *of*.

- **In the end** means 'after a long period of time' or 'eventually'. It is never followed by *of*.

half/a quarter

✘	✔
I've written the half of my essay.	I've written ~~the~~ <u>half</u> (of) my essay.
We've only got half of a kilometre to go.	We've only got <u>half</u> ~~of~~ a kilometre to go.
I've been living here for two and half/quarter years.	... for two and <u>a</u> half/quarter years.

- Don't use *the* before **half** except when talking about a particular half of something, e.g. *The second half of the match was pretty boring.*

- You can say **half** or **half of**, but **half** is more common.

- Use **half** (not **half of**) in front of measurement words like *kilometre, litre* or *hour*.

- After numbers, **half** and **quarter** take an indefinite article, e.g. *two and <u>a</u> half metres; four and <u>a</u> quarter years.*

one in ten/nine out of ten

✘	✔
It was a one out of a million chance.	It was a one <u>in a</u> million chance.
Three in four cats prefer 'Moggie' cat food.	Three <u>out of</u> four cats prefer ...

- Use the preposition *in* to talk about very small proportions, e.g. *one or two in ten.*

- Use the prepositions *out of* to talk large proportions, e.g. *99 out of 100.*

worth/value

✘	✔
The museum is certainly worth to see.	... is worth <u>seeing</u>.
The current worth of the property is £100,000.	The current <u>value</u> of the property ...

- **it's worth doing something; something is worth doing.** These phrases take an *-ing* form, not an infinitive.

- **worth** is usually used as a preposition, e.g. *The car is **worth** £100.* The noun related to **worth** is **value**, e.g. *The **value** of the car is £100.*

9 ▶ Water, water everywhere

In this unit you will practise:

- Discussing water resources and water use
- Comparing water consumption for different activities
- Skimming, scanning
- Completing a table; classification; sentence completion; multiple choice

Exam Focus
Speaking: Part 3
Speaking/Writing
Reading skills
Reading: Exam tasks

Lead-in

1 Work with another student to discuss which activity in each of the following pairs uses the most water.

1 taking a bath *80 litre*   3 one day's cooking *20 litres*
  taking a shower *60 litre 5min* one day's drinking *2 litres*
2 washing dishes by hand *5 lt.*   4 washing the car   *450 lit*
  using a dishwasher *35 litres* ─ watering the garden *1 500 litres*

Check your answers on page 217 and write in the number of litres for each activity.

2 The bar chart below shows how much water (in litres) is needed to produce various foods. Use the information in the following sentences to complete the bar graph.

- It takes nearly **50% more** water to produce a glass of **milk** than it does to produce a serving of pasta.
- It takes over **six times as much** water to produce a serving of chicken **as it** does to produce a glass of milk.
- Producing a serving of tomatoes takes **less than a quarter** of the water needed to produce a serving of pasta.
- Producing a serving of oranges takes **nearly twice as much** water as producing a serving of tomatoes.

How much water does it take to produce one serving of:

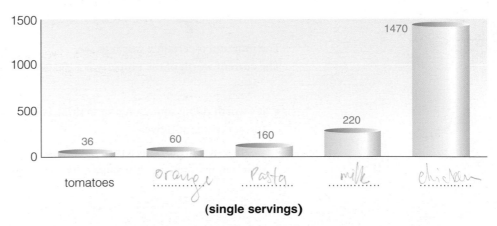

(single servings)

3 Write four sentences comparing the amount of water needed in each pair of activities in Exercise 1.

Begin: *Taking a shower uses …*
or *It takes … to take a shower …*

Refer back to the language of comparisons (pages 33–34) and fractions and percentages (page 67) if necessary.

Focus on speaking *Water issues*

▶ Part 3: Discussion

1 Discuss these points with another student.

1 Do you generally use water carefully or do you use it without thinking?
2 Are there ever any restrictions on water use in your country?
3 What are some of the ways of saving water in the home?

2 Work with a partner to answer as many of these questions as possible. Follow the instructions on page 74 to find the answers to the Water Quiz.

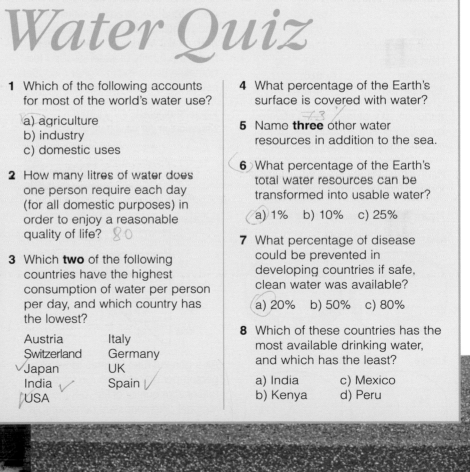

Water Quiz

1 Which of the following accounts for most of the world's water use?

a) agriculture
b) industry
c) domestic uses

2 How many litres of water does one person require each day (for all domestic purposes) in order to enjoy a reasonable quality of life? 80

3 Which **two** of the following countries have the highest consumption of water per person per day, and which country has the lowest?

Austria   Italy
Switzerland   Germany
Japan   UK
India   Spain
USA

4 What percentage of the Earth's surface is covered with water?

5 Name **three** other water resources in addition to the sea.

6 What percentage of the Earth's total water resources can be transformed into usable water?

a) 1%   b) 10%   c) 25%

7 What percentage of disease could be prevented in developing countries if safe, clean water was available?

a) 20%   b) 50%   c) 80%

8 Which of these countries has the most available drinking water, and which has the least?

a) India   c) Mexico
b) Kenya   d) Peru

Focus on reading 1 *Water: Earth's most precious resource*

SKIMMING/SCANNING

Find the answers to the quiz questions on page 73 as quickly as possible by skimming and scanning the following text and tables.

1 Skim the text so that you have a general idea of what it's about. Read the *title*, the *headings* for Figures 1–4, and look quickly at each *table*.
2 Read the first question from the quiz.
3 Scan the text to find the section which contains relevant information, and locate the answer. NB Don't expect to find the exact words in the question. Look for topic words and parallel expressions.

WATER: Earth's most precious resource

Over the last 300 years, world population has increased sevenfold, but water use has increased by 35 times. Since 1950, the amount of annually renewable fresh water available per human being has fallen by more than half.

Figure 1: Contribution to Earth's total water resources in %

Sea	97.3
Glaciers	2.1
Underground aquifers	0.6
Lakes and rivers	0.01
Atmosphere	0.001
Biosphere	0.0006

Although 70% of the Earth is covered by seawater and a further 3% by ice, neither of these is easily transformed into usable water. Less than 1% of the Earth's total water resources is usable for drinking, farming or industry.

Figure 2: Water consumption by sector

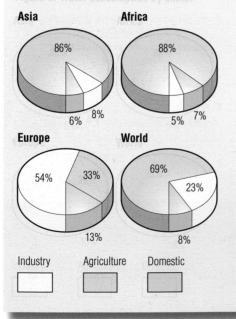

Asia 86% 6% 8%

Africa 88% 5% 7%

Europe 54% 33% 13%

World 69% 23% 8%

Industry   Agriculture   Domestic

While domestic users in rich countries tend to be wasteful in their use of water, regarding it as essentially free and plentiful, they play only a small part in total water use. On the other hand, the quality of water needed for domestic use is much higher than that needed for industry or farming.

Figure 3: Domestic daily water consumption per inhabitant in litres

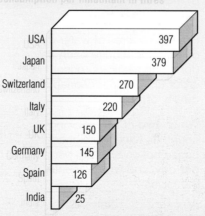

USA	397
Japan	379
Switzerland	270
Italy	220
UK	150
Germany	145
Spain	126
India	25

As a general rule, 80 litres of water per person per day are enough for a reasonable quality of life, but the regional differences are considerable. An American uses 400 litres, while an inhabitant of Burundi may have to survive on 10 litres or less. Consumption is much higher where pipelines are laid than in regions where water has to be carried from a well. Thus the provision of piped water

services – while highly desirable from a health point of view – greatly increases water use, putting a further strain on scarce resources.

Figure 4: Percentage of the population with access to drinking water

USA/Europe 100%   India 75%   Mexico 69%   Peru 58%

Liberia 48%   Congo 38%   Kenya 28%

It is difficult to establish precise figures for access to safe drinking water, but it is thought that 1.3 billion people worldwide do not have this basic service. Not surprisingly, the problem is much worse in rural areas than in towns. Thus 82% of urban areas had access to safe water in 1990, compared with only 63% in rural areas. Dirty water is the world's biggest health risk, accounting for as much as 80% of disease in the Third World. The WHO* estimated that 10 million people were dying annually from polluted drinking water at the beginning of the 1990s.

*World Health Organisation

Focus on reading 2 *The Ecology of Hollywood*

1   The tasks below are based on the text *The Ecology of Hollywood* on pages 76–77. Before you start, look through the reading passage quickly in order to form a general picture.

INTRODUCING EXAM TASKS 1
▶ Completing tables, diagrams, flow charts

2   In this task, you have to complete a table, using information from the text. In this version, you can also write 'not given' if the information needed is not in the text.

TASK APPROACH

- Study the instructions and the table or diagram. Read any headings or labels and make sure you understand the *organisation*. Notice what kind of information is needed.
- Scan the text until you find the first key topic. Highlight it and read the information.
- Make sure you use words from the passage in your answers.

Questions 1–4
Complete the table by filling in the missing information or writing 'not given'.

The table below summarises information about four methods of obtaining water in California.

Project	Los Angeles Aqueduct	Extension to Los Angeles Aqueduct	Colorado River Aqueduct	Californian Aqueduct
Year completed	1913	1940	1	*not given*
Length	2	168km	3	720km
Source	Owens Valley	4	Colorado River	*not given*

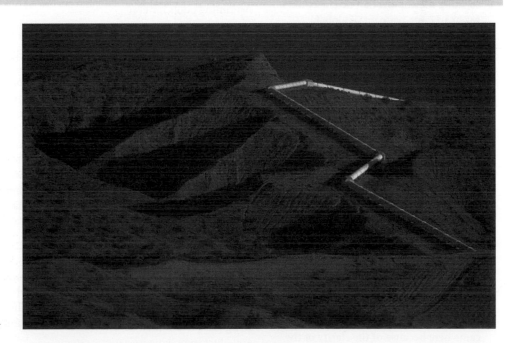

The Los Angeles Aqueduct

The Ecology of HOLLYWOOD

1 Los Angeles is an unlikely city. Built over a major seismic fault, on the edge of one of the world's most inhospitable deserts, the city has developed like the extension of a Hollywood movie set, a sprawling urban fantasy which many people feel should not really exist. Scientists have estimated that the land and water in the area could naturally support 200,000 people, not the 15 million that live there.

2 Since the 1880s, Los Angeles has been transformed from a sleepy cattle town with a population of 4,000, to a seething metropolis that now accounts for nearly one per cent of global greenhouse emissions. It is the car culture par excellence, with nine million cars contributing to the ubiquitous smog and air pollution and 40 per cent of the population suffering from respiratory problems due to vehicle emissions. Surprisingly, LA is now becoming the forum for some of the most progressive environmental thought in the USA.

3 The city is full of contradictions. Often regarded as the apotheosis of consumerism and material extravagance, it is seen as the essence of anti-nature. Paradoxically, people often move to Los Angeles because of nature; attracted by its climate, the snow-capped mountains, the ocean and the beaches. The movie industry came here because of the clarity of the light, the 270 days of sunshine per year and the diversity of location close by.

4 The fantasy has always depended on one fundamental resource – water. No metropolis on the planet has looked farther afield for its supply than LA has, and the fact that there are "no more rivers to bring to the desert" is a cause of much concern. The natural water table was exhausted after four decades in the 1890s. In 1913, when the controversial Los Angeles Aqueduct was first opened, diverting water over 350 kilometres from Owens Valley, chief engineer William Mulholland proclaimed that it would supply Hollywood's lawns and swimming pools for ever.

5 Within ten years, the city needed more. In 1940, the aqueduct was extended 168 kilometres north to Mono Lake, while the following year southern California was able to tap into Arizona via the Colorado River Aqueduct. However, neither supply has been without problems. In 1964, the US Supreme Court settled in favour of Arizona's claim to supply from the Colorado River, and LA's entitlement was reduced by about 50 per cent. And in the 90s, with the water level in Mono Lake falling to dangerously low levels, LA was ordered to reduce its water intake from this source as well. The city is also dependent on the State Water Project, which brings more than a trillion gallons of water per year along the 720-kilometre Californian Aqueduct, supplying irrigation systems for the vast agricultural base of the San Joaquim Valley. This effectively removes half the water that would otherwise flow into the San Francisco Bay area, altering the flow of fresh and saltwater in the Sacramento Delta, with inevitably harmful consequences for fish and wildlife.

6 Almost a third of the water feeding Los Angeles is now obtained by extraction from underground aquifers*. However, a combination of illegal dumping, run-off from commercial fertilisers and leakage from garbage landfills, has left some 40 per cent of the wells in southern California contaminated above federal limits. To compound the problem, half of the considerable winter rainfall, which would permeate the soil and recharge the aquifers, is swallowed by concrete drainage systems and diverted into the Pacific. Since intensive farming methods require around 200,000 litres of water to produce what an average Californian eats in a day, the issue of water supply is never far away. Desperation has led to some ambitious proposals, ranging from a plastic pipeline from Alaska to towing icebergs from Antarctica.

7 What few Angelinos are aware of today is that the city is actually built on a river. The so-called LA river, which stretches 92 kilometres from The Valley down Long Beach, passing through Hollywood studios and Chinatown, is the central natural feature of the city. At one time, it was shaded by sycamores, oaks and willows. However, as the city was paved over, the winter floods created a threat to economic expansion and, in the 1930s, work began to erase the river altogether. "The Army Corps of Engineers built a concrete trough, put the river inside it and fenced it off with barbed wire," explains Jennifer Price, an environmental writer. "The river became the ultimate symbol of LA's destruction of nature."

8 Inevitably, the concrete flood-control system had disastrous ecological consequences, destroying wetland areas which provided an important staging area for migratory birds on the Great Pacific Flyway. The empty concrete channel is now used as an area for training municipal bus drivers to turn around, and it has been suggested that it be used as a freeway during the dry season. Fittingly, it is best known today as the location for Hollywood car chases.

9 However, plans are now underway to restore the river, recreate wetland areas to attract birds, and establish nature walks, cycle paths and equestrian trails. Led by the Friends of the LA River, a pressure group formed by poet and filmmaker Lewis McAdams, the project has pulled people together from government agencies, environmental groups and neighbourhood associations, all working together in what is being seen as a symbolic attempt to heal the split between the population and the landscape of the city.

10 Being a prime example of nature's confluence with human culture, Los Angeles clearly provides the perfect platform to examine this interaction and make progress towards a sustainable urban environment. "If we actually rethought how to retain the water that falls from the sky, we wouldn't be so dependent on water sources hundreds of miles away," says Price. Various initiatives have now been implemented in this vein: a huge waste-water recycling plant has been built in Santa Monica while environmental groups like The Tree People are redesigning drainage systems to collect run-off rainwater from buildings, and redirect it into underground aquifers.

11 There is a feeling of optimism about the future of nature in a city which has always been regarded as being in fundamental opposition to it, leading to a more integrated vision of environmentalism in the 21st century. Those involved with the restoration of LA rivers see it as not only important for ecological sustainability and a way of linking disparate communities but also as being of tremendous significance symbolically. "There is a feeling that if you can fix the LA river, you can fix the city," believes Price. "And if you can fix this city, it seems possible that you can fix any city."

*aquifer: a layer of rock or soil that can absorb and hold water

INTRODUCING EXAM TASKS 2
▶ Classification

3 Classification tasks are similar to matching tasks and require a similar approach. Read the following advice.

TASK APPROACH

- When choosing answers from a list, don't expect to find the same words in the text – look for *parallel expressions*.
- Where more than one answer is correct, you can write them in any order.
- Questions may not be in the same order as information in the text.

Questions 5–10
Classify the following methods of obtaining water according to the problem(s) connected with them.

Method of obtaining water	Problem
Los Angeles Aqueduct	5 ....
Extension to LA Aqueduct	6 .... 7 ....
Colorado River Aqueduct	8 ....
Californian Aqueduct	9 ..E....
Extraction	10 ..D....

List of Problems
A Too much water has been taken from this source.
B Taking water from this source has had adverse effects on the environment.
C The supply from this source proved inadequate.
D Much of the water from this source is impure.
E The amount of water which can be drawn from this source is now restricted.

4 Now do the following exam tasks. Read these reminders before doing the sentence completion task.

- The sentences appear in the same order as information in the text.
- Underline key words or phrases in the questions.
- Check the text, remembering to look for parallel expressions. Think about grammar too: not every phrase can complete each statement.

Questions 11–16
Complete each of the following statements with one of the phrases A–J from the box below.

11 Los Angeles is described as an unlikely city because of its

12 Many LA citizens have health problems caused by

13 LA is unique in the distances from which it brings its

14 Farms in the San Joaquim valley benefit greatly from

15 The water shortage could be relieved by utilising more

16 The LA river was destroyed in the interests of the city's

List of Phrases

A water supply.	**F**	drainage systems.
B trade and industry.	**G**	winter rainfall.
C global warming.	**H**	unpromising location.
D the good weather.	**I**	irrigation systems.
E saltwater.	**J**	exhaust fumes.

▶ Multiple choice

Questions 17–20
The list below gives some of the developments planned for, or recently introduced in, Los Angeles.
*Which **FOUR** of these developments are mentioned by the writer of the text?*

A recycling solid waste

B creating paths for walkers and horse riders

C collecting and storing rainwater

D converting the river bed into a freeway

E forming government agencies

F allowing the LA river to flow again

G providing suitable habitats for birds

H planting a variety of trees

The four developments are:

17 ....

18 ....

19 ....

20 ....

Focus on vocabulary

VOCABULARY MATCHING

> **KEY LANGUAGE**
> Introducing sentences
> ▶ ex. 16, p. 197–198
> e.g. *Inevitably, By and large, Paradoxically*, etc.

1 Use the paragraph numbers in brackets to find expressions 1–5 in the text and study the context. Then match the expressions to their meaning a)–e).

1 support *v* (1)
2 inevitably *adv* (5)
3 to compound the problem *phr* (6)
4 underway *adj* (9)
5 disparate *adj* (11)

3 a) to make the situation worse
5 b) completely different in kind
4 c) now happening
1 d) provide the necessities of life
2 e) as you would expect

DERIVED ADJECTIVES

> **KEY LANGUAGE**
> Forming derived adjectives and nouns
> ▶ ex. 14 and 15, p. 197
> e.g. *constitutional, generosity, computerisation*

2 Many adjectives are formed with a suffix (e.g. *-al, -ic*). Study the phrases from the text and say what topic the adjectives in italics refer to. Paragraph numbers are given in brackets. There is a list of topics to choose from below.

e.g. *global* greenhouse emissions – **global** refers to: the whole world

1 a major *seismic* fault (1) F
2 *respiratory* problems (2) H
3 contaminated above *federal* limits (6) D
4 *economic* expansion (7) A
5 disastrous *ecological* consequences (8) C
6 *municipal* bus drivers (8) G
7 *equestrian* trails (9) E
8 a sustainable *urban* environment (10) B

A trade, industry and the management of money 4
B town or city (as opposed to country) 10
C plants, animals, people and their environment 8
D the government of a town or city or the public services it provides 6
E horse riding 7
F earthquakes 1
G central government (US)
H breathing 2

> ▶ **LANGUAGE FACT**
> Derived adjectives are extremely common, particularly in academic writing. Adjectives formed with *-al* are overwhelmingly more common than adjectives formed with any other suffix.

The LA river – a popular movie location

10 ▶ Hazard warning

In this unit you will practise:
- Discussing natural hazards and their impact
- Describing a sequence of events; expressing opinions
- Labelling a diagram; completing notes; multiple choice
- Describing a process: introductory sentences, marking stages

Exam Focus
Speaking skills
Speaking: Parts 2, 3
Listening: Sections 3, 4
Writing: Task 1

Lead-in

1 a **Work with another student to discuss this question.**

Have you ever experienced any of the natural hazards below?
If so, tell your partner what happened.
If not, say which you'd *least* like to experience, and why.

> *Earthquake   Volcano   Bush fire   Drought*
> *Tsunami   Tropical cyclone   Flood   Landslide*

b **Put the following words under the correct heading: 'Volcano' or 'Earthquake'.**

> *tremor   active   erupt   aftershock   crater*
> *extinct   seismic   fault line   dormant   epicentre*

KEY LANGUAGE
Expressing cause and result:
cause, result from/result in;
lead to, etc.
▶ ex. 17, p. 198–199
e.g. *The Newmarket tornado*
resulted in property damage
worth £1,000,000.

2 **Experts grade natural hazards according to the factors listed below. Which two have the most severe impact do you think? Which one has the least severe impact?**

- length of event
- area affected
- loss of life
- economic loss
- social effect
- long-term impact

You can check your answer against the official ranking of these events on page 217.

'I think they're saying "tsunami" – whatever that means.'

Focus on listening 1 *Predicting a volcanic eruption*

▶ Section 3
▶ Labelling a diagram

You will hear a conversation between two students about an assignment on volcanoes. Before you begin, study the diagram and questions carefully.

Questions 1–10
*Label the diagram below. Write **NO MORE THAN THREE WORDS** for each answer.*

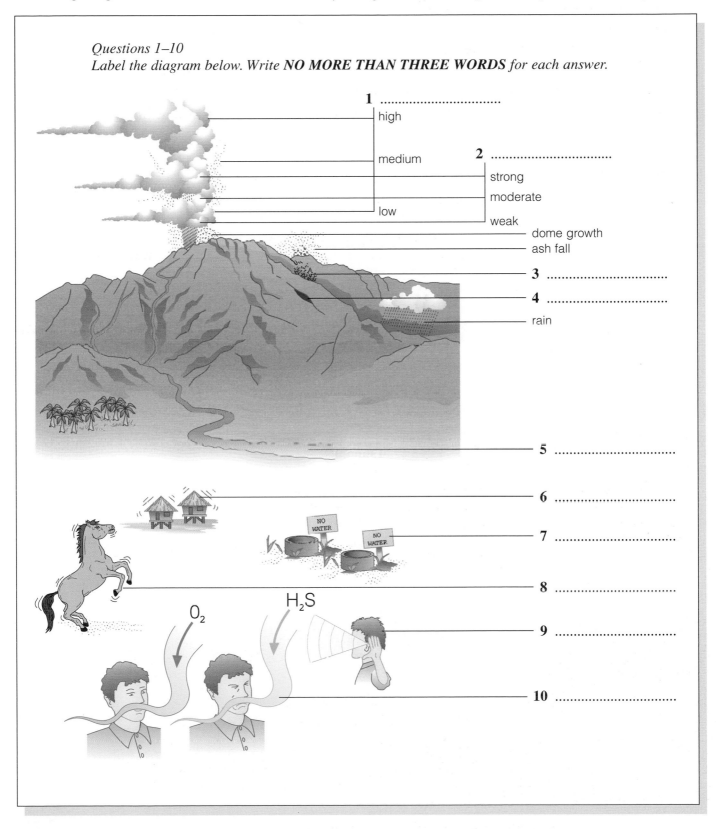

Focus on listening 2 *Tsunami*

▶ Section 4
▶ Labelling a diagram; note completion; multiple choice

Before you listen, look through the questions and remember the approach for each task type.

Listen to part of a lecture on tsunami and answer Questions 1–10.

Questions 1–3
Label the diagram of a water wave below. Write the appropriate letters A–F against Questions 1–3.

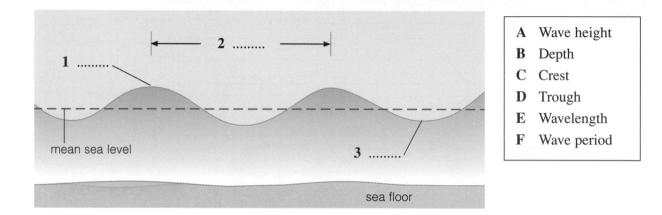

A Wave height
B Depth
C Crest
D Trough
E Wavelength
F Wave period

Questions 4–9
*Complete the notes. Use **NO MORE THAN THREE WORDS** or **A NUMBER** for each answer.*

Tsunamis

Main cause:	4	....
Percentage occuring in Pacific Ocean:	5	....
Typical wave height in open ocean:	6	....
Country where largest tsunami ever was recorded:	7	....
Average wavelength in Pacific:	8	....
Travel at speeds up to:	9	.... kph

Question 10
Choose the appropriate letter A–C.

10 What was the result of the Crescent City tsunami?

    A Many people were killed or injured.

    B Many buildings were flooded.

    C Many high-rise buildings were destroyed.

Focus on writing *Describing a process*

► Task 1

TASK APPROACH:
DESCRIBING A PROCESS

1 Read the following advice on describing processes.

- Study the diagram and make sure you understand how the process works. Look for a point where you can begin your description. Is there an end or is it a cycle?
- Begin with an **introductory sentence**, which summarises the whole process.
- Choose a tense which is appropriate for the topic: present, past or future.
- It may be helpful to divide your description into paragraphs if there are distinct stages in the process.
- Use the notes on the diagram, but try to express them in your own words, where possible.
- Remember to use **sequence expressions** to link the stages.

INTRODUCTORY SENTENCES

2 a Introductory sentences need to summarise a process or cycle as a whole. Look at the diagram of the global water cycle below. Which of the following sentences A–C would serve as the best introduction to a description of the cycle? Why?

A There is water in the clouds and in the sea.
B Water moves in a continuous cycle.
C Snow falls from the clouds to the mountain tops.

The water cycle

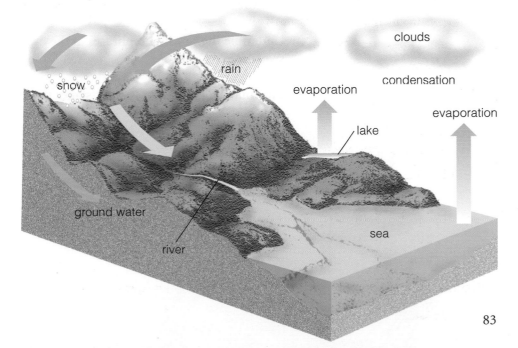

b   Write the correct introductory sentence from page 83 on the dotted line in the description of the water cycle below.

MARKING THE STAGES IN A PROCESS

3   Study the diagram of the global water cycle on page 83 and complete the gapped description below. Use the verbs below in active or passive forms, as appropriate.

> reach   fall   absorb   rise   run   cause   release   blow

The water cycle

....

The heat of the sun **1** .... water to evaporate from seas, rivers and lakes. In addition, water vapour **2** .... from the soil and from plants. As the water vapour then **3** .... into the atmosphere, it cools and condenses into clouds. The clouds **4** .... by winds until they **5** .... high ground. At this stage, the water droplets **6** .... back to earth as rain, hail or snow. After rain has fallen on land, it either evaporates into the air or it **7** .... by soils and plants. Some of it also **8** .... into rivers and lakes and eventually reaches the sea.

4   What tenses are used in the description of the water cycle? Why?

5   Underline the words and phrases in the description which indicate the sequence of events.

6   The following expressions mark stages in a process. Answer the questions.

> First,   Next,   Then,   Meanwhile,   Later,   During this process,   Afterwards, At this stage,   Subsequently,   Eventually,   Finally,

1   Which expressions mark stages which happen at the same time?
2   Which one marks a stage which happens after a long time?
3   Which two would **not** be used in describing a cycle like the water cycle? Why?

GUIDED WRITING TASK

7 Write a short description of the carbon cycle using the diagram and notes below. Try to include several of the sequence expressions on page 84.

Begin: *Carbon is used repeatedly in a process called the carbon cycle.*

The carbon cycle

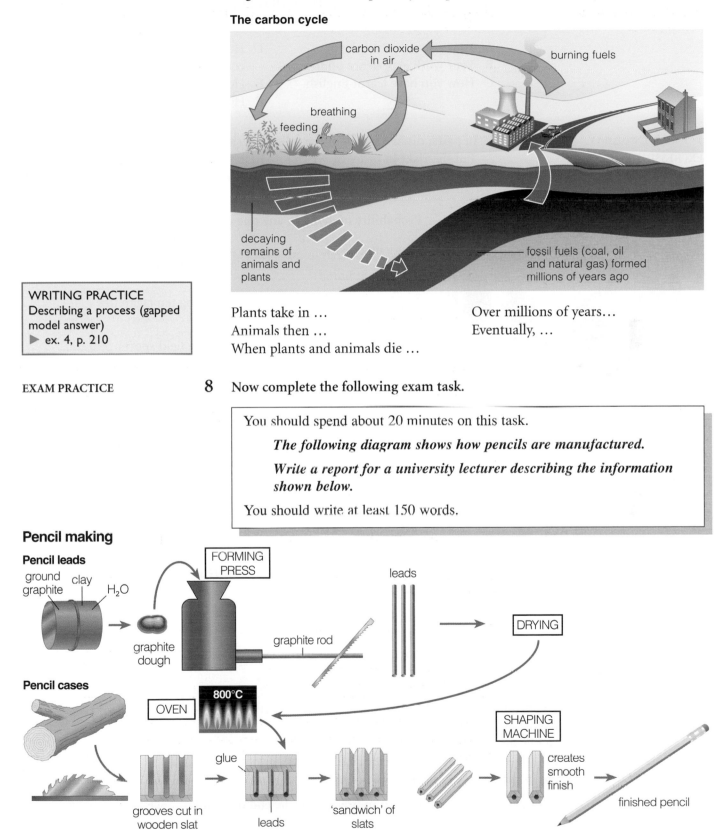

Plants take in …
Animals then …
When plants and animals die …

Over millions of years…
Eventually, …

WRITING PRACTICE
Describing a process (gapped model answer)
▶ ex. 4, p. 210

EXAM PRACTICE

8 Now complete the following exam task.

> You should spend about 20 minutes on this task.
>
> *The following diagram shows how pencils are manufactured.*
>
> *Write a report for a university lecturer describing the information shown below.*
>
> You should write at least 150 words.

Pencil making

Pencil leads
ground graphite   clay   H₂O

FORMING PRESS

graphite dough

graphite rod

leads

DRYING

Pencil cases

OVEN

800°C

grooves cut in wooden slat

glue

leads

'sandwich' of slats

SHAPING MACHINE

creates smooth finish

finished pencil

Focus on speaking *Sequencing*

▶ **Part 2: Individual long turn**
DESCRIBING A SEQUENCE
OF EVENTS

1 Work in pairs. Choose one of the topics below and make brief notes of the stages you need to describe. Then tell your partner about it, remembering to use a range of sequence expressions.

A Your education up to now.
B Your work experience up to now.
C How you have learnt English.

D How you qualify to drive in your country.
E How you arrange a holiday abroad.
F How you plan a party.

▶ **Part 3: Discussion**
EXPRESSING OPINIONS
AND GIVING REASONS

2 a In pairs, discuss which of the following risks are most likely to kill you. Put the risks in order by writing 1–10 in the spaces provided (1 = most probable). Be prepared to give reasons for your choices.

Probability of dying in any one year from various causes			
Accident at work	....	Hit by lightning	....
Accident at home	....	Influenza	....
Accident on road (driving in Europe)	....	Smoking ten cigarettes a day	....
Earthquake (living in California)	....	Playing field sports	....
Floods (living in Bangladesh)	....	Wind storm (living in northern Europe)	....

SOURCE: Coburn and Spence, 1992

WRITING PRACTICE
Expressing an opinion (exam task)
▶ ex. 5, p. 211

b Compare your answers with the table on page 217. How accurate was your perception of risk? What can you say about the risks posed by natural hazards?

Spot the error

Most of these sentences contain common errors, some of which come from *Error Hit Lists.*
Identify and correct the errors.

1 The country is experiencing serious economic problems. (HL10)
2 At first, the machine must be switched on. (HL10)
3 It's more economic to travel by bus than by train. (HL10)
4 News of the event didn't reach the city until several hours after. (HL10)
5 The report has taken a year to complete, but it's available at last. (HL10)
6 Firstly I enjoyed the course, but gradually I began to lose interest. (HL10)
7 There has been an increase of spending on childcare. (HL2)
8 The landslide caused a big amount of damage. (HL4)
9 There was a report about the earthquake on the television. (HL6)
10 It rained every day, and in the end we decided to go home. (HL8)

You can check your answers by referring to the section in brackets at the end of each sentence.
HL = *Error Hit List*

ERROR HIT LIST

economic/economical/financial

✘	✔
Travelling by public transport is easy and economic.	… easy and <u>economical</u>.
Underdeveloped countries need economical support.	… <u>economic</u> support.
He's got serious economics problems.	… serious <u>financial</u> problems.

- **economical** describes something which is cheaper to buy or use than something similar, e.g. *Coach travel is an **economical** alternative to rail travel.*
- Use **economic** to talk about the way a country's money is produced, spent and controlled, e.g. *The Labour party is proposing a number of **economic** reforms.*
- **financial** means 'connected with money'. Use it to talk about the way people and organisations use and control their money, e.g. *The company got into **financial** difficulties; I had to draw up a **financial** plan.*

at first/firstly/first

✘	✔
There are two problems. At first, we have no money.	<u>First of all/Firstly/First</u> …

- **First**, **firstly** and **first of all** introduce the first item in a list or sequence. The next item in a sequence is normally introduced by **then** or **next**, and in a list by **second/secondly**, etc.
- **At first** means at the beginning of an event or period, especially when the situation changes, e.g. *We liked living abroad at first, but we got homesick later.*

at last/lastly

✘	✔
At last, I'd like to thank everyone for coming tonight.	<u>Lastly</u>, I'd like to …

- Use **lastly** like **finally** to introduce the last in a sequence or list.
- Use **at last** when something good happens after a long period of waiting, e.g. ***At last** the government is doing something about unemployment.*

after/afterwards

✘	✔
I left school and went abroad a month after.	… a month <u>later</u>.
There was thunder and after it began to rain.	… and <u>then/afterwards</u> it began to rain.

- When you mention a time in the past that is measured from an earlier time in the past, don't use **after**. Use **later** instead, e.g. *They met in July and married two years later.*
- Don't use **after** on its own as an adverb. Use **afterwards**, **later**, etc. instead. **After** can be used in informal styles in phrases like *immediately after* and *not long after*.

87

11 ▶ Use it or lose it

In this unit you will practise:

- Talking about learning and memory
- Prediction; skimming; scanning; reading for detail
- Multiple choice, sentence completion; matching; True/False/Does Not Say
- Vocabulary: word families

Exam Focus

Speaking: Parts 2, 3

Reading skills

Reading: Exam tasks

Lead-in

1 Study the words on page 217 for exactly two minutes. Then turn back to this page and write as many words as you can remember in the spaces below.

MEMORY TEST: PART 1

1	6	11	16 ....
2	7	12	17 ....
3	8	13	18 ....
4	9	14	19 ....
5	10	15	20 ....

2 Now answer the following questions.

1 How did you get on? Which words were easiest to remember? Why?
2 Does writing things down help you to remember them?
3 What other techniques (if any) did you use to remember the words?
4 If you had to learn another set of words, would you do it differently?

3 Work with another student. Discuss how you normally remember the following:

- things you need to buy
- someone's birthday
- an important telephone number
- what you need to say in a telephone conversation
- things you have to pack for a holiday
- someone's name after you've been introduced
- directions for getting somewhere
- new English vocabulary

Part 2 of the Memory Test comes later in the unit. If you add together your scores for the two parts, you will see how your total score compares with the average for these tests (see page 94).

Focus on reading 1 *Sleep*

PREDICTION

1 Making guesses about the content of a text by looking at the heading, subheading and any visuals will help you read more efficiently.

Look at the newspaper headline below and say what you think the article is going to be about.

Sleep better than midnight oil on eve of exams

NB Headlines often rely on fixed phases and colloquialisms. If you are unsure about the meaning of this headline, look up the idiom *to burn the midnight oil.*

SKIMMING

2 Skim the article quickly to check or correct your prediction. Note that the text below is shorter than an exam passage.

By Mark Henderson
Science Correspondent

STUDENTS who stay up all night to cram for an exam are doing themselves more harm than good, according to research into the link between sleep and memory published yesterday.

Scientists at Harvard Medical School discovered that people who deprive themselves of sleep so that they can study until the last minute are unlikely to remember anything that would improve their performance, while suffering the crippling effects of fatigue.

The scientists found that the brain needs good-quality sleep immediately after practising a task if it is to learn to improve at it. Those who substitute study for sleep, particularly those who miss deep or "slow-wave" sleep, will get little benefit from their extra effort.

Instead, they may perform worse than expected because tiredness is a major cause of poor decision-making.

The findings, published in *Nature Neuroscience*, add to a growing body of evidence that sleep is vital to the learning process.

In the study, a team led by Robert Stickgold, assistant professor of psychiatry at Harvard Medical School, asked 24 volunteers to practise a "visual discrimination task" that involved identifying the orientation of diagonal lines on a computer screen.

Half the volunteers were then kept awake all night, while the other half had a normal night's sleep. To eliminate the effects of fatigue on the sleep-deprived group, both groups then slept normally for two further nights. They were then tested again on the same exercise.

Among the group who slept normally, the volunteers showed a marked improvement. Those who had not slept showed none, despite the two nights of sleep to catch up.

The results, Professor Stickgold said, suggest that a good night's sleep immediately after learning is "absolutely required" to embed new skills in the memory. "We think that the first night's sleep starts the process of memory consolidation," he said. "It seems that memories normally wash out of the brain unless some process nails them down. My suspicion is that sleep is one of those things that nails them down."

From *The Times*

SCANNING

3 Scan the article to find the answers to these questions as quickly as possible.

1 What was the subject of the scientists' research?
2 Where did the research take place?
3 Where can the results of the study be found?
4 How many people volunteered to help with the study?
5 What kind of task were they asked to do?

READING FOR DETAIL **4** Exam reading passages often discuss causes and effects, and you may need to identify and match these in order to answer a question.

Find the relevant sections of the article on page 89 and read them carefully in order to match the causes and effects.

Causes

1 Students stay up all night studying.
2 Scientists have carried out research.
3 Some volunteers stayed awake all night.
4 The volunteers who had stayed awake slept. normally for the next two nights.
5 Some volunteers slept normally.
6 Learning is followed by good night's sleep.

Effects

A They showed an improvement in the task.
B The effects of fatigue were eliminated.
C New skills are retained in the memory.
D They showed no improvement in the task.
E They do not improve their performance in the exam.
F More is known about the effects of sleep on learning.

1 .... 2 .... 3 .... 4 .... 5 .... 6 ....

Focus on reading 2 *Use it or lose it*

► Multiple choice; sentence completion; matching; True/False/Does Not Say

1 Questions 1–16 on pages 91–93 are based on the following reading passage. Glance through the text first before you look at them.

Use it or lose it: keeping the brain young

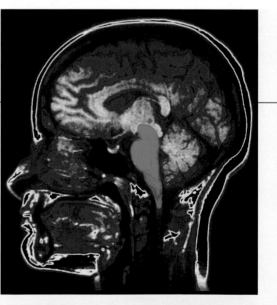

1 You hear the same complaint all the time as people get older: "My memory is terrible." Is it all in the mind, or do real changes take place in the brain with age to justify such grumbling? The depressing answer is that the brain's cells, the neurons, die and decline in efficiency with age.

2 Professor Arthur Shimamura, of the University of California at Berkeley, says there are three main ways in which mental function changes. The first is mental speed, for example how quickly you can react to fast-moving incidents on the road. Drivers in their late teens react quickly but tend to drive too fast, while the over sixties are more cautious but react more slowly. The near-inevitable slowing with age also partly explains why soccer players are seen as old in their thirties, while golf professionals are still in their prime at that age. This type of mental slowing results from a reduction in the efficiency with which the brain's neurons work.

3 The fact that adults find it harder to learn musical instruments than children points to a second type of mental loss with age – a reduction in learning capacity. The parts of the brain known as the temporal lobes control new learning, and are particularly vulnerable to the effects of ageing. This means that, as we get older, we take longer to learn a new language, are slower to master new routines and technologies at work, and we have to rely more on diaries and other mental aids.

4 "Working memory" is the third brain system which is vulnerable to the effects of ageing. Working memory is the brain's "blackboard", where we juggle from moment to moment the things we have to keep in mind when solving problems, planning tasks and generally organising our day-to-day life. Absent-mindedness occurs at all ages because of imperfections in the working memory system – so, for instance, you may continually lose your glasses, or find yourself walking into a room of your house only to find that you cannot remember what you came for.

5 Such absent-mindedness tends to creep up on us as we age and occurs because our plans and intentions, which are chalked up on the mental blackboard, are easily wiped out by stray thoughts and other distractions. Stress and preoccupation can also cause such absent-mindedness, in addition to age-related changes in the brain. The frontal lobes of the brain – located behind the forehead and above the eyes – are where the working memory system is located. Like the temporal lobes, which handle new learning, the frontal lobes are more vulnerable to the ageing process than other parts of the brain.

6 The news, however, is not all bleak. Although neurons reduce in number with age, the remaining neurons send out new and longer connecting fibres (dendrites) to maintain connections and allow us to function reasonably well with only relatively small drops in ability.

7 This and other evidence suggests that the principle "use it or lose it" might apply to the ageing brain. Professor Shimamura studied a group of university professors who were still intellectually active, and compared their performance on neuropsychological tests with that of others of their age group, as well as with younger people. He found that on several tests of memory, the mentally active professors in their sixties and early seventies were superior to their contemporaries, and as good as the younger people.

8 Research on animals provides even stronger evidence of the effects of stimulation on the brain structure. Professor Bryan Kolb, of the University of Lethbridge in Canada, has shown that animals kept in stimulating environments show sprouting and lengthening of the connecting nerve fibres in their brains, in comparison with animals kept in unstimulating environments.

9 The beneficial effects of continued mental activity are shown by the fact that older contestants in quiz shows are just as fast and accurate in responding to general knowledge questions as younger competitors, suggesting that at least part of their intellectual apparatus is spared the effects of ageing because of practice and skill.

10 Such findings lead to the intriguing possibility of "mental fitness training" to accompany jogging and workouts for the health conscious. Research in Stockholm by Professor Lars Backman and his colleagues has shown that older people can be trained to use their memory better, with the effects of this training lasting several years.

11 Just as people go bald or grey at different rates, so the same is true for their mental faculties. Why this should be the case for memory and other mental functions is not yet clear, but physical factors play a part. If Professor Shimamura is right, then the degree to which people use and stretch their mental faculties may also have a role to play.

By Ian Robertson in *The Times*

EXAM PRACTICE
▶ Multiple choice

2   The following question is designed to test your global understanding.

> ▶ **EXAM BRIEFING**
>
> **Reading module, multiple-choice questions**
> When multiple-choice questions have more than one correct answer, they may count as one question or more, depending on how difficult they are. When they count as one question, as in the example below, you need to get all parts correct in order to get a mark.

Question 1

*Which **THREE** of the following are given in the text?*

A   a detailed description of the structure of the brain

B   an account of the effects on ageing on the brain

C   a report about the results of several research projects

D   a description of several methods of testing mental ability

E   an explanation of how mental decline can be limited

▶ Sentence completion

3 In this task, you need to match the causes and effects described in paragraphs 1–8 of the text on pages 90–91. Underline key words or phrases in the questions and scan the text to find information about them.

REMINDER

• The questions are usually in the same order as information in the text.

Questions 2–6
Complete each of the statements with the best ending (A–H) from the box on the right. Write your answers in the spaces provided.

2 As the neurons in the brain become less efficient, …

3 As the temporal lobes of the brain are affected by ageing, …

4 If a person is under stress, …

5 When the frontal lobes of the brain are affected by ageing, …

6 If an animal's brain is kept active and stimulated, …

List of Endings

A absent-mindedness may become more frequent.

B people go bald or grey at different rates.

C reactions become slower.

D new connecting nerve fibres develop.

E the performance of some university professors was studied.

F it becomes harder to pick up new skills.

G older quiz competitors do better than younger ones.

H there is a gradual deterioration in the working memory.

2 ……… 3 ……… 4 ……… 5 ……… 6 ………

▶ Matching

4 This task was introduced in Unit 3. These questions focus on information in paragraphs 7–11 of the text.

REMINDERS

• In the text, underline or highlight each person listed (A–C).
• Read each section quickly and notice where the information begins and ends.
• Choose a section – e.g. one of the shorter ones – and read it carefully. Then look for matching information in the list of achievements.

Questions 7–11
Look at the following people (A–C) and the list of achievements (7–11) below. Match each achievement to the appropriate person.

A Professor Shimamura
B Professor Bryan Kolb
C Professor Lars Backman

7 Investigated the memories of different groups of people.
………

8 Established the effectiveness of memory training. ………

9 Identified a number of areas in which mental function may change. ………

10 Investigated the development of nerve fibres in the brain. ………

11 Did a study including observation of the long-term effects on his subjects. ………

▶ True/False/Does Not Say

Questions 12–16
Do the following statements agree with the information given in the passage?
Write

TRUE   *if the statement is true according to the passage*
FALSE   *if the statement is false according to the passage*
DOES NOT SAY   *if the information is not given in the passage*

Example	*Answer*
As people get older, their brain cells become less efficient.	**TRUE**

12   Absent-mindedness is not necessarily a sign of ageing.   ....

13   Animal brains benefit from stimulation as human brains do.   ....

14   Research indicates that physical training can help to improve memory.   ....

15   Taking part in quizzes is the best way to stimulate the brain.   ....

16   Scientists now understand why people's mental faculties decline at different rates. ....

Focus on vocabulary *Word families*

Complete the following table with the correct parts of speech. Most of the answers appear in the texts in this unit.

Verb	Noun	Adjective
suspect	1	2
decide	3	4
compare	5	6
7	8	long
9	benefit	10
11	ageing	12
13	memory	14
vary	15	16

Focus on speaking *Memories*

▶ Part 2: Individual long turn

1 Work in pairs to do this practice task. Choose one of the following topics and talk about it to your partner for two minutes. Your partner should ask one or two questions at the end.

1 Your first job
2 Getting into trouble at school
3 A prize you won
4 Your first girlfriend/boyfriend
5 Your best childhood friend
6 A difficult journey

KEY LANGUAGE
Articles
▶ ex. 18, p. 199–201
e.g. in Greece, in the UAE at school, at the school

---

2 Choose one of the following topics and tell your partner about changes which have taken place since you were a child. Again, try to talk for about two minutes.

1 Your country
2 Your home town
3 School
4 Holidays
5 Crime
6 Marriage

3 Follow the instructions for the second part of the Memory Test and then check your results.

MEMORY TEST: PART 2

Instructions: Turn to page 218 and study the diagrams for exactly two minutes. Then turn back to this page and see how many you can reproduce in the space. You can reproduce them in any order.

Scoring: Give yourself a mark for every word you remembered in Part 1, and every diagram correctly drawn in Part 2. Add the marks together for your total score.

Your score .... (Average score: 17)

SUPERIOR (upper 10 per cent)	23–32
GOOD (next 20 per cent)	19–22
FAIR (next 30 per cent)	16–18
POOR (lowest 40 per cent)	0–15

▶ Part 3: Discussion

4 Work in pairs to discuss the following questions.

1 Was there a difference between your scores for the two parts? If so, what might this suggest?
2 How important is memory in the IELTS exam?
3 Is it a good idea to 'cram' for an exam, i.e. to try and learn a lot in short time just before the Big Day? Why/Why not?

12 ▶ You live and learn

In this unit you will practise:

- Talking about school, studies and education
- Multiple choice; note completion; sentence completion
- Describing diagrams and tables: identifying key information; avoiding repetition
- Presenting and justifying an opinion: thesis-led approach
- Topic vocabulary and word stress

Exam Focus
Speaking: Parts 1, 2, 3
Listening: Sections 2, 4
Writing: Task 1
Writing: Task 2

Lead-in

1 Categorise the following words according to whether they relate mainly to *school* (S) or *college/university* (U). Check any meanings you're not sure of.

headmaster	lecturer	seminar
professor	undergraduate	fresher
degree	form	thesis
class	lesson	secondary
pupil	tutorial	teacher
detention	homework	campus

2 What's the difference between the following pairs of words?

1 a) term
   b) semester

2 a) department
   b) faculty

3 a) curriculum
   b) syllabus

PRONUNCIATION: WORD STRESS

WE'RE TREATING HER FOR WORD STRESS.

3 Examples A–C show three different word stress patterns. The circles represent the number of syllables, and the large circle shows which syllable is stressed.

A O o   e.g. German, science   ....

B o O o   e.g. Norwegian, computing   ....

C O o o   e.g. Arabic, algebra   ....

Find four examples of each stress pattern from the words in Exercises 1 and 2.

▶ LANGUAGE FACT

Stress in long words
There is a useful rule for words of three syllables or more with the following endings:
-ity -iety -logy -graphy -sophy -onomy -etry -ian -ate
Most of these words are stressed on the second syllable **from the end**.
e.g. *poetry* O o o *society* o O o o *university* o o o O o o

Focus on speaking 1 *Schooldays*

▶ Part 1: Interview

TASK APPROACH

1 Read the following advice about answering questions.

- Make sure you answer the question that is asked, not another, similar question!
- Don't give one-word answers. Give full answers with reasons, if possible, e.g.
  Q: Which subject did you find hardest at school?
  A: Well, I suppose the most difficult subject for me was maths. That's because I'm hopeless at figures. I even make mistakes when I'm using a calculator! So I always did very badly in maths tests at school.

2 Work in pairs to ask and answer questions about the following points.

Student A
1 What / enjoy about schooldays?
2 Favourite subject(s)?
3 How much homework / each night?
4 Worst exam?

Student B
1 What subject / studying/hoping to study?
2 How long / course?
3 Why / choose that course?
4 What job?

> **Useful language**
>
> The (*main*) **reason** I enjoyed … was that …
>
> The (*main*) **thing** I liked / enjoyed about … was …   That's because …
>
> The **best / worst thing** about … was … because …
>
> **One of the problems** about / with … was …

▶ Part 2: Individual long turn

3 Work in pairs, each taking one of the topics below, and prepare to speak for about a minute. Listen carefully while your partner is speaking, but don't interrupt. When your partner has finished, ask one or two questions.

> **Student A: describe a teacher who has had an important influence on your education.**
>
> **You should say:**
>
> > where they taught you
> > what subject they taught
> > what you liked about their teaching
>
> **and explain in what way this teacher influenced you.**

> **Student B: describe a skill you learnt successfully.**
>
> **You should say:**
>
> > what skill you learnt
> > when and where you learnt it
> > how you learnt it
>
> **and explain what helped you to learn successfully.**

Focus on listening 1 *The golden rules of listening*

▶ Section 2

THE REASON WHY WE HAVE TWO EARS AND ONLY ONE MOUTH IS SO THAT WE MAY LISTEN MORE AND TALK LESS.

DIOGENES

1 Discuss the following statements. Say if you think they are True or False, and why.

1 People may resist listening to others who blame or get angry with them.

2 People who have something they can't wait to say are good at listening.

3 Some people listen too much because they're afraid of revealing themselves.

4 Talking is more important than listening.

5 People who feel very emotional about issues make good listeners.

6 People are less likely to hear messages which agree with their view of themselves than messages which challenge those views.

You can check your answers on page 217.

EXAM PRACTICE
▶ Multiple choice; note completion

REMINDER

2 Listen to a short radio talk on the skill of listening and answer the questions below.

• When you have to choose answers from a list of about six or more options, it's especially important to study the list of options carefully in advance.

Questions 1 and 2
Circle TWO letters A–F.
Which **TWO** topics will be covered in the programmes?

A taking notes in a lecture

B taking part in a discussion

C writing a letter of enquiry

D preparing a job application

E understanding body language

F complaining on the telephone

KEY LANGUAGE
Collocations
▶ ex. 19, p. 201

Questions 3–10
Complete the notes below. Use NO MORE THAN THREE WORDS for each answer.

THE GOLDEN RULES OF LISTENING
• *Stop talking.*
• *Make a special effort to listen carefully when situation is* **3** ....
• *Relax – listening less effective when you're* **4** ....
• *Make it clear speaker has your* **5** ....
• *If you need* **6** .... , *explain what you are doing and why.*
• *Try not to let personal prejudices influence* **7** ....
• *Listen with reason and with* **8** ....
• *Your aim is to understand, not to* **9** ....
• *Be aware of what speaker* **10** ....

LANGUAGE CHECK
What is the difference between *affect* and *effect*?
e.g. *The way you're feeling can affect your listening ability.*
Error Hit List, p. 121.

Focus on listening 2 *Making the most of your memory*

▶ Section 4

REMINDERS

> **KEY LANGUAGE**
> *The ... the* **comparatives**
> ▶ ex. 20, p. 201
> e.g. **The older** *you are,* **the more**
> **likely** *this is to happen.*

1 Read this advice on dealing with a listening text.

- Before you listen, read through the instructions and questions.
- Know exactly what you have to do and what you need to listen for.
  Think about the following questions:
  1 How many words do you think you will need to write for each
    question?
  2 What clue do you have about the answers to Questions 3 and 4?
  3 What kind of word (e.g. verb/noun) must follow each Question 5–9?
  4 What is the maximum number of words you can use in your answers?
  5 What answers can you guess for Questions 5 and 6?

EXAM PRACTICE
▶ Note completion; sentence
completion; multiple choice

2 Listen to the lecture and complete Questions 1–10 below.

Questions 1–4
Complete the lecture notes. Use **NO MORE THAN THREE WORDS** *for each answer.*

> <u>The five main memory systems:</u>
>
> Encoding
> 1 ....
> Retrieval
> 2 ....
> Visual

> <u>PQRST stands for:</u>
>
> 3 ....
> Question
> Read
> 4 ....
> Test

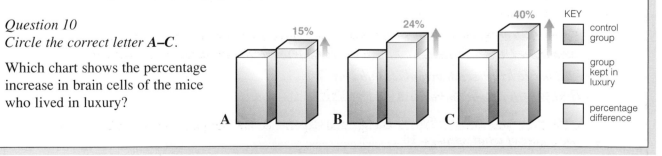

Questions 5–9
Complete the sentences. Use **NO MORE THAN THREE WORDS** *for each answer.*

Before reading an article, you should look **5** ....

When you have read an article carefully, you should **6** ....

'Implicit memory' allows us to learn information without **7** .... to it.

For this system to work efficiently, it is essential not to **8** ....

It is better to test yourself on things you **9** ....

Question 10
Circle the correct letter **A–C**.

Which chart shows the percentage
increase in brain cells of the mice
who lived in luxury?

15%   24%   40%   **KEY**
control group
group kept in luxury
percentage difference

A   **B**   **C**

TASK ANALYSIS

3 How helpful were the pre-listening questions in preparing you for the task?
Did you find some questions more difficult than others? Which ones?

Focus on speaking 2 *Teachers and children*

▶ Part 3: Discussion

Work in pairs to discuss these questions. Make sure you give reasons for your opinions.

1 What's the most important quality in a good teacher?
2 Do well behaved children deserve more of a teacher's attention than badly behaved children?
3 Should a teacher encourage children to treat him/her like a friend?
4 Which is more important for children: freedom of expression or formal correctness?

Focus on writing 1 *Presenting an opinion*

▶ Task 2

REMINDERS

1 Read the following advice.

- Analyse the **key points** of the question.
- Think of ways of **disagreeing** and **discussing implications**. (See page 69.)
- Make a **paragraph plan** so your argument is well structured.
- Use linking expressions to link sentences and paragraphs in a logical manner.

2 a Read the task below. What are your views on the subject?

b Identify the key points you will need to address. Make some notes of the key evidence you will discuss. You will need this later when you attempt the task.

You should spend about 40 minutes on this task.

Present a written argument or case to an educated reader with no specialist knowledge of the following topic.

Too much emphasis is placed on testing these days. The need to prepare for tests and examinations is a restriction on teachers and also exerts unnecessary pressure on young learners.

How far do you agree or disagree with this view?

You should use your own ideas, knowledge and experience and support your arguments with examples and relevant evidence.

You should write at least 250 words.

THESIS-LED APPROACH

3 We looked at an *argument-led* approach in Unit 6 (page 54). Study this alternative model for a *thesis-led* approach.

4 Answer the following questions.

1 What is the main difference between the two approaches?
2 Which approach is more suitable when you agree/disagree strongly with a stated opinion (and can justify your view in some detail)?
3 Which approach is more suitable when your argument needs to be more balanced?

> **PARAGRAPH PLAN**
>
> <u>Opening paragraph</u>
> • Introduce the topic.
> • State your thesis (point of view).
>
> <u>Middle sections</u>
> • Justify your opinion.
> • Start a new paragraph for each point.
>
> <u>Closing paragraph</u>
> • Restate your point of view.

PLAN

5 Prepare a paragraph plan for the task on page 99, based on this approach.

JUSTIFYING YOUR OPINION

6 In Task 2, you may be asked to agree and disagree with a statement. When justifying your opinion, you may need to link ideas using expressions of concession or contrast. Study the expressions in the box and answer the questions below.

Useful language

although / even though
Although she did well in the exam, she didn't get a distinction.
He was arrested **even though** he had an alibi.

despite / in spite of
Despite its poor record, the government was re-elected.
The company's profits have increased **in spite of** the recession.

however
He claimed to be a doctor. In reality, **however,** he had no medical qualifications at all.

nevertheless
It was only a minor accident. **Nevertheless,** there could be serious repercussions.

while / whereas
While things are improving, there's still a long way to go.
Some people favour devolution, **whereas** others are bitterly opposed to it.

on the other hand
The new factory will provide employment. **On the other hand,** it may damage the environment.

---

1 What is the difference in usage between *despite/in spite of* and *although*?
2 Which three expressions are usually followed by a comma?
3 Which expression can be used to balance two facts or ideas when presenting an argument?

7 Complete the following sentences and link the ideas using suitable expressions from the *Useful language* box on page 100.

1 Football hooligans receive a lot of publicity. There are millions of spectators who cause no trouble at all.
2 Many people feel that censorship is unacceptable in a free society. It's undeniable that children need some form of protection from …
3 Medical advances are extending the human lifespan. Not everyone wants …
4 Smoking is known to cause … People have the right to …
5 City life undoubtedly has many advantages such as … City dwellers face many problems, including …

8 Read the following sentences and make the necessary corrections.

1 Nevertheless the economic situation is improving, full recovery is still some months away.
2 Despite I agree with the idea in principle, I can foresee some practical problems.
3 He failed the exam in spite the fact he had studied very hard.
4 Although modern vaccines have helped in the fight against disease, but they occasionally have harmful side effects.

EXAM PRACTICE **9** Now write your answer to the task.

Focus on writing 2 *Diagrams and tables*

▶ Task I

1 Read the following advice.

REMINDERS

- Before you begin, analyse the graph carefully and **identify key information**.
- When writing your answer, **avoid repetition** by varying your language.
- Begin with an **introductory statement** and end by **drawing a conclusion** about any overall trends.

IDENTIFYING KEY INFORMATION

2 Study the chart in the exam task on page 102 and answer the following questions. In which subject(s) did:

1 pupils of both sexes have most success?
2 pupils of both sexes have least success?
3 boys and girls have very similar results?
4 girls have most success? (Percentage?)
5 girls have a much better pass rate than boys? Compare the two pass rates in the subject where the difference between the girls and the boys was the greatest.
6 boys have a much better pass rate than girls? Compare the two pass rates in the subject where the difference between the boys and the girls was the greatest.

AVOIDING REPETITION

3 Think of another way of saying the each of the following. If you need help, look at the expressions in the box below.

1 do badly (in an exam)
2 nearly twice as many
3 achieve a good grade
4 exam pass rate
5 percentage
6 significantly (more, etc.)
7 comparable
8 approximately

> *figure   percentage of successful candidates   roughly   much   get poor results   almost double   equal   do well*

EXAM PRACTICE

You should spend about 20 minutes on this task.

The graph below shows the percentages of pupils who passed their school leaving exams, by subject and sex, during the period 1993–94.

Write a report for a university lecturer describing the information shown below.

You should write at least 150 words.

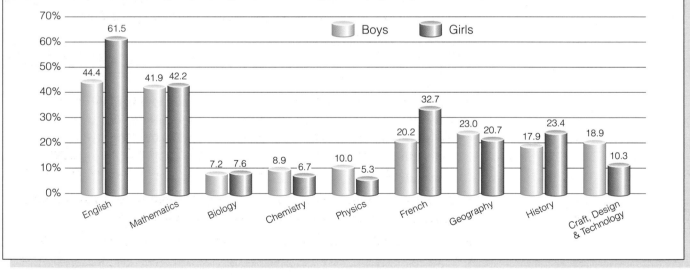

Pupils passing school-leaving exams, by subject and sex, 1993–94

WRITING PRACTICE
Interpreting statistics (guided practice)
▶ ex. 6 p. 211

ERROR HIT LIST

distinction/difference

✘	✔
You must make a difference between visual and verbal memory.	... make a <u>distinction</u> between ...
I've noticed a difference about his attitude recently.	... a difference <u>in</u> ...

- Use the phrase **to make** or **draw a distinction between** when you want to say that two things must be seen as separate and different.

- The noun **difference** takes the prepositions *in* or *between*.

differ/vary

✘	✔
British English varies from American English in several ways.	British English <u>differs</u> from ...
Courses differ about length and cost.	Courses differ <u>in</u> ...

- The verb **to differ** is used to say that two or more things have different qualities or features. It can be used without an object, e.g. *Opinions differ*. It can also take the prepositions *in* and *from*, e.g. *A differs from B. They differ in height.*

- The verb **to vary** is always used to refer to the way several things of the same type are different. It takes the preposition *in*, e.g. *Courses vary in length and cost.*

university

✘	✔
My brother went to the university.	... went to ~~the~~ university.
I hope to study in the university.	... <u>at</u> university.
My sister is in university, studying medicine.	... <u>at</u> university ...
I am a student at a university.	I am a <u>university student</u>.
I am studying physics at University of London.	... at <u>the</u> University of London.

- Notice the prepositions in the phrases **be/study at university** and **go to university**. Notice, too, that these phrases do not include the definite article.

- You can use **university** before a noun, e.g. *a university campus, university studies.*

- Notice the use of the definite article in the two phrases: **London University** and **the University of London.**

make/do

✘	✔
Try not to do too many mistakes.	<u>make</u> a mistake/an error
I made this exercise for homework.	<u>do</u> an exercise/a test/homework
We had very little progress at first.	<u>make</u> progress
Please take an effort to be on time.	<u>make</u> an effort/an attempt
If you make your best, we'll be satisfied.	<u>do</u> your best
We must make the most out of our time.	make the most ~~out~~ of something

13 ▶ Bones to phones

In this unit you will practise:

- Discussing communication systems
- Recognising participle phrases
- Matching; multiple choice
- Comparing and contrasting
- Vocabulary: introducing examples

Exam Focus

Speaking: Part 3

Reading skills

Reading: Exam tasks

Speaking: Parts 2, 3

Lead-in

1 Work with another student. Can you identify each form of communication below?

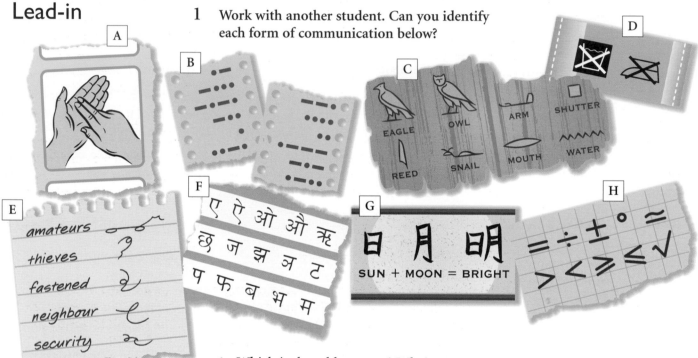

1 Which is the odd one out? Why?
2 What do the most ancient (**C**) and the most modern (**D**) have in common?
3 What other everyday examples like **D** can you think of?

2 a With your partner, put the following inventions in chronological order.

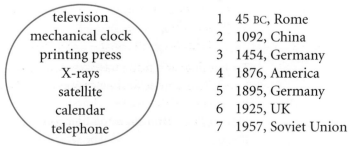

television
mechanical clock
printing press
X-rays
satellite
calendar
telephone

1 45 BC, Rome
2 1092, China
3 1454, Germany
4 1876, America
5 1895, Germany
6 1925, UK
7 1957, Soviet Union

b Which two of the above inventions have been the most significant, and which the least significant, in your opinion?

Focus on reading 1 *Communication devices*

1 Each of the following short texts is concerned with storing or communicating information. Read each text and guess which invention it refers to.

A

This device, first introduced in 1947 in America, did not come into general use until the 1980s. Since then, models have become progressively smaller and lighter, making them far more convenient to use. The original analogue operating system was replaced by digital networks in the 1990s, providing greater security for users. More than 24 million Britons, nearly half the population, now own one, and the device has even become something of a fashion accessory for the young.

B

Invented in Germany in 1500, this useful gadget became smaller and thinner as technology improved. At first regarded purely as 'ladies' fashion', it began to be worn by men after its successful use by soldiers in the First World War. In the 20th century, Switzerland took over from England and America as the dominant manufacturing country.

D

This familiar item of business equipment dates back to 1910, when it was regularly used by newspapers to send and receive pictures. It was expected to become a common household appliance, and millions of dollars were spent on its development in the 1920s. However, it was another 40 years before it came into general office use.

C

This important medium of communication, first became available in Greece in the second century BC, replacing papyrus rolls, which could be up to 35 metres in length. The new invention was far more convenient to use, being both portable and easy to access at any point. Having remained dominant for more than two millennia, it may now be under threat from item E.

E

This has been called the most liberating invention of the late 20th century. Having originated in technology developed in the early 1960s, it evolved through a miracle of international co-operation into the system we know today. Initially used only by scientists, it was released to the public in 1991, and by 1996 the number of users was doubling every 18 months.

Check your answers on page 217.

RECOGNISING PARTICIPLE CLAUSES

2 Participle clauses are short versions of longer clauses, conveying the same meaning more economically. They have the effect of making a text denser, so that it requires more careful reading. This is relevant to the IELTS Reading paper because participle clauses are a feature of academic writing (see *Language fact* on page 106).

The two main types of participle clause are:

1 *-ing* clauses, which have an active meaning.
   - *This was replaced by digital networks, **providing** greater security.*
     (***providing*** = which provided)
   - ***Having examined** the arguments in favour, we can consider the opposing views.*
     (***Having examined*** = Now that we have examined)

2 *-ed* clauses, which have a passive meaning.
   - *This device, first **introduced** in 1947, did not come into general use until the 1980s.*
     (*first **introduced*** = which was first introduced)

3 Underline four more *-ing* clauses and four more *-ed* clauses in the texts above, and say how they could be expressed more fully.

4 Rewrite the following sentences using participle clauses.

1 He produced an essay which was based on information which he had downloaded from the Internet.
2 The paper, which contains the results of the survey, is about to be published.
3 The damage which was caused by the flood will take years to be repaired.
4 Once he had finished his speech, the President answered the reporters' questions.
5 When he realised that he had lost the confidence of his team, the manager resigned.

KEY LANGUAGE
Common verbs in -ed and -ing clauses
▶ ex. 21, p. 202
Participle clauses are also relevant to IELTS writing skills.

> ## ▶ LANGUAGE FACT

Participle clauses in academic writing

- Participle clauses are more common in academic writing than in other written forms, with -ed clauses being the more common of the two.
- The verbs most commonly used in these constructions in academic writing are:
  -ing clauses: *being, containing, using, concerning, having, involving*
  -ed clauses: *based, given, used, caused, concerned, made, obtained, produced, taken*

From *The Longman Grammar of Spoken and Written English*

Focus on reading 2 *Bones to phones*

1 Questions 1–18 on pages 108–109 are based on the following reading passage. Glance through the text before you start.

Bones to phones

Radio survived, the pneumatic mail didn't. Books are still here, but the Inca quipu *aren't. Why do some media die while others live on, asks Margaret Wertheim.*

A With no books, no TV, no Internet, just how did our forebears exercise their minds around the campfire back in Palaeolithic times? One pastime seems to have been bone-notching. Across Europe and the Middle East, early humans took to etching parallel lines and crosses into pieces of bone. Why they did this is still a mystery, though present thinking is that the bones served as tally sticks or even a form of lunar calendar. Whatever their purpose, the bones were clearly important, or they would not have been used for so long – about 90,000 years. "I doubt very much that any form of media we have today will survive that long," declares Bruce Sterling with heartfelt admiration.

B Sterling, a Texas-based science-fiction writer, is a man who should know about such matters. He has spent much of the past five years sifting through the dustbins of history in search of dead media. He and fellow writer Bruce Kadrey are assembling an archive of the dead and dying. Their only criteria are that a device must have been used to create, store or communicate information, and that it must be deceased – or at least down to its last gasp.

C Appropriately, for a project about the transience of media, the Dead Media Project is housed on the Internet. Sterling and Kadrey set the ball rolling, but ultimately it is a communal effort, relying on a cadre of selfless workers around the globe who scour historical sources for arcane, obscure, forgotten and abandoned media. Most of these are not academic historians, just self-professed obsessives.

D At present, the official archive, known as the Dead Media Working Notes, contains more than 400 listings. Take, for example, the *inuksuit* – huge stone relics that dot the Arctic landscape of North America. Their builders, the Inuit, used them as travel guides. By learning the shapes of individual sculptures and the sequences in which they appeared, the Inuit could travel vast distances over unfamiliar ground without getting lost. Then there are the *lukasa*, used by the Luba people of Zaire. These hand-held wooden objects, which were studded with beads or pins or incised with ideograms, were used to teach lore about cultural heroes, clan migrations and sacred matters. Yet the symbols they carried were not direct representations of information, but designed to jog the user's memory.

E In the category called "Dead Physical Transfer Systems", one group stands out – the multifarious systems designed to deliver mail. Pigeon posts have been around for 4,000 years, starting with the Sumerians. More recently, at the end of the nineteenth century, many cities boasted pneumatic mail systems made up of underground pipes. Telegrams and letters shot through the tubes in canisters propelled by compressed air. But perhaps the most bizarre postal innovation was missile mail. On 8 June 1959, at the behest of the US Post Office Department, the submarine USS Barbero fired a missile containing 3,000 letters at the Naval Auxiliary Air Station in Mayport, Florida. The postal service's website quotes an official at the time saying: "Before man reaches the Moon, mail will be delivered within hours from New York to California, to Britain, to India or Australia by

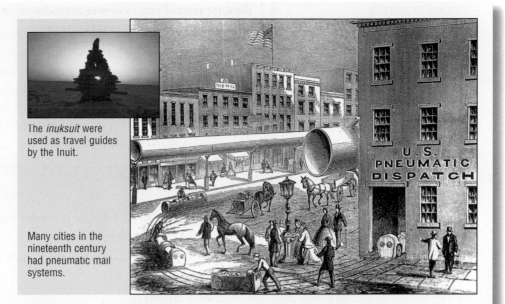

The *inuksuit* were used as travel guides by the Inuit.

Many cities in the nineteenth century had pneumatic mail systems.

guided missile." Sadly, the trial did not spark off a postal revolution.

F With his knowledge of media fossils and what has lived on, has Sterling noticed any qualities that select for survival? "It really depends on the society that gave birth to it," he says. "It helps a lot if it is the nerve system of how government information is transmitted." At the very least, he argues, successful media need a close association with some form of power in society. The Inca *quipu* illustrates the point. The Inca did not write, but kept records on complex arrangements of coloured, knotted strings, some weighing up to twenty kilograms and carrying tens of thousands of knots. These knots were tied by an official class – the Inca equivalents of historians, scribes and accountants.

G Unfortunately, the *quipu* did not survive long, but were burnt by the Spanish invaders. This demonstrates, as Sterling puts it, that media can be murdered. He believes that but for the Spanish, *quipu* could have been taken a great deal further. They are his favourite dead media. "One of the things that really fascinates me is that they were networks," he says.

"They had directories and even sub-directories, and all this just with strings and knots."

H Kadrey has noted another feature of long-lasting media: they tend to be simple. There are systems for sending messages with light, which have been invented time and again, starting with the Babylonians, Romans and Imperial Chinese, who operated a network of fires along the Great Wall. Before the invention of electrical telegraphy, the Russians, Czechs, British and Australians all experimented with optical telegraphy. These attempts may vary in their levels of sophistication but they're all based on the same simple idea. "All a person needs is a shiny thing and the Sun," says Kadrey.

I Another shining example that draws the admiration of both Sterling and Kadrey is that old standby, the book. "I have this argument all the time," Kadrey says. "So many people today claim that the book is dead. I don't believe it for a minute," he says. "It's a very powerful technology. Books are so dumb, just ink on a page, but they've lasted so long!"

EXAM PRACTICE
▶ Matching

TASK APPROACH

2 One version of this task was introduced in Unit 5. In this second version, the headings pick out key information.

- Always study the example, if there is one, to help guide your approach, either looking for the main idea in each section or scanning for specific detail.
- When headings pick out key information, read the first section of the text carefully **before** you look at the list of headings.
- Look through the list of headings and choose the best answer. Make sure you choose a heading which focuses on key information, not a minor detail.

Questions 1–8
*The reading text has nine paragraphs (**A–I**). Choose the most suitable heading for each paragraph from the list of headings below.*

List of Headings

i   It's also possible to destroy media

ii   Examples of unsuccessful dead media

iii An experimental medium which was not developed

iv   A long-lasting but mysterious dead medium

v   The first item collected for the Dead Media Project

vi   A visual aid for teaching

vii How are dead media defined?

viii The belief that this medium is dead is mistaken

ix   Academic uses of the Dead Media Working Notes

x   A design feature shared by several successful media

xi   The importance of a medium's role in society

xii Where the Dead Media Project can be found

1	Paragraph A	....
2	Paragraph B	....

Example	Paragraph C	*Answer* **xii**

3	Paragraph D	....
4	Paragraph E	....
5	Paragraph F	....
6	Paragraph G	....
7	Paragraph H	....
8	Paragraph I	....

▶ Matching   **3**   Refer to the *Task approach* on page 28 if necessary.

Questions 9–15
Look at the following media (A–J) and the list of notes (9–15) below.
Match each note to the appropriate medium.

List of Media

A bone-notching	**E** pneumatic mail	**I** electrical telegraphy
B Inuit *inuksuit*	**F** missile mail	**J** the book
C Luba *lukasa*	**G** Inca *quipu*	
D pigeon post	**H** optical telegraphy	

Example	*Answer*
its inventors were very optimistic about its future	**F**

  9   a widely used system in the 19th century, operating below ground level ....

 10   their meaning depended on their form and the order in which they were placed ....

 11   made only by a certain group in the society ....

 12   may have been used to record years, months and their divisions ....

 13   various experimental systems using the same basic principle ....

 14   a system which has been used for four millennia ....

 15   used as a reminder of aspects of cultural history and religion ....

▶ Multiple choice   **4**   Remind yourself of the three key questions you should ask yourself in choosing
                                    the correct answer. Refer to the *Task approach* on page 45 if necessary.

Questions 16–18
Choose the appropriate letter A–D.

 16   What is the main role of Sterling and Kadrey in the Dead Media Project?

   A   They have collected the majority of the dead media in the archive.
   B   They were responsible for initiating the research.
   C   They are writing a book about the subject.
   D   They travel round the world searching for dead or dying media.

 17   What is Sterling's opinion about the Inca *quipu*?

   A   They represent the most important records of the time.
   B   They were unnecessarily complicated.
   C   They will never be fully understood.
   D   They had potential for further development.

 18   Which medium is mentioned as having been especially long lasting?

   A   bone-notching   **B**   pigeon post   **C**   Inca *quipu*   **D**   the book

Focus on vocabulary *Introducing examples*

1   Giving examples is a useful way of supporting or clarifying statements in an argument. The most common phrases used are *for example* and *such as*, but there are several other ways of introducing examples.

Underline the expressions used to illustrate examples in the following sentences.

1   The archive contains many fascinating media. Take, for example, the Inuit *inuksuit* ...
2   In the category called 'Dead Physical Transfer Systems', one group stands out – the various systems designed to deliver mail.
3   Successful media need a close association with some form of power in a society. The Inca *quipu* illustrate the point.
4   The article discusses a range of dead media: bone-notching, Inuit *inuksuit* and Luba *lukasa*, to name but a few.

2   Add examples to support the following statements, using some of the expressions above.

1   Technology is moving so fast that it's hard for the older generation to keep up with the latest innovations.
2   Mobile phones are undoubtedly useful, but they also have their disadvantages.
3   Not every so-called labour-saving device actually makes life easier.
4   There are a number of concerns about children who spend too long at their computers.
5   There have been many wonderful inventions in the last hundred years.

> **KEY LANGUAGE**
> *Doubt*
> ► ex. 22, p. 202
> e.g. *I doubt very much that any form of media we have today will survive that long.*

Focus on speaking *Comparing and contrasting*

1   When comparing the following methods of communications, what factors would you consider (e.g. *speed, convenience*)?

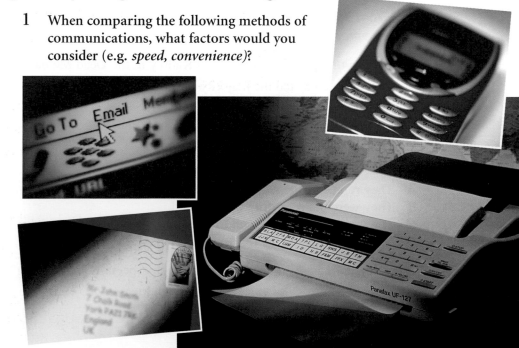

2   Work in pairs to extend this mindmap.

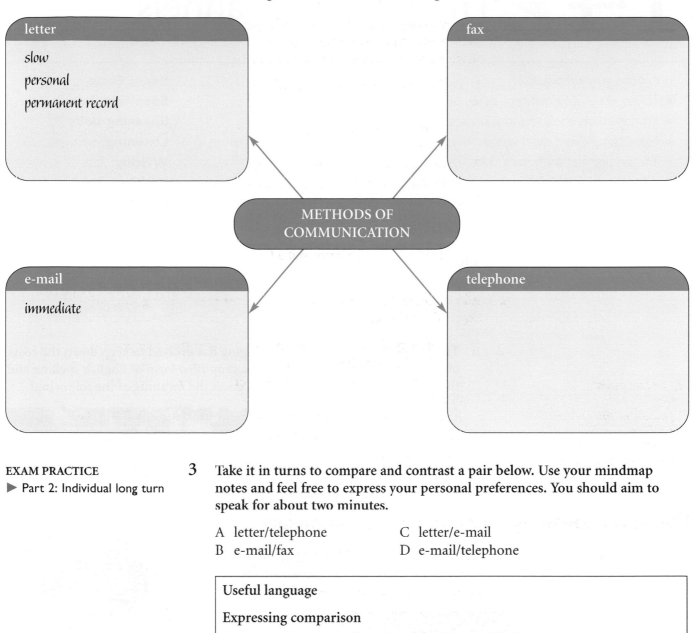

letter
slow
personal
permanent record

fax

METHODS OF COMMUNICATION

e-mail
immediate

telephone

EXAM PRACTICE
▶ Part 2: Individual long turn

3   Take it in turns to compare and contrast a pair below. Use your mindmap notes and feel free to express your personal preferences. You should aim to speak for about two minutes.

A   letter/telephone   C   letter/e-mail
B   e-mail/fax   D   e-mail/telephone

Useful language

Expressing comparison

Both … and …	*Both* letters *and* faxes provide a written record.
as … as	It's *as* quick to write a memo *as* to send an e-mail.
be equally …	E-mails and memos can *be equally* effective as means of communication.

Expressing differences

comparatives	It's slightly *cheaper* to send a fax *than* make a phone call. Letters take a lot *longer than* faxes to arrive.

Contrasting

but / while / whereas	Communication by fax is almost instant, *whereas* letters can take days to arrive.

14 ▶ The proper channels

In this unit you will practise:
- Talking about information media
- Pronunciation: spelling and sounds; silent letters
- Note completion; short-answer questions; multiple choice; labelling a diagram
- Interpreting and presenting data
- Presenting an opinion; opening and closing paragraphs

Exam Focus
Speaking: Parts 2, 3
Speaking skills
Listening: Sections 1, 3
Writing: Task 1
Writing: Task 2

Lead-in

1 Look at the quote. Can you understand what it says? When is this kind of code used?

> GV A MN A FSH N U FD
> HM 4 A DY TCH A MN 2 FSH
> N U FD HM 4 A LFTM.
> MAO ZEDONG

2 a The modified spelling of text-messaging has evolved to keep down the costs of using mobile phones. It relies on a simplified form of English spelling and the use of certain symbols. Can you guess the meaning of the following?

1 THRU
2 2MORO
3 THNQ
4 WILSPK 2U
5 CUL8R

b Another way of expressing yourself electronically is through the use of 'emoticons'. Do you know what the following emoticon symbols mean? If you don't, can you guess?

1 :-) 2 :-(3 ;-) 4 :-/ 5 :-@

PRONUNCIATION:
SILENT LETTERS

3 a How is the word *thru* in Exercise 2a above normally spelt? Which letters are silent, i.e. not pronounced?

b Most of the following words have silent letters. Circle them.

answer	combat	island	muscle
behind	doubt	ignorant	psychologist
calm	golfer	knife	receipt
climb	half	listen	wrist

If you are not sure, look the word up in a dictionary.

PRONUNCIATION: SOUNDS

4 Good dictionaries use phonemic symbols to show the pronunciation of a word. For example:

/ɑː/   is the sound in *hard*
/ɒ/   is the sound in *hot* or *wash*
/ɔː/   is the sound in *poor* or *all*

The letter 'a' can be pronounced in a number of ways. Put the following words in the correct column according to the way the letter 'a' is pronounced.

calm	*half*	*raw*	*watch*
class	*law*	*swallow*	*water*
command	*past*	*walk*	*what*
drama	*quality*	*wander*	
fall	*quantity*	*warn*	

1	**2**	**3**
/ɑː/ as in *far*	/ɒ/ as in *wash*	/ɔː/ as in *all*

Focus on speaking 1 *Communication problems*

1 Look at the following extracts A–D. Take two minutes to read them, then answer these questions.

1 Which forms of communication/technology do they discuss?
2 Which problems do they discuss?
3 Which problem do you think is the most serious?

A Dr Pine said: 'Put simply, the more television children watch, the more presents they want. The lone-viewing data suggests that by watching television with their child, a parent can lessen the impact of adverts, probably by helping the child develop a little healthy scepticism.'

B Mobile phones are unlike previous fads because they undermine tradition and authority. There is no way to monitor the wide social circle within which a student might phone at school. Students sense this, hence the attraction of the mobile phone. Justine, 15, who goes to a school in central London, says: 'When I have my phone, I can do what I want.'

C Many managers are starting working an hour earlier to cope with the volume of e-mails. They don't know whether they are relevant or not until they have been opened. If they are away for a day, many managers feel threatened by the volume of e-mails, particularly because an instantaneous response is expected. That puts a lot of pressure on.

D The symbols have evolved to keep down the cost of mobile phone text-messaging and e-mailing, speed up the response time and inject emotion into concise missives.
Teachers say that the new shorthand style associated with e-mails is making their job of improving literacy skills even harder.

EXAM PRACTICE
► Part 3: Discussion

2 Discuss these points in pairs. Try to think of arguments both for and against.
- There are good reasons for children to carry mobile phones.
- Toy manufacturers should be banned from targeting children with their advertisements.
- It's no longer important to learn correct spelling and punctuation.
- E-mail is the most efficient means of communication these days.

Focus on listening 1 *Media survey*

KEY LANGUAGE
Topic vocabulary: the media
▶ ex. 23, p. 203

▶ Section I

EXAM PRACTICE

▶ Note completion; multiple choice

Questions 1–3
Complete the form below.
Write **NO MORE THAN THREE WORDS** *or* **A NUMBER** *for each answer.*

MEDIA SURVEY

Details of Respondents

Respondent No: 6

Name: *Philip*   **1** ....

Age: **2** ....

Occupation: **3** ....

Questions 4–6
List **THREE** *sections of the newspaper that he reads regularly.*
Write **NO MORE THAN THREE WORDS** *for each answer.*

4 ....

5 ....

6 ....

Questions 7–10
Circle the correct letters **A–C**.

7 Preferred TV programmes

    A comedies

    B documentaries

    C dramas

8 Main source of information

    A radio

    B TV

    C newspaper

9 Main use of computer

    A for computer games

    B for coursework

    C for accounts

10 Main use of Internet

    A for sending e-mail

    B for surfing the Web

    C for banking

Focus on listening 2 *Couch potatoes*

► Section 3

**REMINDERS: QUESTIONS
WITH DIAGRAMS**

1 Read the following advice.

- Study the diagram(s) and notice the important features:
  e.g. **heading scale** (percentages, years, etc.) **Key**
- Try to describe the main features in your mind to help you listen more
  effectively.
  e.g. pie charts: *a quarter, just over half, roughly a third,* etc.
        bar charts and graphs: *a steep fall, a steady rise; rose steadily,* etc.

EXAM PRACTICE
► Labelling, multiple choice

2 Complete Questions 1–10 on this page and page 116.

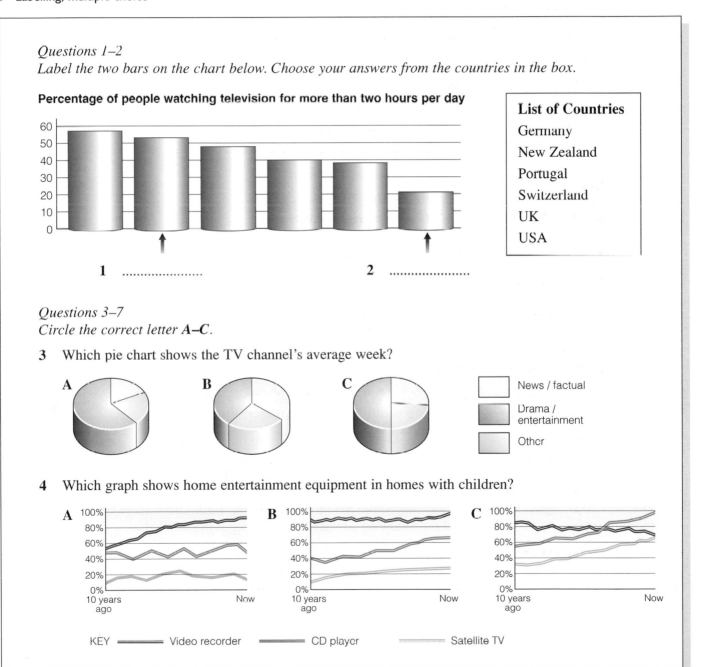

Questions 1–2
Label the two bars on the chart below. Choose your answers from the countries in the box.

Percentage of people watching television for more than two hours per day

List of Countries
Germany
New Zealand
Portugal
Switzerland
UK
USA

1 ....

2 ....

Questions 3–7
Circle the correct letter A–C.

3 Which pie chart shows the TV channel's average week?

A   B   C

☐ News / factual
▨ Drama / entertainment
☐ Other

4 Which graph shows home entertainment equipment in homes with children?

A   B   C

KEY ——— Video recorder ——— CD player ——— Satellite TV

5 Why does Jonathan think that television is so important to children?

   A They don't have much else to do in their free time.

   B They like to watch the same programmes as their friends.

   C It's a way of escaping from their parents' demands.

6 How many British children have televisions in their bedrooms?

   A less than half

   B about half

   C more than half

7 How many British children have access to computers in their bedrooms?

   A less than half

   B about half

   C more than half

Questions 8–10
*Circle **THREE** letters A–F.*
What **THREE** reasons did children give for not reading books?

A Not interesting   **E** Information is out of date

B Too expensive   **F** Too much effort

C Parents don't buy books   **G** Not enough pictures

D Not fashionable

Focus on writing 1 *Dealing with different data*

INTERPRETING AND
PRESENTING DATA

You will sometimes have to present information from more than one diagram. Read the following advice before you begin the task below.

▶ Task 1

TASK APPROACH

- Study each diagram individually to get the overall picture.
- Be clear about what information each diagram contributes to the subject.
- Look for opportunities to compare data *between* diagrams as well as *within* diagrams.
- When there is a lot of data, be very selective in deciding what to report.

NB Try not to use the exact words of the question. (See page 102.) How else could you say *between 1987 and 1997* or *where people got news*, for example?

> You should spend about 20 minutes on this task.
>
> ***The graphs below show where people first got their news, both about the world and about local events, between 1987 and 1997.***
>
> ***Prepare a report for a university lecturer describing the information shown below.***
>
> You should write at least 150 words.

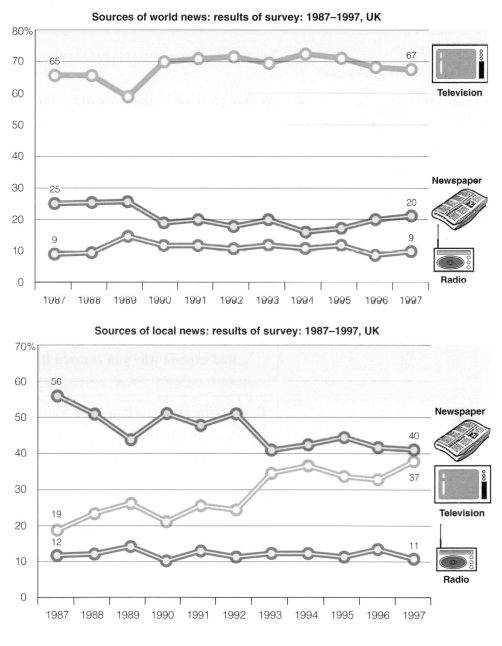

Figures do not include other sources or people who responded 'Don't know'.

Focus on speaking 2 *The Internet*

1 **In pairs, discuss the following questions.**

1 If you use the Internet, which reasons do you use it for most? If you don't use the Internet yet, which applications would you find most useful?

e-mail	*news / current affairs*
financial information	*random surfing*
hobbies / interests	*shopping*
movie information	*sports reports*
music information	*work / school research*

2 In a survey, there were four top reasons mentioned by over 80 per cent of Internet users. Which do you think they are?

You can check your answers to Question 2 on page 217.

EXAM PRACTICE
▶ Part 2: Individual long turn

REMINDERS

2 **Work in pairs, each taking one of the topics below.**

- Spend a few moments thinking about what you're going to say, perhaps using a mindmap to make notes. Then tell your partner about your topic for one to two minutes.
- Listen carefully while your partner is speaking but don't interrupt. When your partner has finished, ask one or two brief questions.

A Describe a book you enjoyed reading.

> **You should say:**
>
> > **what the book was**
> > **what it was about**
> > **when you read it**
>
> **and explain why you enjoyed it.**

B Describe an important letter you received.

> **You should say:**
>
> > **who the letter was from**
> > **what it was about**
> > **why it was important**
>
> **and explain how you felt about it.**

Focus on writing 2 *Beginning and ending*

OPENING PARAGRAPHS

1 Your opening paragraph makes an immediate impression on the examiner, so it's important that it's clear, well constructed and appropriate. Before you can write your first paragraph, you need to:

- analyse the question
- decide how you are going to tackle your answer
- make a paragraph plan

In your opening paragraph, you will need to provide a general introduction to the topic for a non-expert reader. Depending on the approach to structure you choose (see Units 6 and 12), you may or may not need to state your point of view in your opening paragraph.

INTRODUCING THE TOPIC

2 Look at the following topic and read three students' introductions A–C. Then answer Questions 1–3.

> *Does television have a beneficial or a harmful influence on children?*

A

Television was one of the most important inventions of the 20th century. Early sets only had small black and white screens, but later colour TVs became common, and nowadays you can even buy pocket-sized sets to carry with you.

B

Research shows that young people can be influenced by watching violence on television. For example, a 14-year-old killed a number of his classmates after watching the film 'Terminator'.

C

It is undeniable that television, like the Internet, can be a powerful educational tool. On the other hand, there are a number of reasons to be concerned about the effect it can have on children.

1 Which introduction begins with a specific example rather than a general overview?
2 Which introduction presents a balanced view of the issues involved?
3 Which introduction fails to address the essay topic?

STATING YOUR POINT
OF VIEW

3 In a thesis-led argument, you will need to give a clear indication of your general response to the topic in your opening paragraph. Which of the following, A–C, gives the clearest indication of the writer's overall opinion?

A

There are various conflicting views about the effects of television on the viewer, and I intend to give a brief outline of the main arguments.

B

Many people believe that television has a negative impact on children, but my view is that, like any other medium, it can have a positive and powerful effect.

C

One of the arguments in favour of television is that it can be a powerful educational tool, and there is certainly some evidence for this.

CLOSING PARAGRAPHS

4 Your final paragraph should briefly summarise the main points of your argument and give a conclusion that's clear and convincing to the reader.

> **Useful language**
>
> In conclusion,   To sum up,   To summarise,
> In the last analysis,   On balance,

Read these closing paragraphs for the topic on page 119 and answer Questions 1–3.

A
From my point of view, the government should also introduce more programmes specifically designed for children to watch.

B In conclusion, TV sometimes brings good things for children to watch, such as general knowledge and news, but most children are not interested in these things.

C *To sum up, children need to be exposed to television because it is part of our cultural life, but they should be supervised until they are old enough to make judgements about what they watch.*

1 Which paragraph introduces unnecessary (and probably irrelevant) information?
2 Which paragraph brings the writing to an abrupt ending?
3 Which paragraph provides a thoughtful and balanced conclusion?

EXAM PRACTICE
▶ **Task 2**

5 You should spend about 40 minutes on this task.

> Present a written argument or case to an educated reader with no specialist knowledge of the following topic.
>
> ***According to a recent study, the more time people use the Internet, the less time they spend with real human beings. Should we worry about the effect this is having on social interaction or should we see the Internet as a way of opening up new communication possibilities worldwide?***
>
> ***What are your views?***
>
> You should use your own ideas, knowledge and experience and support your arguments with examples and relevant evidence.
>
> You should write about 250 words.

ERROR HIT LIST

news/media/press

✘	✔
The news are no better today.	The news <u>is</u> no better today.
There's a news that will interest you.	There's <u>a piece of</u> news that …
Television is a powerful media.	Television is a powerful <u>medium</u>.
Several reports have appeared in press.	… in <u>the</u> press.

- **the news** is an uncountable noun. To refer to specific information, use *a news item, a piece of news* or *an item of news*.

- **the media** refers to all the organisations which provide information, especially the newspapers, television and radio. It takes a definite article and can be followed by a singular or plural verb. The singular of **media** is **medium**.

- **the press** refers to all newspapers and reporters, considered as a single group. It takes a definite article and can be followed by a singular or plural verb. **in the press** = in the newspapers.

after all/finally

✘	✔
After all, I would like to sum up the arguments …	<u>Finally</u>, I would like to sum up …
They fought the case for years, but after all they lost.	… <u>in the end</u> they lost.

- Don't use **after all** to introduce the final point. Use *finally/lastly*.

- Don't use **after all** to mean 'after a long period of time'. Use *in the end/eventually*.

- **After all** can be used to remind someone of a fact they should consider, e.g. *I think we have every right to protest. **After all**, we live in a democracy.*

affect/effect

✘	✔
The ageing process effects the memory.	The ageing process <u>affects</u> …
Smoking can have a serious effect to the health.	… can have a serious effect <u>on</u> …

- **affect** is a verb meaning 'to have an effect on something'.

- The noun **effect**, meaning 'change' or 'result', takes the preposition **on**.

- The verb **effect** is very formal and means 'cause to happen', e.g. *The new law is designed to **effect** a change in employment.*

15 ▶ Beyond gravity

In this unit you will practise:

- Discussing space exploration and space tourism
- Predicting; skimming/scanning
- Multiple choice; matching; True/False/Does Not Say; labelling a diagram
- Vocabulary: parts of speech; word partners

Exam Focus
Speaking: Part 3
Reading skills
Reading: Exam tasks

Lead-in

Do this quiz with another student.

1 When was the launch of the first artificial satellite?

    a) 1948   b) 1957   c) 1961

2 Which country sent the first man into space?

    a) USA   b) Soviet Union   c) China

3 Which event in 1969 was watched on television by one-third of the world's population?

4 By the year 2000, how many people had travelled into space?

    a) 100   b) 200   c) 300

5 Unmanned spacecraft have landed on two planets. Which ones?

6 Which three of the following have taken part in space exploration?

    a) Skylab   b) Soya 10
c) Space Shuttle   d) Tourist 1   e) Mir
    f) Wobble Space Telescope

7 What is the longest continuous time a human being has spent in space so far?

    a) 57 days   b) 227 days   c) 437 days

8 Pegasus, launched in 1990, was the smallest and cheapest US rocket to date. What was the budget for its development?

    a) $10 million   b) $45 million
    c) $300 million

9 Each space mission releases tonnes of polluting gas into the atmosphere. True or False?

You can check your answers on page 217.

Focus on speaking *The final frontier*

1 Read the extracts below and discuss the questions which follow with a partner.

A

SPACE FOR SALE

Dennis Tito, 59, a former US space station engineer and multimillionaire, has become the globe's first space tourist. He blasted off from the Baikonur Cosmodrome in Kazakhstan, with two Russian cosmonauts, aboard a giant Soyuz rocket. "The citizen explorer", as he was called, paid $20 million for a week's all-inclusive holiday on the creaky Mir space station. (Shopping: limited; menus: dull; excursions: none.)

B

The Ultimate Adventure

"I am the most enthusiastic supporter of space tourism and I hope it will happen whilst I am still around," says former Apollo astronaut, Buzz Aldrin who, more than 30 years ago, walked on the Moon. On his website, Aldrin insists that "space tourism is the next evolutionary step in the adventure tourism market". He talks of his plans for a place which people could visit in orbit, "a container, a habitat, a hotel – in time some word will emerge that best describes what I mean. Maybe Star Lodge. I like that term."

1 What is the common theme in the two texts?
2 What's your opinion of Dennis Tito's holiday?
3 If money were no object, would you want to be a 'citizen explorer'?
4 Do you believe that space tourism will become a reality in the next 20 years?

EXAM PRACTICE
▶ Part 3: Discussion

2 Discuss the following questions in pairs.

1 How do you feel about the idea that people may soon be living in colonies in space? Would you like to be one of the pioneers? Why/Why not?
2 Some people say that space exploration is a waste of money. Do you agree or not? If so, how do you think the money should be spent?
3 What qualities do you think would be required of a space traveller?

Focus on reading *Surviving in space*

PREDICTING

1 Read the headline and subtitle of the text on page 124. Then, with another student, discuss the possible health risks astronauts could face during long space missions.

SKIMMING/SCANNING

2 Look through the text fairly quickly to find the general areas of risk that are mentioned. Compare your findings with another student.

> **KEY LANGUAGE**
> *-ing* forms vs infinitive
> ▶ ex. 24, p. 203–204
> e.g. *To get answers, Goldin established the NSBRI. Understanding their biological effects ...*

Surviving in Space

A voyage to Mars may be every astronaut's dream,
but the health risks are formidable.

By MICHAEL E. LONG

Motion sickness afflicts more than two-thirds of all astronauts upon reaching orbit, even veteran test pilots who have never been airsick. Though everyone recovers after a few days in space, body systems
5 continue to change. Deprived of gravity information, a confused brain engenders visual illusions. Body fluids surge to chest and head. The heart enlarges slightly, as do other organs. Sensing too much fluid, the body begins to excrete it, including calcium, electrolytes and blood
10 plasma. The production of red blood cells decreases, rendering astronauts slightly anaemic. With the loss of fluid, legs shrink. Spinal discs expand, and so does the astronaut – who may gain five centimetres and suffer backache. Though the process may sound terrible,
15 astronauts adjust to it, come to enjoy it and seem no worse for wear – at least for short missions such as space shuttle flights that last a week or two.

During longer flights, however, physiology enters an unknown realm. As director of Russia's Institute for
20 Biomedical Problems from 1968 to 1988, Oleg Gazenko watched cosmonauts return from long flights unable to stand without fainting, needing to be carried from the spacecraft. "We are creatures of the Earth," Gazenko told me. "These changes are the price of a ticket to space."

25 Americans, returning from months-long flights on Mir, the Russian space station, also paid the price, suffering losses in weight, muscle mass and bone density. NASA geared up to see how – even if – humans would survive the most demanding of space ventures, a mission to Mars, which
30 could last up to three years. "We don't even know if a broken bone will heal in space," said Daniel Goldin, NASA's administrator. To get answers, in 1997 Goldin established the National Space Biomedical Research Institute (NSBRI), a consortium of experts from a dozen leading universities
35 and research institutes. NSBRI will study biomedical problems and by 2010 will present NASA with a "go" or "no go" recommendation on a Mars mission.

Jeffrey Sutton, leader of the medical systems team at the NSBRI, has treated the head trauma, wounds, kidney stones
40 and heart rhythm irregularities that one could encounter on the way to Mars. On the spacecraft he envisions, Mars-bound in the year, say, 2018, there may lurk harmful bacteria or carbon monoxide. No problem. The deadly substances will be detected by smart sensors – microprocessors no
45 bigger than a thumbnail – that roam autonomously through the spacecraft, communicating their finds to a computer that warns the crew.

To cope with infection, Sutton plans a factory to make drugs, even new ones, to cope with possible organisms on
50 Mars. Miniature optical and ultrasound devices will image body and brain, while a small X-ray machine keeps track of any bone loss. Smart sensors embedded in clothing will monitor an astronaut's vital functions. The crew will be able to craft body parts, Sutton says, precisely tooled to an
55 astronaut's personal anatomy and genome stored in computer memory. Researchers are building artificial liver, bone and cartilage tissue right now.

Lying in wait beyond the Earth's atmosphere, solar radiation poses additional problems. Coronal mass ejections
60 fling billions of tons of electrically charged gas into space, relegating Earth's volcanic eruptions to mere hiccups. Nevertheless, NASA officials are confident that accurate monitoring will warn astronauts of such events, allowing the crew to take refuge in an area where polyethylene shielding
65 will absorb the radiation.

A second kind of radiation, cosmic rays from the Milky Way or other galaxies, is a more serious threat – possessing too much energy, too much speed for shielding to be effective. "There's no way you can avoid them," says Francis
70 Cucinotta, manager of NASA's Johnson Space Centre. "They pass through tissue, striking cells and leaving them unstable, mutilated or dead. Understanding their biological effects is a priority."

Another major concern is the psychological health of astronauts. And there's a new stressor on a three-year Mars Mission – people, other members of the crew. NASA found that the stresses of isolation and confinement can be brought on rapidly simply by giving people few tasks. Mir astronaut Andrew Thomas described how six astronauts were confined in a 12-foot square room for a week. "If you give them little to do, stress can be achieved in a couple of days," says Thomas.

Will NSBRI meet Daniel Goldin's 2010 deadline for a decision on Mars? "Yes, we will, perhaps even before. We're very confident," says Laurence Young, the director of NSBRI. Meanwhile, some of NSBRI's research may bear fruit on Earth. The institute has made one discovery that promises to save many people at risk of sudden cardiac death, usually brought on by a heart-rhythm disturbance called ventricular fibrillation. This kills 225,000 people in the US each year.

Richard Cohen, head of the NSBRI cardiovascular team, explained that zero gravity may – emphasising "may" – incite this condition in astronauts. So the team invented a non-invasive diagnostic device that measures extremely tiny changes in heart rhythm. The team found that the device can be used as part of a standard stress test to identify patients at risk. Then pacemaker-like devices can be implanted to regulate the rhythm anomalies. "This technology has the potential to save hundreds of thousands of lives," says Cohen. "NASA can be proud."

Such discoveries are no accident, says Michael E. DeBakey, a cardiovascular surgeon who has saved many hearts himself. "The key word is research. When I was a medical student and a patient came to the hospital with a heart attack, things were mostly a matter of chance. Today there's a better than 95 per cent chance of surviving. Now that all comes from research. The unfortunate thing is that there are people, even some scientists, who look at the money that goes to NASA and say we could use that money to support our work. That's very short-sighted. The more research that's done in any area of science, the better off everyone is going to be."

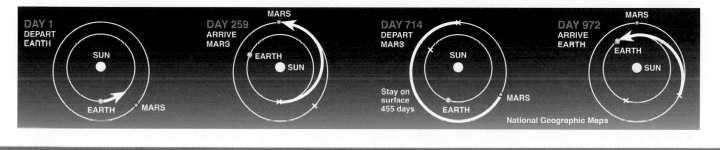

National Geographic

EXAM PRACTICE
▶ True/False/Does Not Say

3 Now complete the four tasks in this section.

Questions 1–6
Do the following statements agree with the information in the passage?
Write

TRUE	*if the statement is true according to the passage*
FALSE	*if the statement is false according to the passage*
DOES NOT SAY	*if the information is not given in the passage*

1 Everyone who travels in space suffers from feelings of motion sickness initially. ....
2 Astronauts are likely to increase in height while in space. ....
3 It's important for astronauts to exercise in order to keep their muscles fit. ....
4 Scientists have found a way of protecting astronauts from solar radiation. ....
5 If astronauts are given tasks to do, they quickly begin to suffer from stress. ....
6 Scientists aim to develop technology that can recognise psychological states. ....

▶ Multiple choice

REMINDER
- Make sure there is evidence in the text for the options you choose.

Questions 7–9
According to the text, which **THREE** *of the following are part of the role of the*
National Space Biomedical Research Institute (NSBRI)?

A To develop technology for monitoring astronauts' health in space.
B To study the effects of weightlessness during short space missions.
C To advise NASA on whether to launch a future Mars mission or not.
D To improve the design of spacecraft in order to reduce the risk of injury to astronauts.
E To assess and select suitable astronauts for long space flights.
F To find ways of dealing with medical emergencies on board a spacecraft.

7 .... **8** .... **9** ....

▶ Labelling a diagram

REMINDERS
- Study the instructions and the diagram, including any labels that are given. Think about the information which is missing. Can you make any guesses?
- Scan the text until you find each topic, and study the information carefully.
- Make sure you use exact words from the passage in your answers.

Questions 10–12
Complete the diagrams.
Choose **NO MORE THAN THREE WORDS** *from the passage for each answer.*

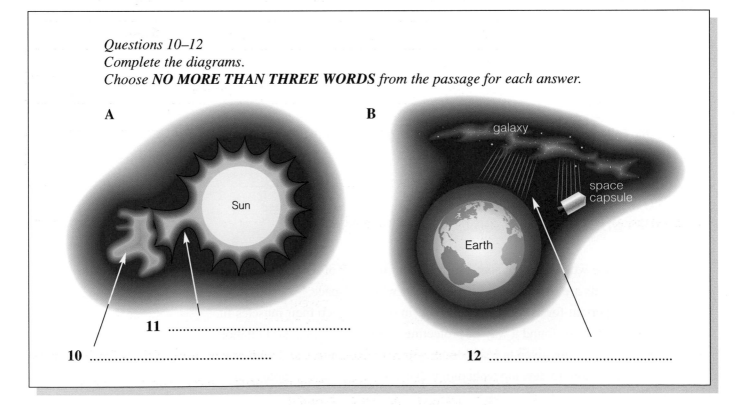

A

Sun

11 ....

10 ....

B

galaxy

space capsule

Earth

12 ....

▶ Matching

REMINDERS
- In the text, underline or highlight the experts listed.
- In the list of opinions, underline or highlight key words and phrases.

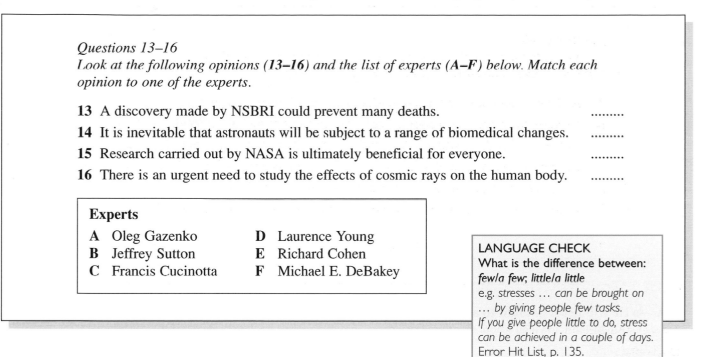

Questions 13–16
*Look at the following opinions (**13–16**) and the list of experts (**A–F**) below. Match each opinion to one of the experts.*

13 A discovery made by NSBRI could prevent many deaths. ....

14 It is inevitable that astronauts will be subject to a range of biomedical changes. ....

15 Research carried out by NASA is ultimately beneficial for everyone. ....

16 There is an urgent need to study the effects of cosmic rays on the human body. ....

Experts

A	Oleg Gazenko	**D**	Laurence Young
B	Jeffrey Sutton	**E**	Richard Cohen
C	Francis Cucinotta	**F**	Michael E. DeBakey

LANGUAGE CHECK
What is the difference between:
few/a few; little/a little
e.g. *stresses … can be brought on … by giving people few tasks.*
If you give people little to do, stress can be achieved in a couple of days.
Error Hit List, p. 135.

Focus on vocabulary

PARTS OF SPEECH

1 Complete the table by adding the noun form of the following verbs.

Verb	Noun	Verb	Noun
1 expand		6 confine	
2 adapt		7 survive	
3 adjust		8 invest	
4 dense		9 disturb	
5 renew		10 diagnose	

WORD PARTNERS

2 Say what the following adjectives refer to or are connected with, e.g. *aural = the sense of hearing.*

1 optical 5 physiological 9 gastric
2 solar 6 cardiac 10 orthopaedic
3 cosmic 7 psychological
4 astronomical 8 psychiatric

3 Match each adjective from Exercise 2 with one or more of the following nouns.

eclipse warfare illusion telescope arrest ulcer surgeon illness
rays features profiling hospital

16 ▶ Falling forward

> In this unit you will practise:
> - Talking about the future/predictions
> - Note completion; multiple choice; labelling a diagram; completing a table
> - Explaining how something works; describing function/structure
> - Presenting an opinion; summarising sentences
>
> **Exam Focus**
> **Speaking:** Parts 1–3
> **Speaking skills**
> **Listening:** Sections 3, 4
> **Writing:** Part 1
> **Writing:** Part 2

Lead-in

1 **Read predictions A–G below and answer the following questions.**

   1 Why were predictions A–D ill-advised?
   2 Why are we bad at predicting the future? Look especially at predictions E–G.

A **❛He will never amount to anything.❜**
(Albert Einstein's high school report, c. 1890)

B **❛We have struck an iceberg, but there is no danger. The ship is unsinkable.❜**
(Captain's announcement to passengers, *Titanic*, 1912)

C **❛Man will never set foot on the Moon.❜**
(British astronomer, 1957)

D **❛I think there is a good market for about five computers.❜**
(IBM chief executive, 1958)

E **❛The Americans may have need of the telephone but we do not. We have plenty of messenger boys.❜**
(British official, 1876)

F **❛No mere machine can replace an honest and reliable clerk.❜**
(Remington company official, on turning down the rights to manufacture the typewriter, 1896)

G **❛There will probably be a mass market for no more than a thousand motor cars in Europe. There is, after all, a limit to the number of chauffeurs who could be found to drive them.❜**
(Spokesman for Daimler-Benz, 1900)

I never think of the future — it comes soon enough.
ALBERT EINSTEIN

2 **The illustration on page 129 represents a typical vision of the future in the 1950s. How accurate was this vision? Answer the following questions by referring to the image.**

   1 Which predictions have failed to come true?
   2 Which aspects of modern life were not foreseen?

Focus on speaking 1 *Predicting the future*

1 Writing in 2001, the science-fiction writer, Brian Dana Akers, made a number of predictions for the 21st century. These he divided into four categories:

A Definite   B Almost certain   C Probable   D Possible

The list below represents some of Brian Dana Akers's predictions. Work in pairs to discuss which of the four categories A–D to put them in. Be prepared to give reasons for your answers.

KEY LANGUAGE
Expressing probability
▶ ex. 25, p. 205–206
It's (highly) likely/probable .../
There's a remote possibility
that .../In all probability, etc.

- Fewer species
- More countries
- Longer lives
- Global warming
- First contact with an alien civilisation
- More city dwellers
- Computers everywhere

- Massive, rapid change
- Nuclear war or meltdown
- Alternative energy replaces fossil fuels
- More people
- Space exploration and colonies in space
- Fewer languages

You will hear how Brian Dana Akers categorised his predictions in *Focus on listening 1*.

EXAM PRACTICE
▶ Part 3: Discussion

2 Discuss these points.
- Are you generally optimistic or pessimistic about the future?
- Do you believe that we will ever contact beings from other planets?
- Do you think computers will eventually replace human workers?
- Do you think that the environment will change dramatically because of global warming?

Focus on listening 1 *Reality or science fiction?*

▶ Section 3

REMINDER

Read the advice on note completion.

- Read through the notes and try to predict the answers – this will help you tune in to the topic and vocabulary so you will be able to listen more effectively.

Questions 1–10
*Listen to the telephone conversation between two students and answer Questions **1–10**. Complete the notes. Write **NO MORE THAN THREE WORDS** or **A NUMBER** for each answer.*

- Immense changes – political, **1** .... , etc.
- Changes caused by forces of demography and **2** ....
- Species disappearing faster than they're coming **3** ....
- **4** .... languages spoken today expected to die out.
- Earth's long-term capacity estimated at **5** ....
- Trend will continue towards **6** .... countries.
- New energy economy theoretically possible by **7** ....
- Space exploration depends on **8** ....
- Countries likely to enter the space race: China, **9** ....
- Factors making nuclear war possible:
  – availability of nuclear know-how
  – number of **10** ....
  – quantity of nuclear weapons

> We try our best to walk forward.
> There is no turning back, there is no standing still.
> Walking is controlled falling. With each step, your foot catches you just in time. Try taking a step at a time in the right direction.
> BRIAN DANA AKERS

Focus on writing 1 *Explaining how something works*

▶ Task I

TASK APPROACH

1 Read the following advice.

- Study the diagram(s) carefully and make sure you understand the process.
- Start with a brief description of the structure and function of the equipment.
- Continue by describing the process step-by-step.

GUIDED PRACTICE

2 Study the diagram of a canal lock on page 131. Read the first section of the model answer and fill in gaps 1–4, using words or phrases from the *Useful language* box.

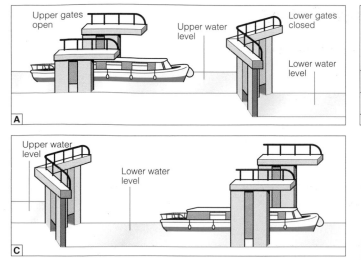

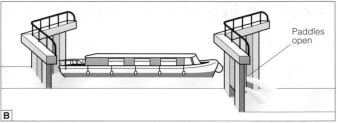

A canal lock is a system which 1 .... boats to move from one water level to another. It 2 .... a section of canal, large enough to take one or more boats, with gates at each end. The gates have valves 3 .... 'paddles', which 4 .... lowering the water level in the lock.

Useful language

Function

a tool	which allows / enables … to + inf.
a device	(which is used) for + -ing
a system	which prevents / stops … from + -ing

Structure

It consists of …   (is) called …   (is) shaped like …   (is) made of …
(is) divided into … sections
The …. (is / are) connected to …   by …

---

3 Look at the diagram again and answer the following questions.

1 What needs to happen for a boat to move down to a **lower** water level?
2 What needs to happen for a boat to move up to a **higher** water level?

4 Complete the explanation of how a canal lock works. Write about 100 words.

When a boat needs to move to a lower water level, the upper gates …

Spot the error

Five of the sentences below contain errors. Identify and correct the errors.

1 I think it's highly likely that the tax on cigarettes will be increased.
2 If you don't complete your last assignment, you probably will fail the course.
3 They say there's 90% probability of snow later today.
4 What is the likelihood of the company making a profit, in your view?
5 There seems to be very little prospect of achieving a lasting peace in the area.
6 According to me, it's unlikely that the government will be re-elected.
7 I believe there is a high chance of finding a cure for AIDS in the next few years.
8 The possibility of a reduction in interest rates is small, in my opinion.
9 It's unlikely for a new form of energy to be found in the near future.
10 I don't think there's much likelihood of our local team reaching the finals.

Check your answers by referring to *Key language* Exercise 25 on page 205.

Focus on listening 2 *The techno-house*

▶ Section 4

REMINDERS

- Study the diagram and try and describe it in your mind. Think about topic vocabulary.
- Look at the labels which are given and also the gaps. Can you guess any answers?

Questions 1–3
*Choose the appropriate letter **A–C**.*

1 In Britain …

    A most new houses include the latest technology.

    B the technology for high-tech houses is not available.

    C few people are interested in buying high-tech houses.

2 An important concern for British homebuyers is that a house …

    A is in a suitable place.

    B has a modern design.

    C is environmentally friendly.

3 How do Integer Project buildings compare with conventional houses?

    A They cost more to buy.

    B They can be built more quickly.

    C They are more complicated to construct.

Questions 4–6
*Label the diagram of the Millennium House. Write **NO MORE THAN THREE WORDS** for each answer.*

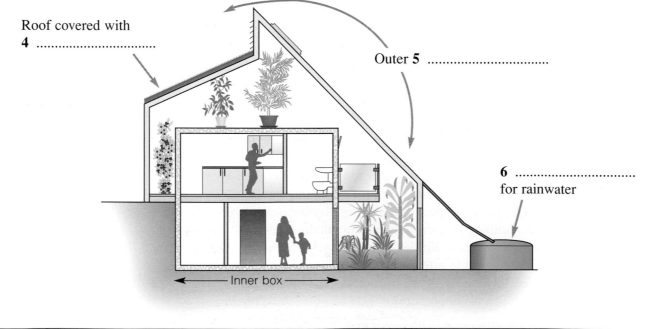

Roof covered with
4 ....

Outer **5** ....

6 ....
for rainwater

Inner box

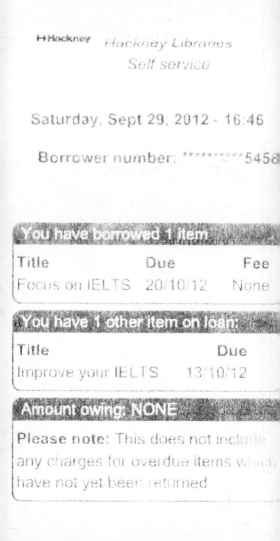

⊢Hackney *Hackney Libraries*
Self service

Saturday, Sept 29, 2012 - 16:46

Borrower number: **********5458

You have borrowed 1 item

Title	Due	Fee
Focus on IELTS	20/10/12	None

You have 1 other item on loan:

Title	Due
Improve your IELTS	13/10/12

Amount owing: NONE

Please note: This does not include any charges for overdue items which have not yet been returned

Thank you for using this service

Questions 7–10
*Complete the table using **NO MORE THAN THREE WORDS** for each answer.*

Company	Building(s)	Features
Berkeley Homes	Housing development	• Computers control heating and lighting. • Water is recycled and heated by **7** ....
Laing Homes	**8**	• Heating, TV and security system can be operated from the **9** .... via a website.
Redrow Homes	'House for the Future'	• The **10** .... is moveable, so shape and size of rooms can be changed. • Water and waste are recycled.

Focus on speaking 2 *Personal goals*

DISCUSSING FUTURE GOALS
▶ Part 2: Individual long turn

REMINDERS

• Try using a mindmap to make notes.
• Think of as many aspects of your topic as possible.

In this practice task, you need to think about a personal goal you have for the future. Work in groups of three to five. You should each choose one of the following topics. You will need to speak for about one minute.

Describe one of the following:

• **The place** you would like to live
• **The job** or career you would like to have
• **A country** you would like to visit
• **Something** you would like to own
• **A skill** you would like to learn

You should say what is special about your chosen goal and explain your reasons for choosing it.

'Stop moaning. If she wants to be an air hostess it's up to us to help her.'

Focus on writing 2 *Summarising sentences*

1   It is often helpful to summarise the main points you have made as a way of introducing the next stage of the argument. Look at the *Useful language* box below for examples of this language.

> **Useful language**
>
> *Having* looked at / discussed   a number of problems / benefits   *we should now consider …*
>
> *Given*   the problems / factors which have been outlined,   *we can turn to the question of …* / *we need to ask …*

2   Summarising sentences are often used to 'signpost', that is to give the reader an indication of the direction your argument is taking.

Complete the following sentences in a logical way.

1   Having discussed the benefits of single-sex education, we should consider …
2   Given the expense of subsidising school lunches, we must ask …
3   Having examined the case for the death penalty, …
4   … we need to ask whether taking a gap year is such a good idea.
5   … we can now turn to the arguments of more traditional educators.
6   … we have to examine the case presented by those who oppose speed limits.

EXAM PRACTICE
▶ **Task 2**

3   Read the following reminders and then write your answer to the task below.

REMINDERS

- Make notes before you begin, perhaps using a mindmap.
- Decide on your choice of approach, depending on your reaction to the point of view expressed.
- Revise ways of expressing disagreement by challenging a claim, pointing out a false conclusion or asking a rhetorical question (pages 68 and 69).
- Check your work, especially for your most frequent mistakes, before you finish.

> You should spend about 40 minutes on this task.
>
> Present a written argument to an educated reader with no specialist knowledge of the following topic.
>
> > *Advances in science and technology and other areas of society in the last 100 years have transformed the way we live as well as postponing the day we die. There is no better time to be alive than now.*
> >
> > *To what extent do you agree or disagree with this opinion?*
>
> You should use your own ideas, knowledge and experience and support your arguments with examples and relevant evidence.
>
> You should write at least 250 words.

ERROR HIT LIST

few/a few; little/a little

✗	✔
We need to discuss few problems that have arisen. Unfortunately, there's a little that can be done.	We need to discuss <u>a</u> few … … there's a <u>little</u> that can be done.

- Used with articles, **a few** and **a little** mean 'some', e.g. *Would you like a little soup? Have you got a few minutes to spare?*

- Used without articles, **few** and **little** have the meanings 'not many', 'not much', 'not enough', e.g. *There's **little** hope of finding survivors. **Few** places on Earth are as beautiful.*

- **very few** and **very little** give an even more negative meaning: 'hardly any', e.g. ***Very few** people speak my language. There's **very little** time left.*

middle position adverbs: *probably/definitely; always/usually,* etc.

✗	✔
You definitely should go there … I sometimes have been asked to give advice. There probably is an easy solution to the problem.	You <u>should definitely</u> … I <u>have sometimes</u> been asked … There <u>is probably</u> an easy solution …

- Middle position adverbs include *probably, definitely, even, really* and adverbs of **frequency** (*always, usually,* etc.); **time** (*already, still,* etc.); and **degree** (*almost, hardly,* etc.).

- These adverbs usually go in front of the main verb, e.g. *I already know the answer.*

- When the main verb is *be*, they go immediately after it, e.g. *We're always pleased to help.*

- When there is more than one auxiliary verb, they go immediately after the first one, e.g. *We'll soon be leaving. I have often been asked that question.*

in spite of/despite

✗	✔
Despite the economy is weak, some companies are still making a profit.	<u>Although</u> the economy is weak, … Despite the economy <u>being</u> weak, … Despite <u>the fact that</u> the economy is weak, …

- **In spite of** and **despite** are followed by a noun or *-ing* form. They mean the same as **although** + clause.

- They are prepositions (not conjunctions) and cannot introduce a clause.

nevertheless

✗	✔
The dangers of cigarettes are well known, nevertheless people continue to smoke.	The dangers … well known<u>.</u> <u>Nevertheless</u>, people continue …

- **nevertheless** is a formal word meaning 'despite the fact which has just been mentioned'. It's normally used at the beginning of a sentence.

17 ▶ Avoiding gridlock

In this unit you will practise:

- Discussing traffic and transport topics
- Short-answer questions, classification, True/False/Does Not Say
- Matching, sentence completion, completing a diagram
- Vocabulary: verbs expressing increase and decrease

Exam Focus

Speaking: Part 3

Reading: Exam practice 1

Reading: Exam practice 2

Lead-in

1   Match the descriptions A–E to the pictures below and give reasons for your answers.

> A   Male driver under 25 years old
> B   Female driver under 25 years old
> C   Middle-aged male driver
> D   Female driver more than 35 years old
> E   Older driver (55+)

2   How has the artist characterised each driver? What potential road safety hazards are illustrated?

3   Discuss the following questions with another student. Refer to the list of driver types A–E on page 136.

> 1   Who is **the safest** driver?
> 2   Who is **the most dangerous** driver?
> 3   Who is **most likely to drink and drive?**

WRITING PRACTICE
Presenting and comparing data (guided practice)
▶ ex. 7, p. 212–213

4   With your partner, discuss which is a more significant factor in road accidents: gender or age?

You will find the answers to most of the questions in the text below.

Focus on reading 1 *Smashing stereotypes*

Smashing Stereotypes

In a study titled *Male and Female Drivers: How different are they?* Professor Frank McKenna of the University of Reading looked at the accident risk between men and women.
5   He found that men drive faster, commit more driving violations, and are more inclined to drink and drive. They look for thrills behind the wheel, while women seek independence. And, although anecdotal evidence might suggest otherwise,
10 women are not starting to drive as aggressively as men.

The question of whether, as drivers, women differ from men is important, because it could affect insurance premiums, which are closely
15 geared to accident statistics.

Despite the increase in women drivers, McKenna's researchers found no evidence that this is changing accident patterns. It seems that age is far more important than gender in the car. It is
20 the biggest single factor in accident patterns, and, while inexperienced new drivers of both sexes are more likely to be involved in accidents, the study found striking new evidence to confirm that young men drive less safely than any other group.

25 The survey shows that men and women aged 17 to 20 are most likely to be involved in bend accidents – men almost twice as often – but the difference decreases as drivers mature.

Nearly half of all accidents involving young men
30 and one-third of those involving young women take place when it is dark. Again, there is a steady decrease in such accidents as drivers grow older, but gender differences remain significant until drivers reach the age of 55.

35 Although there is little difference between men and women in the distance they keep from the car in front, there are differences across age groups. Young drivers show less regard for the danger of following more closely, and young men are likely to
40 'close the gap' as an aggressive signal to the driver in front to speed up or get out of the way.

Men consistently choose higher speeds than women of the same age and driving experience. "This could be because men seek a thrill when they
45 drive," says McKenna. "Speed choice is one of the most important causes of accidents. But breaking the speed limits is regarded by men as a minor offence."

Contrary to public belief, young drivers, as a
50 group, are more likely to avoid drinking alcohol if they are driving, while men in the 30 to 50 age group admitted to drinking the most alcohol before driving.

Men are most likely to nod off, probably because
55 they are willing to drive for longer periods without a break – driver fatigue is a significant factor in accidents.

According to Andrew Howard, of the Automobile Association, "We have to combat the group that
60 speeds for thrills. The key is how men are brought up to look at the car. It is this which needs to be addressed."

INTRODUCING EXAM TASKS
▶ Short-answer questions

1 These are generally straightforward questions requiring short factual answers taken from the text, For example, you may have to give a year or quantity, or to write up to three words. For some questions, you may need to write more than one answer to get a mark.

TASK APPROACH

- Check the **instructions** to see exactly what kind of answer is required.
- Use **skimming skills** to find the relevant section and then **scan** the text to find the information you need.
- Make sure that you don't write more than three words. If your answer is too long, look for words that can be omitted.

Questions 1–3
*Answer the following questions. Write **NO MORE THAN THREE WORDS** for each answer.*

1 What is women's motivation for driving? ....

2 Which group of drivers has grown in number in recent years? ....

3 What is the most significant factor in accident patterns? ....

Question 4
4 After what age do men and women drive equally safely at night? ....

EXAM PRACTICE
▶ Classification

2   **Read the following advice before doing this task.**

REMINDERS

- The questions are not in the same order as the information in the text.
- Study the questions and underline key words or phrases.

Questions 5–9
Classify the following statements (5–9) as applying to

> **A**   men in general
> **B**   young men in particular
> **C**   both young men and young women

Example	*Answer*
They are the most likely to have accidents while driving.	**B**

5   They may follow another car closely to make the driver go faster.   ....

6   They are more likely to have accidents due to tiredness.   ....

7   They are the least likely to drink and drive.   ....

8   Driving gives them a feeling of excitement.   ....

9   They are the most likely to have accidents on bends.   ....

▶ True/False/Does Not Say

3   **Now complete the final task of the exam practice.**

Questions 10–15
Do the following statements agree with the information in the text?
Write

TRUE	*if the statement agrees with the information given*
FALSE	*if the statement disagrees with the information given*
DOES NOT SAY	*if there is no information about this*

10   There is a common belief that women are becoming more aggressive drivers.   ....

11   The results of the study may influence the cost of motor insurance.   ....

12   Young women are most likely to have accidents when driving at night.   ....

13   Men do not consider it very serious to exceed the speed limit.   ....

14   Women are more prone to accidents at junctions than men.   ....

15   Andrew Howard thinks there is little that can be done to reduce accidents.   ....

Focus on speaking *On four wheels*

▶ Part 3: Discussion

Work in pairs to discuss one or more of the following mini topics. Try to think of reasons for and against each point of view.

1   The world would be a better place without cars.
2   We should build more motorways.
3   Basic driving skills should be taught at school.
4   The minimum age for driving should be 25.

Focus on reading 2 *Avoiding gridlock*

1   Answer the following questions in pairs before reading the text.

1   What is 'gridlock'? Find out if your partner knows. If not, check in a dictionary.
2   What causes gridlock?
3   How can gridlock be avoided?

▶ EXAM BRIEFING

Reading module

Reading texts come from a variety of sources, including British, Australian and American English. If you are used to British or Australian English, you may notice occasional differences in spelling and vocabulary in American texts, but these should not affect your understanding.

Avoiding Gridlock

A Beginning from the earliest sledges, people have sought ways to move themselves, messages and goods from place to place. By 1900, speeds of up to 120 miles per hour were possible on land. The spread of steamships, the introduction of railways and the development of bicycles were among the transforming innovations of the nineteenth century. The scope of transportation in industrial countries was further widened in the twentieth century with the mass production of the automobile and the development of air travel.

B Since the end of World War Two, motor vehicle production has risen almost linearly. As a result, the global car fleet now numbers more than 500 million. In the United States, the number of household vehicles increased at six times the rate of the population between 1969 and 1995.

However, while road traffic dominates the transportation system, air transportation is the fastest growing segment. And as road and air travel have grown, rail has become relatively less important. (See Figure 1.)

C Cities have spread out over larger expanses of land as builders have constructed wide expressways and ample parking to accommodate motor vehicles. Asked in a survey to identify the top influence shaping the American metropolis, a sampling of urban historians, social scientists and architects chose the highway system and dominance of the automobile as the number-one influence. As cities sprawl, cars become essential while transit, bicycling and walking become less practical. In the Czech Republic, for instance, car use has surged and public transit use has fallen as the number of suburban hypermarkets ballooned from one to fifty-three between 1997 and 2000.

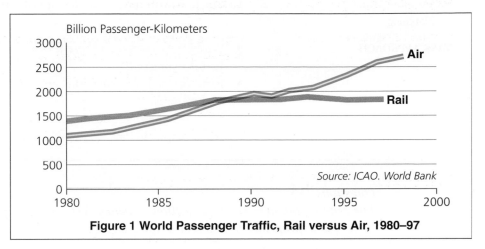

Figure 1 World Passenger Traffic, Rail versus Air, 1980–97

D Advances in transport technology have brought benefits, but growing vehicle fleets and escalating fuel use have also created problems. Researchers estimate that nearly a million people are killed on the world's roads each year, and most of them are pedestrians. Motor vehicles impede other forms of traffic and cause delays. Congested roads in São Paulo have prompted the wealthiest residents to take to the skies, boosting the city's helicopter fleet to the third largest in the world, after New York and Tokyo.

Roads also cause profound changes to ecosystems. A great deal of land in car-dependent cities is lost to roads and parking lots. Water quality and quantity both suffer in proportion to the amount of paved roads and parking that cover a watershed. Plants and animals are killed during road construction as well as by vehicles. And roads promote the dispersal of species that are not native to a given area, and alter the physical and chemical environment.

E The single largest contributor to the costs of transportation borne by society in many countries is illnesses and deaths from air pollution. One challenge, therefore, is to tackle immediate health threats from the most polluting vehicles. By adopting policies that promote cleaner technologies, governments can take one important step towards solving this problem.

F Today transportation planners increasingly recognize that building more roads does not necessarily solve traffic problems. Michael Replogle, a transportation specialist, came up with this analogy: "Adding highway capacity is like buying larger pants to deal with your weight problem." As new roads attract more cars, regions that have invested heavily in roads have fared no better at easing traffic than those that have invested less. Measures to diversify transportation options include regulations to curb car traffic, price incentives to reduce motor vehicle use and boost alternatives, and changes in urban design that enhance the viability of cycling, walking and public transit.

G Individuals make choices every day about different transportation modes, based, in part, on perceptions about safety and comfort. Poorly maintained cycling and public transport networks are therefore less appealing than the private car. High-income residents of Mexico City, surveyed in a recent study of travel behavior, said they feared robberies on buses and that they would use public transportation only if it were safe, well organized and comfortable.

People are also influenced by the car's image of freedom, power and modernity. To many young people, getting a driver's license is a rite of passage. In one survey in England,

young adults were asked: "Imagine that you were only able to have one of the following two rights – the right to vote in an election, or the right to obtain a driving license – which would you choose?" Some seventy-two per cent chose the license.

H But views and behaviors may change, as congested roads thwart the car's promise of individual freedom and power. The category "traffic congestion and urban sprawl" was the major concern of both urban and suburban Americans, and nationwide it tied with "crime and violence" as the top worry according to five public-opinion surveys around the country.

I The automobile came to dominate the world's roads in the last century, the age of oil. Today, with the environmental and social costs of road traffic well documented, and with natural gas and renewable sources of energy beginning to replace oil, we can envision a new generation of transportation systems. Vehicles could be cleaner, and cities could be made more attractive and functional, with integrated networks for bicycles, bus, rail and new types of transit. People will need to work together to build this future, and to confront those in government and industry with vested interests in transportation systems that belong to the last century.

From *Making Better Transportation Choices* by Molly O'Meara Sheehan, Worldwatch Institute

EXAM PRACTICE
▶ Matching

2 In this task, you have to match specific information to sections of a text.

TASK APPROACH

- Study the example, if there is one, to see how information from the text is expressed.
- Read through the questions and underline or highlight key words and phrases.
- Consider the first question and use skimming and scanning skills to locate the topic in the text. Remember to look out for parallel expressions.

Questions 1–5
*The reading passage has nine sections labelled **A–I**.*
*Write the appropriate letters **A–I** in the spaces below.*

Example	*Answer*
Which section mentions the manufacture of cars?	**A**

1 Which section describes the attraction of the car for young people? ....

2 Which section compares the growth of the population and car ownership? ....

3 Which section mentions energy sources which have advantages over oil? ....

4 Which section describes how expanding the road network has failed to reduce traffic congestion? ....

5 Which section mentions a city where the rich have begun commuting by air? ....

▶ Sentence completion

3 Now complete the next task in this section.

Questions 6–10
*Choose one phrase (**A–H**) from the list of phrases to complete each sentence below.*
*Write **NO MORE THAN THREE WORDS** for each answer.*

6 The development of modern cities both reflects and contributes to ....

7 Animals and plants may spread to new areas as a result of ....

8 Possible strategies for reducing the use of private cars include ....

9 Improved standards of maintenance would increase the popularity of ....

10 Several surveys suggest that ordinary Americans are becoming very worried about ....

List of Phrases

A transport technology
B public transport
C motor vehicle production
D traffic congestion
E the dominance of the automobile
F changes in town planning
G road building
H new energy sources

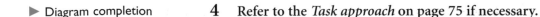

▶ Diagram completion   **4**   Refer to the *Task approach* on page 75 if necessary.

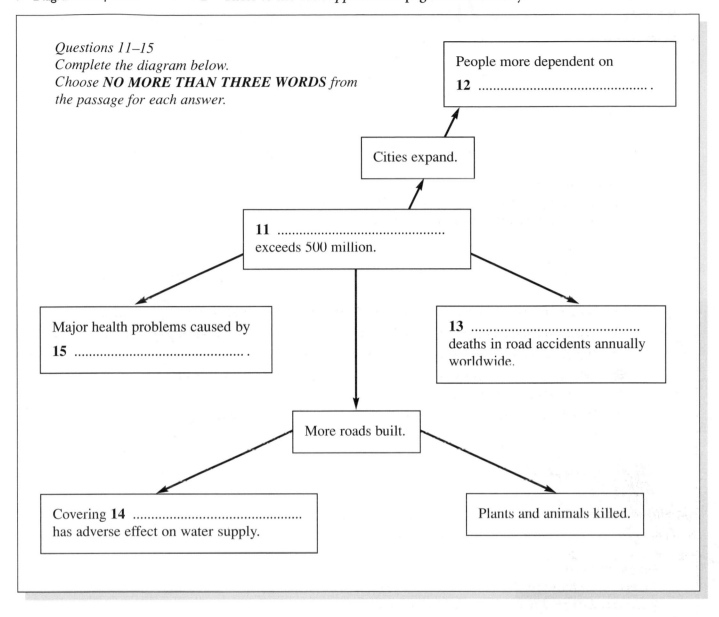

Questions 11–15
Complete the diagram below.
*Choose **NO MORE THAN THREE WORDS** from*
the passage for each answer.

People more dependent on
12 ....

Cities expand.

11 ....
exceeds 500 million.

Major health problems caused by
15 ....

13 ....
deaths in road accidents annually
worldwide..

More roads built.

Covering **14** ....
has adverse effect on water supply.

Plants and animals killed.

Focus on vocabulary *More or less?*

Several of the verbs below come from the reading text on pages 140–141.
Decide whether the general meaning in each case is A or B.

A become or make more, wider, or bigger
B become or make less or smaller

1	balloon	6	escalate	11	sprawl
2	boost	7	fall	12	spread
3	diminish	8	lessen	13	surge
4	drop	9	rise	14	widen
5	dwindle	10	shrink	15	restrict

KEY LANGUAGE
British vs American vocabulary
▶ ex. 26, p. 206
e.g. *automobile (US),*
expressway (US)

18 ▶ Wish you were here

In this unit you will practise:

- Discussing travel and the tourism industry
- Pronunciation: sounds
- Dealing with different data
- Presenting the solution to a problem
- Completing a table and flow chart; sentence completion; labelling a diagram; multiple choice

Exam Focus

Speaking: Parts 1–3
Speaking skills
Writing: Task 1
Writing: Task 2
Listening: Sections 2, 3

Lead-in

'This hotel is renowned for its peace and solitude. In fact, crowds from all over the world flock here to enjoy its solitude.'

AN ITALIAN HOTEL BROCHURE

1 Work with another student. Look at Box A when answering Questions 1–2, and at Box B when answering 3–5.

A

Australia	France	Poland
Austria	Germany	Spain
Canada	Italy	UK
China	Japan	USA

B

Uluru (Ayers Rock) (*N.T. Australia*)	**Niagara Falls** (*Canada/USA*)
British Museum (*London, England*)	**Grand Canyon** (*Arizona, USA*)
CN Tower (*Toronto, Canada*)	**Eiffel Tower** (*Paris, France*)
Disneyland (*Tokyo, Japan*)	**Great Pyramid** (*Giza, Egypt*)
Empire State Building (*New York, USA*)	**Tower of London** (*London, England*)

1 Over the last 50 years, cheap air fares have made long-distance travel commonplace. Which three countries are the most visited tourist destinations in the world?

....

2 Tourism has been marketed as a universal benefit. But not everyone can afford to travel. The citizens of which three countries spend most on tourism?

....

3 Which three tourist sights receive the most visitors every day?

....

4 Which tourist sight would you most like to visit? Why?

5 Which would you be least interested in? Why?

You can find the answers to Questions 1–3 on page 218.

PRONUNCIATION: DIPHTHONGS

2 When two vowels are pronounced together quickly, they form a combined sound called a *diphthong*. For example, /e/ + /ɪ/ produce the diphthong /eɪ/ as in *Spain*.

Put the following words in the correct group, according to their pronunciation.

> *buy   eight   freer   freight   grey   height   light*
> *we're   sphere   weigh   while   year*

1 /eɪ/ as in US**A**, Austr**a**lia   ....

2 /aɪ/ as in Ch**i**na, Dub**ai**   ....

3 /ɪə/ as in Kor**ea**, Kashm**ir**   ....

Focus on speaking 1 *Tourism*

1 Work in pairs. Imagine that foreign tourists regularly visited your local area. Which of the following would you object to most, and why? Number them 1 (most) – 6 (least). Compare your answers with the results of a survey on page 218.

a) Group of tourists take photographs of the local people without asking permission.	....
b) Prices in your local shops double during the tourist season.	....
c) Tourists are disrespectful or inappropriately dressed at an important cultural event.	....
d) Tourists expect you to speak their language.	....
e) Tourists criticise your home and country in front of you.	....
f) Most of the money tourists spend goes to companies based in another country.	....

2 Make three suggestions about ways of making tourism fairer and more acceptable for local people.

Focus on listening 1 *Worldwide Student Projects*

▶ Section 2
▶ Short answers; table/flow-chart completion

*Listen to a short talk on an organisation called Worldwide Student Projects (WSP)
and answer Questions **1–10**.*

Question 1
*Write **NO MORE THAN THREE WORDS** for your answer.*

1   What does WSP aim to promote?   ....

Questions 2–7
Complete the table showing details of the projects.
*Write **NO MORE THAN THREE WORDS** or **A LETTER** for each answer.*

Period	S = Short-term M = Medium-term L = Long-term

LIST OF PROJECTS			
Country	**Period**	**Project**	**Special information**
Japan	S	Village **2**	Some knowledge of Japanese required
Poland	**3**	Renovating children's holiday centre	
Mexico	S	Sea turtle conservation	Accommodation in school with **4** ....
China	**5**	Architecture: planning and design	US$ **6** .... payable on arrival
India	M	Medicine: centre for **7** .... children	

Questions 8–10
*Complete the flow chart. Write **NO MORE THAN THREE WORDS** for each answer.*

You complete an application and send it with **8** ....

↓

We send 'Welcome Pack' with: • General information • Formal **9** .... • A questionnaire for you to return

↓

We use the questionnaire to match you to your job.

↓

10 .... before departure we send full details of your placement.

Focus on writing 1 *Presenting the solution to a problem*

In some questions, you have to consider a problem and either evaluate possible solutions or suggest a solution of your own. The best way to answer this question is to follow the argument-led approach described in Unit 6. Look at this paragraph plan.

NB Conditional structures and expressions of probability are both useful for this task. Refer to Exercises 13 and 25 in the *Key language*, pages 196 and 205.

> **PARAGRAPH PLAN**
>
> *Opening paragraph*
> • Outline the problem in your own words.
> • Discuss its implications.
>
> *Middle sections*
> • Evaluate a number of possible solutions.
> • Include the pros and cons in each case.
>
> *Closing paragraph*
> • Sum up your argument.
> • Give your view as to the best solution(s).

EXAM PRACTICE
▶ Task 2

> You should spend about 40 minutes on this task.
>
> Present a written argument or case to an educated reader with no specialist knowledge of the following topic.
>
> > *Most of the world's poor live in countries where tourism is a growing industry. The issue is that tourism does not benefit the poorest. How can the income generated by tourism benefit the poor? And how can we ensure that tourism does not destroy traditional cultures and ways of life?*
> >
> > *What are your views?*
>
> You should use your own ideas, knowledge and experience to support your arguments with examples and relevant evidence.
>
> You should write at least 250 words.

Focus on speaking 2 *Time off*

EXAM PRACTICE
▶ Part 1: Interview

1 Work in pairs to ask and answer the following questions.

1 How do you usually spend your holidays?
2 What was the best holiday you've ever had?
3 How do you prefer to travel, by road, rail or air?
4 Would you rather go on holiday with one or two friends, or in a group?

▶ Part 2: Individual long turn

2 Work in pairs. Take it in turns to tell each other about the topics below. Speak for one to two minutes. Your partner should listen carefully and ask the 'closing questions' to finish.

REMINDERS

- Take a few moments to make brief notes before you begin, perhaps using a mindmap.
- Make sure you cover all the points on the topic card.

TOPIC 1

Describe a tourist attraction you have visited.

You should say:

what the attraction was
when you visited it
what you saw and did there

and say what you thought of it.

Chichen Itza
Mexico

Closing questions
Would you recommend other people to go there?
Do you enjoy sightseeing in general?

TOPIC 2

Describe a tourist attraction you would like to visit.

You should say:

what the attraction is
what you can see and do there
how you know about it

and say why you would particularly like to go there.

Closing questions
Have you been to a place like that before?
Do you like travelling in general?

▶ Part 3: Discussion

REMINDERS

'Oh lovely, that's a good one of you...'

3 Discuss the following questions.

- Don't give one-word answers – this is an opportunity to demonstrate your fluency.
- Be prepared to express a variety of opinions and to give reasons for them.
- Try to use a range of structures and vocabulary, and to use linking expressions, e.g. *Because, as, since* (reason); *and, as well as, besides* (addition); *although, even though, despite* (concession), etc.

1 What changes have there been in the last 50 years or so in the way people travel?
2 Would you say all the developments in travel and transport have been for the better?
3 Some young people nowadays have a 'gap year' between school and university, when they travel or work in another country. Do you think this is a good idea?
4 What would you do to prepare yourself before you visited another country?
5 What new developments will there be in tourism in future, do you think?

Focus on listening 2 *The end of oil*

▶ Section 3

EXAM PRACTICE

▶ Sentence completion; labelling a diagram; table completion; multiple choice

Listen to this discussion between a student and his tutor and answer Questions 1–10.

Questions 1–3
Complete the sentences.
*Write **NO MORE THAN THREE WORDS** or **A NUMBER** for each answer.*

Andrew's tutor thinks he can achieve a **1** .... if he maintains his progress.

His tutor advises him to avoid the subject of **2** ....

The assignment needs to be **3** .... words long.

Questions 4–6
Label the pie chart.
*Write **NO MORE THAN THREE WORDS** for each answer.*

4 ....

5 ....

6 ....

Questions 7–9
Tick (✓) the relevant boxes in each column.

Country	7 Which countries are producing less oil now than in the past?	8 Which countries use the most gasoline per head?	9 Which countries are increasing their gasoline use most rapidly?
Great Britain			
Canada			
Germany			
India			
Japan			
Mexico			
Saudi Arabia			
South Korea			
former Soviet Union			
USA			

Question 10
*Circle the correct letter **A–C**.*

10   Which solution does Andrew favour?

   A finding new sources of oil

   B developing an alternative to oil

   C imposing taxes on the use of oil

Focus on writing 2 *Dealing with different data*

EXAM PRACTICE
▶ Task 1

You should spend about 20 minutes on this task.

The bar charts below give information on road transport in a number of European countries.

Write a report for a university lecturer describing the information shown below.

You should write at least 150 words.

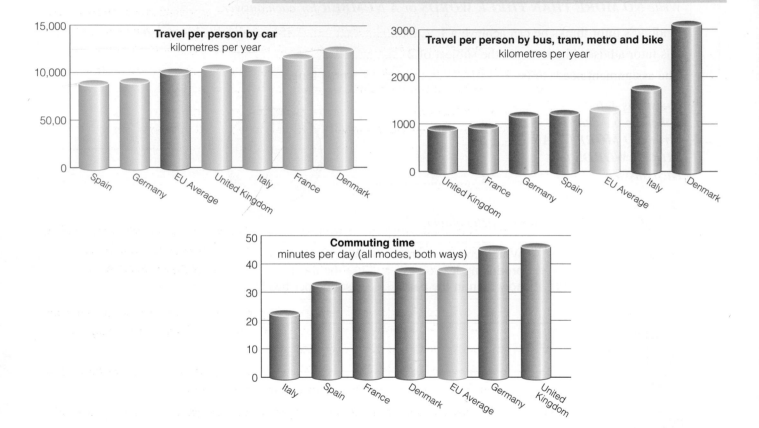

REMINDERS

DON'T

- try to describe every detail. Concentrate on key features and significant trends.
- speculate about reasons. Concentrate on the facts.
- spend longer than 20 minutes on Task 1 in the exam. Task 2 carries twice as many marks.

DO

- begin with an introductory statement.
- think about the clearest way to express information, e.g. *one in three*, *twice as many*, etc.
- look for opportunities to compare information, *between* graphs and charts as well as *within* them.
- think about how to group the information and link points together logically.
- finish with a concluding comment on general trends.

ERROR HIT LIST

journey/trip/travel

✗	✔
You can make journeys to local places of interest.	You can take trips to …
We've done several journeys in Asia.	We've made/been on several journeys …
The travel to college takes about an hour.	The journey to college …
I enjoy foreign travelling.	I enjoy foreign travelling.

- **a journey** is the period of travel between two places, especially over a long distance. Use **go on** or **make a journey** (not *do*), e.g. *Take some food with you for the journey. Every year the Atlantic salmon makes a 2,000-mile journey to warmer zones.*

- **a trip** is a return journey, especially for a short visit. Use **go on, make** or **take a trip.** It occurs in compound nouns such as *day trip, business trip,* etc.

- **travel** (uncountable) is the general activity of moving from place to place, e.g. *Travel broadens the mind.* It occurs in compound nouns such as *air travel, travel sickness,* etc.

reach/arrive

✗	✔
The ladder didn't reach to the window.	The ladder didn't reach to the window.
I first reached this country in 1984.	I first arrived in this country …
The best way to reach your purpose is to persevere.	… to achieve your purpose …

- Use **reach** (without *to*) both literally and figuratively to mean 'be long enough, high enough or large enough to reach a particular point', e.g. *I can't reach the top shelf. Unemployment reached a peak in March.*

- You **reach** a place after a long or difficult journey, e.g. *It was midnight by the time we reached the capital.* Otherwise **arrive (at/in)** or **get to** is more usual.

- Use **achieve** to mean 'succeed in doing something' or 'get the result that you want'.

possibility/opportunity

✗	✔
I'm considering the possibility to buy a car.	I'm considering the possibility of buying …
You will have a possibility of joining in.	… an opportunity for joining in.

- Use **possibility** when you are talking about something that may happen, e.g. *There's a possibility that it may snow later on.* **possibility** is followed by *of + -ing*, or a *that* clause.

- Use **opportunity** to refer to a situation where it is possible for someone to do something, e.g. *If you go to Madrid, you will have an opportunity to visit the Prado.*

- **opportunity** is followed by *for* or *of + -ing* or by *to* + infinitive, e.g. *an opportunity of making money/to make money.*

19 ▶ Face value

In this unit you will practise:

- Discussing facial expressions and gesture
- Skimming/scanning; reading for detail; cohesion
- Short-answer questions; table completion; multiple choice
- Individual long turn and two-way discussion
- Vocabulary: word families, dependent prepositions

Exam Focus

Speaking skills
Reading skills
Reading: Exam tasks
Speaking: Parts 2, 3

Lead-in

1   It is generally agreed that there are a number of basic universally recognised facial expressions. With another student, study the pictures below and identify the seven basic emotions they show. Check your answers on page 218.

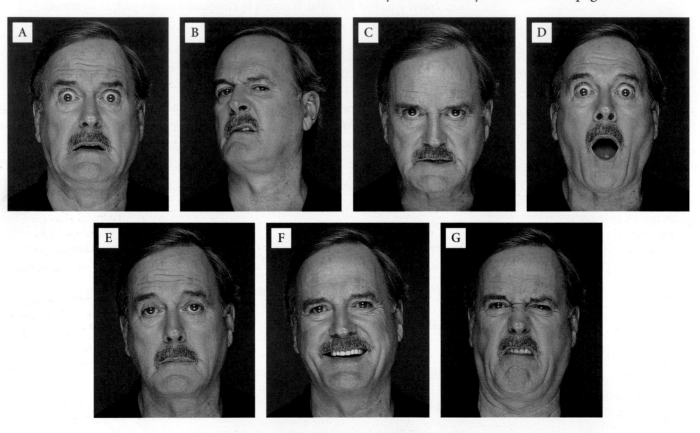

2   **With your partner, discuss the following questions.**

1   Which of the expressions were easiest, and which most difficult to identify?
2   What other signals (e.g. gestures) might accompany these facial expressions? Are they equally universal?
3   On what occasions would it be important to hide the following feelings? Why?

Anger   Fear   Disgust

Focus on speaking 1 *Face the facts 1*

▶ Part 3: Discussion

Discuss the following questions in pairs.

1 How do facial expressions help in everyday communication?
2 What kind of difficulties can arise when people communicate without being able to see each other, by telephone or e-mail for example?
3 Why is it better for children to play with friends than play on a computer?
4 How can you tell if someone is embarrassed? What kind of situations make you feel embarrassed?

Focus on reading 1 *Face the facts 2*

SKIMMING AND SCANNING

1 Each of the extracts (A–D) relates to one of the questions (1–4) above. Read the extracts quickly and answer the following questions.

1 Which extract below relates to each question above? Write the letters next to the questions.
2 Which words or phrases helped you identify the correct extract?

A

When two pedestrians collide, there's none of that anger we see when motorists cross one another's path. The experts say that we don't see aggression when people collide because they're liable to exchange little signs of apology, which you are unable to do when you're trapped inside a car.

The same kind of misunderstandings can easily happen on e-mail. The style of e-mail is terse but informal, so people get annoyed where no rudeness is intended, because they can't see the expression on the face of the person they're communicating with. If they could, the problem would instantly disappear.

B

Facial movements associated with embarrassment act as an apology, with the gaze averted and the eyes moving downwards. A brief smile flickers across the face and the hand often moves to the cheek. This may be accompanied by blushing. The whole response takes about five seconds.

Studies done in court rooms in the United States prove that of the defendants found guilty in court, the ones who blushed and looked embarrassed after the verdicts were read out received shorter sentences than those who appeared unrepentant. Embarrassment on the face is the equivalent of apologising. It helps to show people that you know you've transgressed the rules.

Interestingly, embarrassment seems only to appear at the age of eighteen months, much later than other expressions. It's at this age that a child first gets an awareness of people around it and a social sense.

C

Eye contact and head nods are crucial to our conversations. The single head nod indicates that the nodder has understood what is being said and wishes the speaker to continue. Rapid and repeated head nods indicate that the speaker wishes to speak. Eye contact is also vital, and we spend up to 75 per cent of the time looking at the person we're talking to. We can underline the points we are making by raising our eyebrows or pursing our lips. The eyebrows can also be raised in a kind of visual question mark at the end of a sentence.

D

Most children learn to express themselves naturally through face-to-face communication with their parents and their peers. But in the modern world this kind of contact is diminishing. Instead of playing football and fighting, children are spending increasing amounts of time in front of computers. Numerous studies have shown that this can cause relationship problems later in life. Without the feedback of another's emotions, children risk becoming withdrawn and depressed.

From BBC OnLine Science: *The Human Face*

READING FOR DETAIL	**2**	Do the extracts on page 153 confirm your answers in *Focus on speaking 1* or not? What additional points do they make?

COHESIVE FEATURES	**3**	Say what the words in italics below refer to in the extracts.

1 The *same* kind of misunderstandings … (Text A)
2 If they *could* … (Text A)
3 *This* may be accompanied … (Text B)
4 … *those* who appeared unrepentant. (Text B)
5 … an awareness of people around *it* (Text B)
6 … *this* kind of contact (Text D)

DEALING WITH UNKNOWN VOCABULARY	**4**	You may not be familiar with the following words, but it's possible to work out the general meaning from the context. Explain the general meaning in your own words.

A 1 collide   B 4 unrepentant   C 6 crucial   D 7 peers
   2 liable   5 transgressed   8 feedback
   3 terse

Focus on reading 2 *Face*

The following questions are based on the reading passage *Face* on page 155.

REMINDERS

- Glance through the questions to see what topics they focus on, and what you have to do. Underline any key words that will give you cues to look for in the passage.
- Read through the passage fairly quickly, to form a general picture. Underline any key words you notice that relate to the questions.

Questions 1–5
*Answer the following questions using **NO MORE THAN THREE WORDS** for each answer.*

1 How does facial skin differ from other human skin?   ....

2 Which **TWO** facial muscles are employed when we are afraid?   ....

3 When can human beings first show an expression of happiness?   ....

4 Which part of the face has a limited role as an indicator of mood?   ....

5 Which subject did Gottfried Leibnitz have an important insight into?   ....

FACE
by Daniel McNeil

A We rely on facial signals constantly, yet we cannot define them. We are reading a language we cannot articulate and may not consciously notice. Good face-reading can provide an insight into a person's true feelings. As always, real skill demands practice but anyone can learn a few basics.

B We have twenty-two facial muscles on each side, more than any animal on earth. In common with most muscles, they anchor in bone. Unlike most, they attach to skin, making the face more mobile than the skin on other parts of the body. These muscles form a complex skein, as shown in Figure 1, but some stand out in particular. The *zygomatic major* is the smile-maker. It runs across the cheek to the corner of the mouth, which it pulls upwards. The *corrugator* knits the eyebrows together, causing vertical furrows in between. Most pleasant expressions involve the *zygomatic major*, most unpleasant ones the *corrugator*.

C Other muscles also play important roles. The busiest is the *frontalis*, the curtain-like muscle of the forehead, which causes the eyebrows to rise in expressions of fear or for emphasis. Its opposite number, the *procerus*, causes the eyebrows to descend in sadness. When the mouth is retracted horizontally in fear, we employ the *risorius*. These signals emerge in infancy and on a reliable timetable. The smile and surprise appear at birth, disgust and distress (sadness) between zero and three months, the 'social smile' at one and a half to three months, anger at three to seven months, and fear at five to nine months.

D Anger is a dark look of concentration. The eyebrows descend and the lips tighten. An angry face is a warning. Fear has almost the opposite characteristics. The eyes widen and the eyebrows rise. Surprise resembles fear and often precedes it. Both the eyes and mouth fly open and the eyebrows rise and arch. Disgust centres on the nose, not otherwise a very expressive facial feature. It may partly turn up, wrinkle and contract, as when we sense a bad smell.

E What about telling lies? On the whole we are not very good at detecting lies. Even individuals one would expect to be skilled – judges, policemen and psychiatrists – fail here and score only slightly above average. Prisoners spot lies fairly well, possibly because they live in a world of deceit and must become adroit.

What is the secret? In the eighteenth century, Gottfried Leibnitz suggested that studying the face and voice could improve lie detection – and he was right.

F First, a warning: there is no sure give-away of a lie. Anyone who relies on a lone cue will often be misled, so good lie-spotters seek out several. One key involves smiling. The liar shows fewer genuine smiles and more masking or cover-up smiles and these, along with higher vocal pitch, are the best evidence of deception. True smiles make little starburst crinkles in the skin near the eyes; false smiles tend not to. The phoney smiles may occur too early or too late for the context, halt instantly instead of dying away, or show a slight asymmetry.

Figure 1

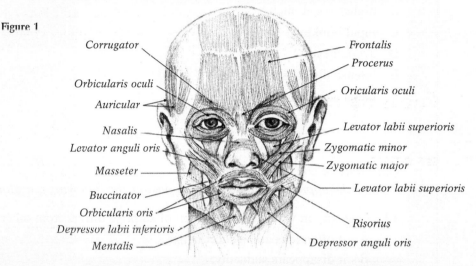

G Honest expressions do not linger. Any expressions that are more than ten seconds long, and most that last longer than five, are probably fake. Intense displays – rage, ecstasy, depression – are exceptions, but even they usually appear as a series of short bursts. Surprise is especially brief. It always lasts less than a second; if it goes on longer, the person is counterfeiting. Unlike other expressions, it also begins and ends abruptly. Many people can mimic the look of surprise, but few capture its flick-switch start and end.

H According to folk wisdom, rapid blinking is a key to lying. While this is true of some lies, unfortunately blinking is a general response to arousal. It can signal excitement, anxiety or other strong emotions. What about averted eyes? We do tend to look down and away out of guilt or shame – as we look straight down with sadness and to the side with disgust. But the eye gaze is an unreliable clue. Liars know some people rely on it and exploit the fact. Curiously, probing for truth can actually blind us to lies. When pressed, some liars increase eye contact and facial animation, convincing questioners of their honesty.

I One secret of facial truth, known to few people, is the micro expression. For an instant or two, the face flashes the emotion it is hiding. Untrained people rarely notice micro expressions, although they spot them on slow-motion videotape. But clinicians detect them readily, and most individuals can learn to recognise them with an hour of training. While the micro is fairly rare, a messier phenomenon, known as the squelch, is much more common. A damning expression starts to emerge, the person senses it and covers it rapidly, usually with a smile. A squelch can occur quickly enough to hide the underlying emotion, but it usually lasts longer than the micro, and even when we cannot see the emotion, we often sense the squelch itself.

J Scientists have now identified six basic expressions – enjoyment, anger, fear, surprise, disgust and sadness. By 'basic expressions', scientists mean expressions that people all over the world can identify from photographs. Movement signals, like those of the eyes, are more difficult to study and have tended to elude research. Even so, numerous expressions spin off from the basic models. Some are matters of degree, like annoyance, which is mild anger. Others are fusions, like contemptuous enjoyment.

K Practice enhances face-reading, and a person may attain varying levels of success with it. But there is one sure path to error: the pseudo-science called physiognomy, which purports to divine character from large chins, long noses and the like. No evidence supports it, modern experts laugh at it. So watch the play of expressions on the face, not the structure. It is a lot more interesting.

Adapted from Times Weekend

Questions 6–10
*Complete the table below using **NO MORE THAN THREE WORDS** for each answer.*

	Sadness	**Fear**	**Anger**	**Surprise**
Eyebrows	6	Rise	Descend	7 ....
Mouth/Lips		8	9	Open
Eyes	Look 10	Widen		Open

Questions 11–13
*Which **THREE** of the following signals are considered to be unreliable as signs of lying?*

A cover-up smiles

B higher vocal pitch

C rapid blinking

D averted eyes

E intense displays of emotion

F facial animation

11 ....   **12** ....   **13** ....

Questions 14–16
*Choose the appropriate letter **A–D** to answer the following questions.*

14 One way in which an expression of surprise differs from other emotions is that …
    A it often appears in short bursts.
    B it disappears suddenly.
    C it lasts a short time.
    D it is easy to imitate.

15 What do micro expressions and squelches have in common?
    A They are both equally difficult to detect.
    B They are both unusual occurrences.
    C They are both connected with concealing an emotion.
    D They are both the subject of current research.

16 Which aspect of the subject have scientists not yet been able to study in detail?
    A Face-reading
    B Physiognomy
    C Basic expressions
    D Movement signals

Focus on vocabulary

WORD FAMILIES

1 Complete the following table by writing in the missing parts of speech.

Verb	Noun	Adjective
annoy	1 *annoyingness*	2 *annoying*
	3 *anxiety*	anxious
collide	4	
5	6	counterfeit
deceive	7	8
emphasise	9	10
exist	11	12
13	14	false
	15	honest
respond	16	17
18	voice	19
20	21	wide
withdraw	22	23

DEPENDENT PREPOSITIONS

2 Fill in the missing prepositions. You can check your answers by referring to similar examples in the reading passage on page 155 as indicated.

1 The latest research provides an insight .... the causes of delinquency. (paragraph A)

2 .... common with most other universities, we are suffering from a reduction in funding. (paragraph B)

3 In babies, the 'social smile' generally appears .... the age of two months. (paragraph C)

4 Eyebrows rise .... expressions of fear, or .... emphasis. (paragraph C)

5 Crime detection was .... its infancy at the turn of the century. (paragraph C)

6 The police investigation centred .... the victim's circle of close friends. (paragraph D)

7 .... the whole, we are not good .... detecting lies. (paragraph E)

8 Some liars increase eye contact, convincing questioners .... their honesty. (paragraph H)

KEY LANGUAGE
Idioms with *face, eyes, ears,* etc.
▶ ex. 27, p. 206

Focus on speaking 2

1 Read the following advice.

- Jot down key words or phrases to jog your memory. Don't write whole sentences.
- Make sure you cover both elements on the topic card: **description** and **explanation**.
- Try to make your subject as interesting as possible. Don't be afraid to use humour!

2 Work in pairs as 'examiner' and 'candidate'. When you've finished Topic 1, change roles for Topic 2.

The examiner should:
1 Read out the instructions below.
2 Allow the candidate one minute to prepare (use a watch if possible).
3 Listen to the candidate's talk without interrupting, and make sure it doesn't exceed two minutes.
4 Ask the closing questions.

> **Instructions to the candidate**
> - *Read the topic below carefully. You will have to talk about it for one to two minutes.*
> - *You have one minute to think about what you're going to say.*
> - *You can make some notes to help you if you wish.*

TOPIC 1

> **Describe your favourite style of dress.**
>
> **You should say:**
>
> **what kind of clothes you like to wear**
> **what fabrics and colours you prefer**
> **what (or who) influences you in your choice of clothes**
>
> **and explain whether clothes are important to you or not.**

Closing questions
What kind of clothes do you feel least comfortable in?
Do you enjoy shopping for clothes?

TOPIC 2

> **Describe a film, theatre or TV performer you admire.**
>
> **You should say:**
>
> **what they look like**
> **what they do**
> **what you like about them**
>
> **and mention a performance you particularly enjoyed.**

Closing questions
Do you see a lot of films/go to many plays/watch a lot of TV? Would you recommend the performance you mentioned to a friend?

▶ Part 3: Discussion

REMINDER

- This is an opportunity to demonstrate your fluency, and also your range of vocabulary and grammar Try to make the most of it!

3   Work in pairs to discuss the following points

Topic 1: Clothes
1   Do you think it's important to wear formal clothes for a job interview? Why/Why not?
2   How much can you judge a person by their appearance, in your opinion?
3   Do you think people should be free to wear whatever they like at work?
4   What do you think about school uniforms? Are they a good idea?
5   Do you think the fashion industry has a bad influence on young people?

Topic 2: Performers
1   Do you think that acting is a good profession for young people to enter? Why/Why not?
2   What would be the advantages and disadvantages of being a famous actor or actress?
3   Do you think there is too much interest in the private lives of famous people?
4   What do you think about well-known TV and movie stars appearing in advertisements?
5   Are there any ways they could use their fame to do good in the world?

20 ▶ Through the lens

In this unit you will practise:
- Interview; individual long turn; two-way discussion
- Note, table and flow-chart completion; multiple choice
- Describing an object
- Pronunciation: word stress

Exam Focus
Speaking: Parts 1, 2, 3
Listening: Sections 1, 4
Writing: Task 1

Lead-in

1 Discuss the following question with another student.

Which medium A–D would you choose for the following purposes, and why?

A    B   C   D

1 to take with you on a week's holiday in the countryside
2 to provide a record of a wedding
3 to keep a child occupied
4 for a portrait of a special person
5 as a subject to study at an evening class

2 Which uses of photography do the following pictures illustrate? Can you think of any more?

€137.204,11 Traditional Normandy house with three bedrooms, kitchen, living room and

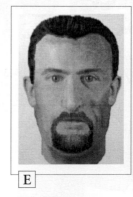

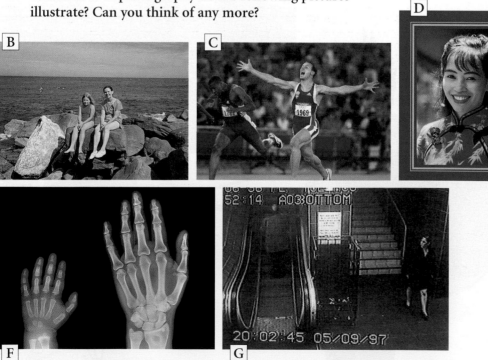

PRONUNCIATION:
WORD STRESS

3 Examples A–D below show four different word stress patterns.

A o O o o photography ....
B O o o studio ....
C o o O o equipment ....
D O o subject ....

Put the following words in the correct group A–D, according to their stress pattern. There should be five words in each group. Check any meanings you're not sure of.

accessory	commercial	landscape	photographer	technology
advertise	develop	negative	portrait	tripod
advertisement	digital	perspective	programme	transparency
cinema	enlargement	photograph	projector	wildlife

Focus on listening 1 *Photography courses*

▶ Section I

*Listen to the telephone conversation between a student and answer Questions **1–10**.*

Questions 1–6
Complete the table below.
Write **NO MORE THAN THREE WORDS** or **A NUMBER** *for each answer.*

PHOTOGRAPHY COURSES				
Course title	**Level**	**Day/Time**	**Length**	**Interview**
Introducing photography	1	Monday 6.30–9.30	10 weeks	NO
Black and white photography	Intermediate	Tuesday 2	10 weeks	YES
Landscape photography	Advanced	Tuesday 6.30–9.00	3	4 ....
The art of digital photography	Advanced	Wednesday 5	6	YES

Question 7
Circle TWO letters A–G.
Which **TWO** of the following subjects are covered in the
Introducing photography course?

A film types   **E** composition

B camera controls   **F** night photography

C camera accessories **G** printing

D lighting

Questions 8–10
Circle the correct letters A–C.

8 What is the fee for the *Black and white photography* course?

    A £85

    B £95

    C £140

9 What does the fee for the *Landscape photography* course include?

    A materials

    B field trip

    C examination fee

10 Which course is it especially important to apply for early?

    A *Introducing photography*

    B *Black and white photography*

    C *The art of digital photography*

Focus on listening 2 *History of cinema*

▶ Section 4   **1** Discuss the quiz questions below with another student.

Film Quiz

1 Where did the history of the camera begin?
  A Arabia   B France   C USA

2 When was the first Oscar ceremony?
  A 1929   B 1949   C 1969

3 Which city has held an international film festival
every year since 1946?
  A Amsterdam (Netherlands)
  B Barcelona (Spain)
  C Cannes (France)

4 Which film actor became President of the USA?

5 Which country has the biggest film industry in
the world?

The answers to the quiz
are on page 218.

2   **Now listen to the recording and answer these questions.**

Questions 1–3
Complete the table using **NO MORE THAN THREE WORDS** *for each answer.*

PRE-HISTORY OF THE MOVIE		
Name of device	**Dating from**	**Details**
Camera obscura	11ᵗʰ century	Originally used to observe solar eclipses. Later used as a **1** .... tool.
Magic lantern	17ᵗʰ century	Ancestor of modern film projector. Mainly used for **2** ....
'Kinetoscope'	1894	Also known as 'peep-hole machine'. Only **3** .... could view film.

Questions 4–7
Complete the flow chart below. Use **NO MORE THAN THREE WORDS** *for each answer.*

LANDMARKS IN CINEMATOGRAPHY

1895   First **4** .... demonstrated in Paris.

↓

1903   First Western screened, 'The Great **5** ....'.

↓

1927   'The Jazz Singer' was the first **6** .... film.

↓

1932   Technicolor introduced and used in a **7** ....

Questions 8–10
Complete this list of factors which made California attractive to film makers.
Write **NO MORE THAN THREE WORDS** *for each answer.*

Constant sunshine
8 ....
9 ....
10 ....

Focus on speaking *Practice interview*

This exam practice section will give you the opportunity to rehearse all three parts of the interview.

Work in pairs as 'examiner' and 'candidate'. Do the tasks for Candidate A in each part first. When you've finished, change roles and do the tasks for Candidate B. Try to simulate exam conditions as much as possible. Read the instructions for each part before you begin

▶ **Part 1: Interview**

The *Introduction and Interview* stage should take four to five minutes.

Examiner: Greet the candidate. Read out the questions below.
Candidate: Close your book and listen carefully to the questions.

Questions for Candidate A

Let's talk first about what you do in your free time.
- Do you have any special hobbies or interests?
- How long have you been interested in .... ?
- What do you enjoy about it?

Let's move on to your future plans.
- What are you planning to do when the IELTS Test is over?
- And what about longer term? Do you have any long-term plans for work or study?
- Where would you like to be living in five years' time?

Questions for Candidate B

Let's talk first about your country.
- You come from .... What's the best thing about living there?
- How do people enjoy themselves in their free time in .... ?
- What places are there for a tourist to visit in .... ?

Moving on now to talk about your studies.
- How long have you been studying English?
- What do you enjoy most about your studies?
- How do you expect to use English in future?

▶ **Part 2: Individual long turn**

The *Individual long turn* should take three to four minutes including one minute for preparation.

Examiner: Read out the top line of the topic card and give the candidate one minute to prepare. Then ask him/her to start speaking. Don't interrupt during the candidate's speaking time. After one to two minutes, ask the closing questions.

Candidate: Read the topic card. You have one minute to prepare. Make notes on a piece of a paper if you wish. You will need to speak for one to two minutes.

Topic for Candidate A

> **Describe a photograph you have taken which is important to you.**
>
> **You should say:**
>> **what the picture shows**
>> **when and why you took it**
>> **where you keep it**
>
> **and explain what is special about it.**

Topic for Candidate B

> **Describe a film you have enjoyed.**
>
> **You should say:**
>> **what it was about**
>> **when and why you saw it**
>> **what special features it had**
>
> **and explain what you especially liked about it.**

Closing questions
Are you a keen photographer?
Do you like looking at other people's photographs?

Closing questions
Do you often watch films?
Do you prefer watching films in the cinema or on video?

▶ Part 3: Discussion

The two-way discussion should take four to five minutes.

Examiner: Begin by asking the following questions. Listen to the candidate's answers carefully. Be prepared to react and ask appropriate follow-up questions.

Candidate: Listen carefully to the examiner. Answer the questions as fully as possible.

Questions for Candidate A
- Is photography becoming more or less popular these days, in your experience?
- Would you agree with the saying: 'The camera never lies'?
- Would you say that photography is an art?

Follow-up questions
- News photographers sometimes take pictures of people in distress, after a disaster, for example. Do you think this is justified?
- Do you think advertising can have harmful effects?

Questions for Candidate B
- Are film stars paid too much money, in your opinion?
- Do you think there's too much violence in modern movies?
- What do you feel about film censorship? Is it necessary?

Follow-up questions
- Do you think television and video will kill the cinema?
- Special cameras are sometimes used to film everything that goes on in the street and in shops. Do you think this is a good idea?

Focus on writing *Describing an object*

▶ EXAM BRIEFING

Writing module, Task 1
One possible task in this section is to *describe an object, event or sequence of events*. This has been less common than other tasks in the past, but things may change!

General strategies
- You are not expected to have technical knowledge or to use specialist vocabulary.
- Your task is description – don't try to give reasons for developments.
- Don't try to describe every detail – concentrate on significant features.

▶ Task 1

1 In the following task, you have to describe a number of developments in camera design over the years. Read the *Task approach* and notes on language before attempting the task.

TASK APPROACH
- Start with a brief overview, outlining the common features, for example: *The basic design of all the cameras shown is the same. They consist of …*
- Look for significant similarities and differences between examples. Try to vary your language whenever possible.
- End with a summarising statement.

VARYING YOUR LANGUAGE

2 In a task like this, which concerns a number of similar developments, you need to avoid overusing the verbs you use to introduce each stage. Think of at least three other ways to say *was invented*.

3 Before attempting the task on page 166, look at the *Useful language* box on the same page.

Useful language: Describing objects

shape

... is
{
(basically / roughly) square / rectangular / cylindrical **in shape**
shaped like a cube / rectangle / cylinder
}

structure

...
{
consists of ...
is divided into ... sections / parts
is made of ...
}

size

... **is** 1 metre
{
long / wide / high
in length / width / height
}

... **is**
{
(slightly / considerably) **bigger / heavier / more complex than** ...
(approximately / less than) **half the size of** ...
(only) **a fraction of the size of** ...
}

EXAM PRACTICE

WRITING PRACTICE
Describing objects
▶ ex. 8 and 9, p. 213–214
Presenting and justifying an
opinion
▶ ex. 10, p. 215

You should spend about 20 minutes on this task.

The diagrams below show stages in the development of the camera since its invention in 1839.

Write a report for a university lecturer describing the information shown below.

You should write at least 150 words.

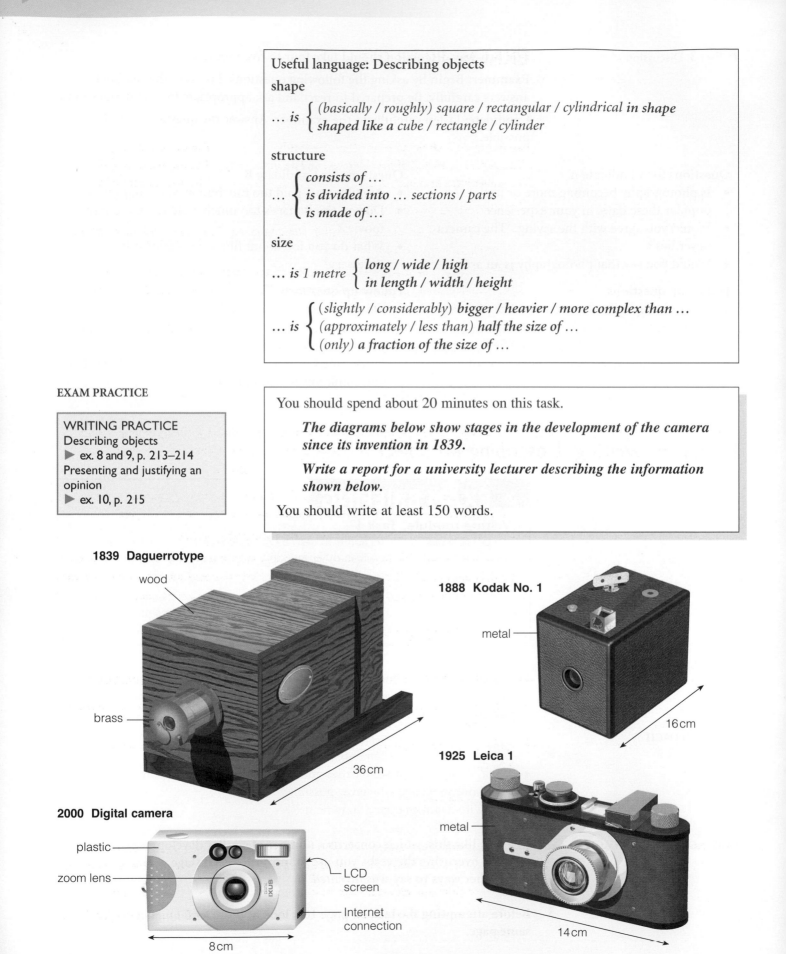

1839 Daguerrotype
wood
brass
36 cm

1888 Kodak No. 1
metal
16 cm

1925 Leica 1
metal
14 cm

2000 Digital camera
plastic
zoom lens
LCD screen
Internet connection
8 cm

ERROR HIT LIST

contain/consist/include

✗

Essays should include no more than 200 words.
The exam is consisted of a written test and an oral.
The wallet was containing £150.

✔

Essays should <u>contain</u> …
The exam <u>consists of</u> …
The wallet <u>contained</u> …

- These verbs cannot be used in progressive tenses.
- Use **contain** to refer to the contents of something, e.g. *The bag **contained** a wallet and car keys. This product **contains** nuts.*
- Use **consist of** / **be made up of** to describe all the parts of something, e.g. *The population **is made up of** three ethnic groups.* The verb *comprise* can also be used, though this is more formal in style.
- Use **include** to mention one or more (but not all) of the parts of a thing, e.g. *The book **includes** a chapter on recent economic trends.*

surely/certainly

✗

Scientists say that temperatures are surely rising.
Unemployment will surely increase as a result.

✔

… are <u>definitely/certainly</u> rising …
Unemployment <u>is bound/</u>
<u>sure</u> to …

- **surely** is used, especially in spoken English, as a way of inviting someone to agree with your point of view, e.g. ***Surely** you don't accept that argument, do you?*
- Use **certainly** or **definitely** to emphasise that something is true.
- To say you are confident that something will happen, use **is/are bound to** / **sure to** or **there is no doubt that**, e.g. *The polls show that the Prime Minister **is bound to** win the election. **There is no doubt that** the Prime Minister will win the election.*

a great deal of/a great many

✗

There have been a great deal of problems.

✔

… <u>a large number of/a great many</u> …

- The phrase **a great deal of** means 'a large amount' and is followed by an uncountable noun, e.g. *It's taken **a great deal of** time to reorganise the office.*
- If there is no need to emphasise the size of a number, use *many* or (informally) *a lot of.*

older/elder/elderly

✗

This type of music is popular with elder people.
The job requires an elderly, more experienced person.

✔

… with <u>older</u> people.
… requires an <u>older</u>, more …

- Only use **elder** and **eldest** to refer to members of a family, e.g. *my **elder** brother.*
- **elderly** is a polite word meaning 'old'; **the elderly** = old people, e.g. *a home for the **elderly**.*

Practice test

LISTENING

TIME ALLOWED: 30 minutes + 10 minutes' transfer time   NUMBER OF QUESTIONS: 40

*All the recordings will be played **ONCE** only.*

The test is in four sections.

SECTION 1   *Questions 1–10*

Questions 1–3

*Circle the correct letters **A–D**.*

> **Example**
> Which country is Anna planning to visit?
>   **A**   Mexico
>   **B**   Mongolia
>   **Ⓒ**   Morocco

1   How long is Anna's trip?
    A   ten days
    B   two weeks
    C   seventeen days

2   What aspect of the climate does Sam think Anna needs to prepare for?
    A   the daytime heat
    B   the cold nights
    C   the possibility of rain

3   What part of the trip does Sam recommend particularly highly?
    A   walking in the mountains
    B   visiting the local markets
    C   camel trekking in the desert

Questions 4–10

Complete the notes below.

*Write **NO MORE THAN THREE WORDS** for each answer.*

<u>What to take on trip</u>

Clothing:
- *comfortable, loose clothes*
- **4** ....
- *sun hat*
- **5** ....

Other:
- **6** ....
- *personal* **7** ....
- *sun cream*
- **8** ....
- **9** ....
- **10** ....

SECTION 2   *Questions 11–20*

Questions 11–13

*List **THREE** groups of people who are at risk from RSI.*

*Write **NO MORE THAN THREE WORDS** for your answer.*

   computer operators

11 ....

12 ....

13 ....

Question 14

14   How many people in the UK are believed to suffer from RSI?   ....

Questions 15–17

Circle the correct letters A–C.

15 Which graph shows the rise in disability claims relating to RSI?

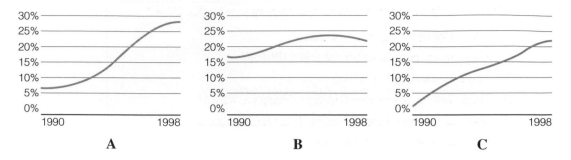

16 According to the speaker, RSI can develop when

    A muscles are used for too long.

    B muscles are not used.

    C muscles are stretched.

17 How often is it advisable to get up from your computer and move around?

    A every ten minutes

    B every half hour

    C every hour

Questions 18–20

*Complete the diagram. Write **NO MORE THAN THREE WORDS** for your answer.*

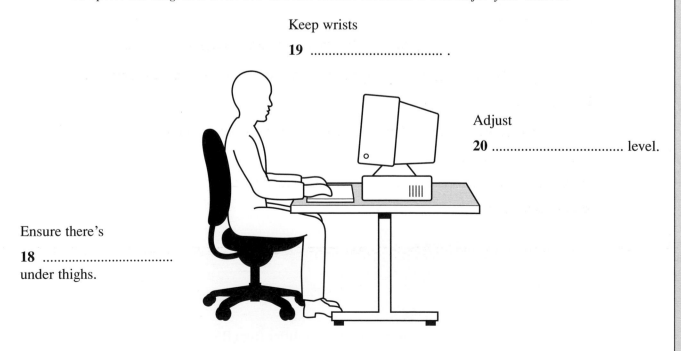

Keep wrists

19 ....

Adjust

20 .... level.

Ensure there's

18 ....

under thighs.

SECTION 3 *Questions 21–30*

Questions 21–24

Circle FOUR letters A–G.

Which **FOUR** of the following does Jeremy predict for 2020?

A Unemployment figures will rise.

B Many more people will work from home.

C The paperless office will arrive.

D There will be an increase in temporary workers.

E Sixty per cent of companies will change completely.

F Most workers will be over 50.

G There will be a shortage of young workers.

Questions 25–27

Circle THREE letters A–G.

Which **THREE** benefits does Caroline gain by flexible working?

A more time for childcare

B a feeling of independence

C more time for leisure activities

D higher earnings

E less distraction

F no commuting

G more interesting work

Questions 28–30

Complete the sentences. Write NO MORE THAN THREE WORDS for each answer.

According to Caroline, one disadvantage of flexible working is that she sometimes feels

28 ....

Jeremy predicts that, in future, the main reason to go to the office will be to

29 ....

In his view, a **30** .... will make it possible

to work anywhere.

SECTION 4 Questions 31–40

Questions 31–33

Complete the following table.

*Use **NO MORE THAN THREE WORDS** or **A NUMBER** for each answer.*

EARLY BRIDGES			
Bridge type	**Material(s) used**	**First examples date from**	**Region**
Arch	stone or brick	**31** .... BC	the Middle East
Suspension	**32** .... and	AD 550	**33** ....
	iron	1826	Wales (UK)

Questions 34–37

Complete the notes on the time line below.

*Use **NO MORE THAN THREE WORDS** for each answer.*

> **The construction of the Clifton Suspension Bridge**
>
> 1831   Design for bridge chosen by **34** ....
>   Work begun, but soon halted by political events.
> 1836   Work resumed.
> 1843   Work stopped when **35** ....
> 1851   Ironwork sold to pay **36** ....
> 1860   Second-hand **37** .... became available.
> 1862   Work resumed.
> 1864   Bridge completed.

Questions 38–40

Complete the table.

*Use **NO MORE THAN THREE WORDS** or **A NUMBER** for each answer.*

BRIDGE PROPOSALS			
Between	**Distance**	**Main difficulty**	**Effect**
Alaska and Siberia	80km	**38**	Construction time limited
Europe and Africa	28km	**39**	New type of bridge structure required
Sicily and mainland Italy	**40** ....km	Funding	

ACADEMIC READING

TIME ALLOWED: 1 hour   NUMBER OF QUESTIONS: 40

READING PASSAGE 1

*You should spend about 20 minutes on **Questions 1–12**, which are based on Reading Passage 1 on pages 173 and 174.*

The Birth of Blue

As a primary colour, blue has been the most difficult for artists and scientists to create.

Artists have always been enchanted by blue, yet fine blues have long been difficult to obtain. Blues are relatively rare in nature, and painters throughout the ages have therefore found themselves at the mercy of what contemporary chemical technology could offer. Some blues have been prohibitively expensive, others were unreliable. The quest for a good blue has driven some crucial technological innovations, showing that the interaction of art and science has not always been a one-way affair.

The first pigments were simply ground-up coloured minerals dug from the earth. But few blue minerals are suitable as pigments – so there are no blues in cave art. Ancient Egyptian artists used blue prominently, however, because they knew how to make a fine artificial pigment, now known as Egyptian blue.

The discovery of Egyptian blue, like that of many other artificial pigments, was almost certainly an accident. The Egyptians manufactured blue-glazed stones and ornaments called *faience* using a technique they inherited from the Mesopotamians. Faience manufacture was big business in the ancient world – it was traded all over Europe by 1500 BC. Faience is made by heating stone ornaments in a kiln with copper minerals such as malachite. Egyptian blue, which was made from at least 2500 BC, comes from firing chalk or limestone with sand and copper minerals, and probably appeared by the chance mixture of these ingredients in a faience kiln.

Scientists recently deduced the secrets of another ancient blue: Maya blue, used for centuries throughout central America before the Spanish Conquest. This is a kind of clay – a mineral made of sheets of atoms – with molecules of the blue dye indigo wedged between the sheets. Using indigo in this way makes it less liable to decompose. No one has made colours this way since the Mayas, and no one knows exactly how they did it. But technologists are now interested in using the same trick to make stable pigments from other dyes.

The finest pigment available to medieval artists was ultramarine, which began to appear in Western art in the 13th century. It was made from the blue mineral *lapis lazuli*, of which only one source was known: the remote mines of Badakshan, now in Afghanistan. In addition to the difficulty of transporting the mineral over such distances, making the pigment was a tremendously laborious business. Lapis lazuli turns greyish when powdered because of impurities in the mineral. To extract the pure blue pigment, the powder has to be mixed to a dough with wax and kneaded repeatedly in water.

As a result, ultramarine could cost more than its weight in gold, and medieval artists were very selective in using it. Painters since the

Renaissance craved a cheaper, more accessible, blue to compare with ultramarine. Things improved in 1704, when a Berlin-based colour maker called Diesbach discovered the first "modern" synthetic pigment: Prussian blue. Diesbach was trying to make a red pigment, using a recipe that involved the alkali potash. But Diesbach's potash was contaminated with animal oil, and the synthesis did not work out as planned. Instead of red, Diesbach made blue.

The oil had reacted to produce cyanide, a vital ingredient of Prussian blue. Diesbach kept his recipe secret for many years, but it was discovered and published in 1724, after which anyone could make the colour. By the 1750s, it cost just a tenth of ultramarine. But it wasn't such a glorious blue, and painters still weren't satisfied. They got a better alternative in 1802, when the French chemist Louis Jacques Thenard invented cobalt blue.

Best of all was the discovery in 1826 of a method for making ultramarine itself. The French Society for the Encouragement of National Industry offered a prize of 6,000 francs in 1824 to anyone who could make artificial ultramarine at an affordable price.

The Toulouse chemist Jean-Baptiste Guimet was awarded the prize two years later, when he showed that ultramarine could be made by heating china clay, soda, charcoal, sand and sulphur in a furnace. This meant that there was no longer any need to rely on the scarce natural source, and ultramarine eventually became a relatively cheap commercial pigment (called French ultramarine, as it was first mass-produced in Paris).

In the 1950s, synthetic ultramarine became the source of what is claimed to be the world's most beautiful blue. Invented by the French artist Yves Klein in collaboration with a Parisian paint manufacturer, Edouard Adam, International Klein Blue is a triumph of modern chemistry. Klein was troubled by how pigments lost their richness when they were mixed with liquid binder to make a paint. With Adam's help, he found that a synthetic resin, thinned with organic solvents, would retain this vibrant texture in the dry paint layer. In 1957, Klein launched his new blue with a series of monochrome paintings, and in 1960 he protected his invention with a patent.

Questions 1–4

Complete the summary below. Choose **NO MORE THAN THREE WORDS** *from the passage for each answer.*

The colours used in cave paintings and other early art were made by crushing .....**1**..... . However, later artists have generally had to rely on the .....**2**..... of the day for their supplies of blue. Among the first examples of the widespread use of blue was in .....**3**..... art. Over the centuries, many more attempts to create acceptable blues have been made, some of which have led to significant .....**4**..... .

1 ....   2 ....   3 ....   4 ....

Questions 5 and 6

*Choose the appropriate letter **A–D**.*

5   What was the main disadvantage in using ultramarine for medieval artists?

   A   It contained a number of impurities.

   B   It was excessively expensive.

   C   The colour wasn't permanent.

   D   The preparation process was hazardous.

6   The discovery of Prussian blue was the result of

   A   using the wrong quantity of an ingredient.

   B   mixing the wrong ingredients together.

   C   including an ingredient that was impure.

   D   using an ingredient of the wrong colour.

Questions 7–12

Look at the following notes that have been made about the types of blue described in Reading Passage 1. Match each description with a type of blue.

Example	Answer
was developed in the early years of the 19th century	**E**

NOTES

7   derived from a scarce natural resource   ....

8   specially designed to retain its depth of colour when used in paint   ....

9   was cheap to produce but had limited appeal for artists   ....

10   made using a technique which is not yet fully understood   ....B....

11   thought to have been produced during another manufacturing process   ..A......

12   came to be manufactured inexpensively in large quantities   ....

Types of Blue

A   Egyptian blue

B   Maya blue

C   ultramarine

D   Prussian blue

E   cobalt blue

F   French ultramarine

G   International Klein Blue

READING PASSAGE 2

You should spend about 20 minutes on **Questions 13–25**, which are based on Reading Passage 2 on pages 177 and 178.

Questions 13–17

*Complete each of the following statements with the best ending **A–I** from the box below.*

13 Napier grass ....

16 Ploughing the land ....

14 The plant called *Striga* ....

17 Sowing black oats ....

15 Growing single crops ....

List of Endings

A reduces losses due to plant diseases.

B can lead to soil erosion.

C causes major financial losses.

D increases soil fertility.

E discourages the growth of weeds.

F helps to retain carbon dioxide.

G destroys harmful insect larvae.

H helps prevent global warming.

I encourages pests to breed.

Questions 18–25

Complete the table below.

*Choose **NO MORE THAN THREE WORDS** from the passage for each answer.*

Area	Strategy	Benefits to farmers
East Africa	**18** .... with food crop.	Lower costs Higher yields
19	Growing mixed crops together.	Higher yields
Madagascar	Transplanting seedlings earlier. Leaving paddy fields unflooded. Replacing chemical fertilisers with **20**	Higher yields
Cuba	Reducing **21** .... Using **22** .... instead of farm vehicles. Growing mixed crops together.	Yields doubled Citizens' **23** .... increased.
Latin America	Zero-tillage	Lower costs Improved **24** .... Higher yields Higher **25** ....

An ordinary miracle

Bigger harvests, without pesticides or genetically modified crops? Farmers can make it happen by letting weeds do the work.

Across East Africa, thousands of farmers are planting weeds in their maize fields. Bizarre as it sounds, their technique is actually raising yields by giving the insect pests something else to chew on besides maize. "It's better than pesticides, and a lot cheaper," said Ziadin Khan, whose idea it is, as he showed me round his demonstration plots at the Mbita Point research station on the shores of Lake Victoria in Kenya. "And it has raised farm yields round here by 60 to 70 per cent."

His novel way of fighting pests is one of a host of low-tech innovations boosting production by 100 per cent or more on millions of poor Third World farms in the past decade. This "sustainable agriculture" just happens to be the biggest movement in Third World farming today, dwarfing the tentative forays into genetic manipulation.

In East Africa, maize fields face two major pests, and Khan has a solution to both. The first is an insect called the *stem borer*, whose larvae eat their way through a third of the region's maize most years. But Khan discovered that the borer is even fonder of a local weed, napier grass. By planting napier grass in their fields, farmers can lure the stem borer away from the maize – and into a honey-trap. For the grass produces a sticky substance that traps and kills stem borer larvae. The second pest is *Striga*, a parasitic plant that wrecks $10 billion worth of maize crops every year, threatening the livelihoods of 100 million Africans. "Weeding *Striga* is one of the most time-consuming activities for millions of African women farmers," says Khan. But he has an antidote: another weed called *Desmodium*. "It seems to release another sort of

chemical that *Striga* doesn't like. At any rate, where farmers plant *Desmodium* between rows of maize, *Striga* won't grow."

"The success of sustainable agriculture is dispelling the myth that modern techno-farming is the most productive method," says Miguel Altieri of the University of California, Berkeley. "In Mexico, it takes 1.73 hectares of land planted with maize to produce as much food as one hectare planted with a mixture of maize, squash and beans. The difference," he says, "comes from the reduction of losses due to weeds, insects and diseases and a more efficient use of the available resources of water, light and nutrients. Monocultures breed pests and waste resources," he says.

Researchers from the Association Tefy Saina, a Madagascan group working for local farmers, were looking for ways to boost rice yields on small farms. They decided to make the best use of existing strains rather than track down a new breed of super-rice. Through trial and error, a new system was developed that raises typical rice yields from three to twelve tonnes per hectare. The trick is to transplant seedlings earlier and In smaller numbers so that more survive; to keep paddies unflooded for much of the growing period; and to help the plants grow using compost rather than chemical fertilisers. The idea has grown like wildfire, and 20,000 have adopted the idea in Madagascar alone.

Few countries have switched wholesale to sustainable agriculture. But Cuba has. The collapse of the Soviet Union in 1990 cut off cheap supplies of grain, tractors and agrochemicals. Pesticide use halved overnight, as did the calorie intake of its citizens. The cash-strapped country was forced to embrace low-input farming or starve. "Today," says Fernando Funes of the Country's Pasture and Fodder Research Institute, "teams of oxen

177

replace the tractors, and farmers have adopted organic methods, mixing maize with beans and cassava and doubling yields in the process, helping average calorie intake per person rise back to pre-1990 levels."

Worldwide, one of the most widely adopted sustainable techniques has been to throw away the plough, the ultimate symbol of the farmer. Ploughing aerates the soil, helping rot weeds and crop residues. But it can also damage soil fertility and increase erosion. Now millions of Latin American farmers have decided it isn't worth the effort. A third of Argentina's farms no longer use the plough. Instead, they fight weeds by planting winter crops, such as black oats, or by spraying a biodegradable herbicide such as glyphosate. "The farmers saw results in a short time – reduced costs, richer soils, bigger grain yields and increased income," says Lauro Bassi of EPAGRI, the agricultural research institute in Santa Catarina state, southern Brazil, which has been promoting the idea.

Zero-tillage also benefits the planet in general. Unploughed soils hang on to carbon that would otherwise escape into the air as carbon dioxide when organic matter rots. "A one-hectare field left unploughed can absorb up to a tonne of carbon every year," says Pretty, "making soils a vital element in preventing global warming."

Sustainable agriculture is no magic bullet for feeding the world. It is an approach rather than a blueprint. Small farms with low yields stand to gain the most and agribusiness the least. But it does offer an alternative for the millions of small farms that have plenty of hands to work the land, but not the skills or financial resources to adopt conventional mechanised farming.

READING PASSAGE 3

You should spend about 20 minutes on **Questions 26–40**, *which are based on Reading Passage 3 on pages 179 and 180.*

Questions 26–30

Complete the sentences below with words taken from Reading Passage 3.

Use **NO MORE THAN THREE WORDS** *for each answer.*

Scientists base their predictions about global warming on evidence from

26 ....

Two weather conditions which are likely to become more common as an indirect result of

global warming are **27** .... and ....

Once infectious disease has become established in an area, its **28** ....
can prove extremely difficult.

Mosquitoes can be effectively destroyed by **29** .... and

30 ....

Is Global Warming Harmful to Health?

Today, few scientists doubt the atmosphere is warming. Most also agree that the rate of heating is accelerating and that the consequences of this temperature change could become increasingly disruptive. Even high-school students can recite some projected outcomes: the oceans will warm, and glaciers will melt, causing sea levels to rise and salt water to inundate low-lying coasts. Yet less familiar effects could be equally detrimental. Notably, computer models indicate that global warming, and other climate alterations it induces, will expand the incidence and distribution of many serious medical disorders.

Heating of the atmosphere can influence health through several routes. Most directly, it can generate more, stronger and hotter heatwaves, which will become especially treacherous if the evenings fail to bring cooling relief. Global warming can also threaten human well-being profoundly, if somewhat less directly, by revising weather patterns – particularly by increasing the frequency and intensity of floods and droughts and by causing rapid swings in the weather. Aside from causing death by drowning or starvation, these disasters promote by various means the emergence, resurgence and spread of infectious disease. That prospect is deeply troubling, because infectious illness may kill fewer people in one fell swoop than a raging flood or an extended drought, but once it takes root in a community, it often defies eradication and can invade other areas.

Mosquitoes Rule in the Heat

Diseases relayed by mosquitoes – such as malaria, dengue fever, yellow fever and several kinds of encephalitis – are among those eliciting the greatest concern as the world warms. Mosquito-borne disorders are projected to become increasingly prevalent because their insect carriers, or "vectors", are very sensitive to meteorological conditions. Cold can be a friend to humans, because it limits mosquitoes to seasons and regions where temperatures stay above certain minimums. Winter freezing kills many eggs, larvae and adults outright.

Excessive heat kills insects as effectively as cold does. Nevertheless, within their survivable range of temperatures, mosquitoes proliferate faster and bite more as the air becomes warmer. At the same time, greater heat speeds the rate at which the pathogens inside them reproduce and mature. As whole areas heat up, then, mosquitoes could expand into formerly forbidden territories, bringing illness with them. Further, warmer nighttime and winter temperatures may enable them to cause more disease for longer periods in the areas they already inhabit.

The extra heat is not alone in encouraging a rise in mosquito-borne infection. Intensifying floods and droughts resulting from global warming can each trigger outbreaks by creating breeding grounds for insects whose desiccated eggs remain viable and hatch in still water. As floods recede, they leave puddles. In times of drought, streams can become stagnant pools, and people may put out containers to catch water; these pools and pots, too, can become incubators for new mosquitoes. And the insects can gain another boost if climate change or other processes (such as alterations of habitats by humans) reduce the populations of predators that normally keep mosquitoes in check.

Opportunists like Sequential Extremes

The increased climate variability accompanying warming will probably be more important than the rising heat itself in fuelling unwelcome outbreaks of certain vector-borne illnesses. For instance, warm winters followed by hot, dry summers (a pattern that could become all too familiar as the atmosphere heats up) favor the transmission of St Louis encephalitis and other infections that cycle among birds, urban mosquitoes and humans.

This sequence seems to have abetted the surprise emergence of the West Nile virus in New York City in 2000. No one knows how this virus found its way into the US. But one reasonable explanation for its persistence and amplification here centers on the weather's effects on *Culex pipiens* mosquitoes, which accounted for the bulk of transmission. These urban dwellers typically lay their eggs in damp basements, gutters, sewers and polluted pools of water.

The interaction between the weather, the mosquitoes and the virus probably went something like this: the mild winter of 1998–99 enabled many of the mosquitoes to survive into the spring, which arrived early. Drought in spring and summer concentrated nourishing organic matter in their breeding areas and simultaneously killed off mosquito predators, such as lacewings and ladybugs, that would otherwise have helped limit mosquito populations. Drought would also have led birds to congregate more, as they shared fewer and smaller watering holes, many of which were shared, naturally, by mosquitoes.

Once mosquitoes acquired the virus, the July heatwave that accompanied the drought would speed up the viral maturation inside the insects. Consequently, as infected mosquitoes sought blood meals, they could spread the virus to birds at a rapid rate. As bird after bird became infected, so did more mosquitoes, which ultimately fanned out to infect human beings. Torrential rains towards the end of August provided new puddles for the breeding of *C. pipiens* and other mosquitoes, unleashing an added crop of potential virus carriers.

Solutions

The health toll taken by global warming will depend to a large extent on the steps taken to prepare for the dangers. The ideal defensive strategy would have multiple components, including improved surveillance systems to spot the emergence or resurgence of infectious diseases; predicting when environmental conditions could become conducive to disease outbreaks; and limiting human activities that contribute to the heating or that exacerbate its effects.

Questions 31–35

Do the following statements agree with information given in Reading Passage 3?

Write:

TRUE	*if the statement is true according to the passage*
FALSE	*if the statement is false according to the passage*
DOES NOT SAY	*if there is no information about this in the passage*

31 Mosquito eggs are capable of surviving dry conditions.

32 Animals which feed on mosquitoes may be adversely affected by global warming.

33 Mosquitoes are becoming increasingly resistant to standard drugs.

34 Higher temperatures are likely to be the most important factor in encouraging diseases carried by mosquitoes.

35 The mosquitoes which transmit West Nile disease breed in rural areas.

Questions 36–40
Complete the flow chart with words taken from Reading Passage 3.
Use **NO MORE THAN THREE WORDS** *for each answer.*

Weather and West Nile Virus

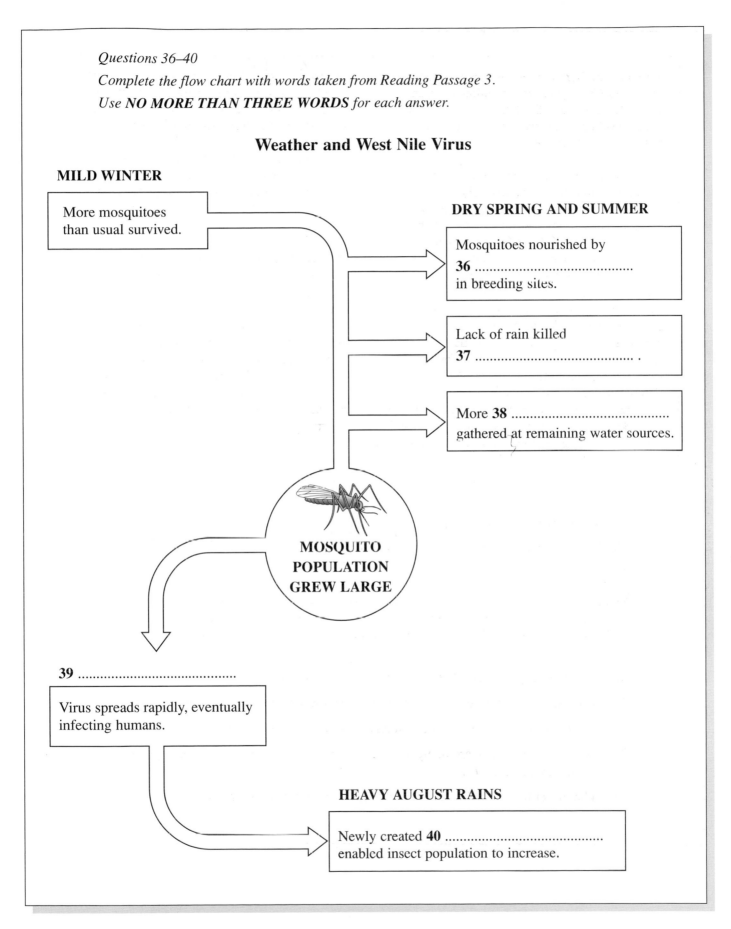

MILD WINTER

More mosquitoes than usual survived.

DRY SPRING AND SUMMER

Mosquitoes nourished by **36** .... in breeding sites.

Lack of rain killed **37** ....

More **38** .... gathered at remaining water sources.

MOSQUITO POPULATION GREW LARGE

39 ....
Virus spreads rapidly, eventually infecting humans.

HEAVY AUGUST RAINS

Newly created **40** .... enabled insect population to increase.

ACADEMIC WRITING

The writing test consists of two tasks. You should attempt both tasks. TIME ALLOWED: 1 hour

WRITING TASK 1

You should spend about 20 minutes on this task.

> *The chart below shows employment figures in different tourism-related industries between 1989 and 1999.*
>
> *Write a report for a university lecturer describing the information shown below.*

You should write at least 150 words.

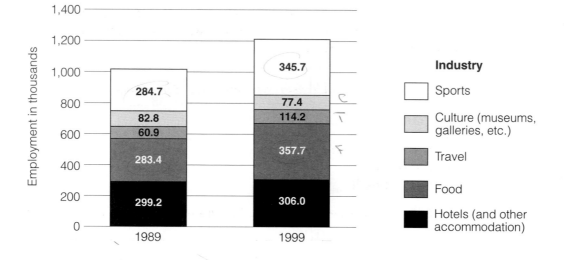

WRITING TASK 2

You should spend about 40 minutes on this task.

·Present a written argument or case to an educated reader with no specialist knowledge of the following topic.

> *Some people argue that the government should give every unemployed person a mobile phone and should make sure they have access to the Internet.*
>
> *They believe this is the best way of using public money to reduce the problem of unemployment.*
>
> *To what extent do you agree or disagree?*

You should use your own ideas, knowledge and experience and support your arguments with examples and relevant experience.

You should write at least 250 words.

SPEAKING

TIME ALLOWED: 11–14 minutes

PART ONE (4–5 minutes)

The examiner will ask you general questions about yourself. For example:

- *What's your name?*
- *Where do you come from?*
- *What are the good things about living there?*
- *Where are you studying English?*
- *How will English be useful in your life?*
- *What do you like doing in your spare time?*
- *What hobbies did you have as a child?*

PART TWO (3–4 minutes, including 1 minute preparation time)

The examiner will give you a topic written on a card. You will have one minute to think about what you're going to say and make notes if you wish. You will then have to talk about the topic for one to two minutes.

Describe a present you bought which gave someone a lot of pleasure.

You should say:

> **what the present was**
> **who it was for**
> **why you chose it**

and explain why the person who received it was so pleased.

After your talk, the examiner will ask one or two brief closing questions. For example:

- *Have you bought this kind of present for anyone else?*
- *Do you prefer giving or receiving presents?*

PART THREE (4–5 minutes)

The examiner will ask general questions related to the topic in Part 2. For example:

Presents for children
- *What kind of presents do children ask for today?*
- *What effect has advertising had on this?*
- *Is there a case for banning advertising directed at children?*

Consumerism
- *Is it better to shop in big supermarkets or in small local shops?*
- *What are the dangers of credit cards?*
- *How can children be encouraged to develop a responsible attitude towards money and spending?*

SAMPLE

IELTS Reading Answer Sheet

Academic
General Training

Module taken (shade one box)

Version number:
Please enter the number in the boxes (one digit per line, starting at the top) and shade the number in the grid beside the box.

0	1	2	3	4	5	6	7	8	9

1		21	
2		22	
3		23	
4		24	
5		25	
6		26	
7		27	
8		28	
9		29	
10		30	
11		31	
12		32	
13		33	
14		34	
15		35	
16		36	
17		37	
18		38	
19		39	
20		40	

Marker's Initials   Band Score   Reading Total

© UCLES 2002

UNIVERSITY of CAMBRIDGE
Local Examinations Syndicate

The British Council

IDP Education Australia
IELTS Australia

SAMPLE

PEN must be used to complete this sheet.

Centre number:

Please write your name below,

then write your four digit Candidate number in the boxes and shade the number in the grid on the right in PENCIL.

Test date (shade ONE box for the day, ONE box for the month and ONE box for the year):

Day: 01 02 03 04 05 06 07 08 09 10 11 12 13 14 15 16 17 18 19 20 21 22 23 24 25 26 27 28 29 30 31

Month: 01 02 03 04 05 06 07 08 09 10 11 12

Year: Last digit of the   0 1 2 3 4 5 6 7 8 9

IELTS Listening Answer Sheet

Version number:
Please enter the number in the boxes (one digit per line, starting at the top) and shade the number in the grid beside the box.

1		19	
2		20	
3		21	
4		22	
5		23	
6		24	
7		25	
8		26	
9		27	
10		28	
11		29	
12		30	
13		31	
14		32	
15		33	
16		34	
17		35	
18		36	
		37	
		38	
		39	
		40	

Marker's Initials   Band Score   Listening Total

IELTS L–R v5

© UCLES 2002

DP452/352

– 2 –

SAMPLE

EXAMINER'S USE ONLY

| EXAMINER 2 TASK 1 | TF | CC | VSS | TOTAL | | GLOBAL BAND |
| EXAMINER 1 TASK 1 | TF | CC | VSS | TOTAL | | GLOBAL BAND |

International English Language Testing System

UNIVERSITY of CAMBRIDGE
Local Examinations Syndicate

The British Council

IDP Education Australia:
IELTS Australia

WRITING ANSWER SHEET

Candidate Name: ....

Candidate Number: ....

Centre Name: .... Date: ....

Module: ACADEMIC   ☐   (Tick as appropriate)
          GENERAL TRAINING   ☐

Version: ....

TASK 1

SAMPLE

EXAMINER'S USE ONLY

EXAMINER 2 NUMBER: ....

EXAMINER 1 NUMBER: ....

CANDIDATE NUMBER: ....

► Key language bank

Exercise 1 (Unit 1)

The suffix -*en* e.g. *less* → *lessen*

1 Each of the adjectives in the box below can be made into a verb by adding the suffix *-en*. Two of them need further changes of spelling – which are they?

bright	*dark*	*hard*	*long*	*loose*	*soft*
weak	*broad*	*fast*	*less*	*light*	*short*
strong	*wide*				

2 Complete the following sentences by adding verbs formed by adding *-en* to adjectives in the box above. Make any other changes necessary.

1 It's easier to blend the butter into the mixture if you .... it first by warming it.

2 According to the weather forecast, it should .... up this afternoon.

3 The council is proposing to .... this road to three lanes instead of two.

4 These exercises are specifically designed to .... the abdominal muscles.

5 Please .... your seat belts for take-off.

6 The danger of developing lung cancer .... as soon as you give up smoking.

7 They say that travel .... the mind, and I hope he'll benefit from his year in South America.

8 The case for the defence was .... when a key witness failed to appear.

► LANGUAGE FACT

-en is the second most common verb suffix in spoken and written English. The most common suffix is *-ze* (*-ise* in British English) which occurs particularly often in academic prose.

Exercise 2 (Unit 1)

Grammatical terms

You need to be familiar with the names for the different parts of speech in English in order to follow the notes in this section, and also to make effective use of a dictionary or grammar reference book.

PARTS OF SPEECH

1 Read the following definitions (1–8) and then choose the correct group of examples (a–h).

1 **noun**
refers to a person, place, thing or an abstract idea, e.g. …

2 **pronoun**
can be used to replace a noun, e.g. …

3 **verb**
refers to an action or a state, e.g. …

4 **adjective**
describes people, things and events, e.g. …

5 **adverb**
used to say when, how or where something happens, e.g. …

6 **article**
has no meaning on its own, and is used before a noun/noun phrase, e.g. …

7 **preposition**
used before a noun or pronoun to indicate place, direction, time, etc., e.g. …

8 **conjunction**
used to join clauses together to make a sentence, e.g. …

a) *well, quickly, yesterday, there*
b) *and, because, although, if*
c) *he, it, her, myself*
d) *Maria, Cairo, train, honesty*
e) *walk, play, decide*
f) *in, at, over, by*
g) *the, a(n)*
h) *easy, expensive, necessary*

OTHER TERMS

2 Match each grammatical term with the correct definition below.

1 auxiliary	......	5 participle	......
2 modal auxiliary	......	6 phrase	......
3 phrasal verb	......	7 clause	......
4 infinitive	......	8 sentence	......

a) the 'base' form of the verb that you find in a dictionary, usually used after *to*

b) a verb with two parts: a main verb and an adverbial particle, e.g. *cut off, take over*

c) a verb used with a main verb to form tenses, negatives, questions: *be, do, have*

d) part of a sentence containing a subject and verb, e.g. <u>They left</u> (because) <u>it was late.</u>

e) a group of words with a subject and verb that express a complete statement, question, etc. *Dinner is ready. Have you booked the ticket?*

f) an auxiliary verb which is used with a main verb to show a particular attitude such as possibility or obligation, e.g. *may, might, could, should*

g) a form of the verb that can be used to form tenses or as an adjective, e.g. *working, moving; damaged, cooked*

h) a group of words which do not form a complete clause or sentence, e.g. *a box of chocolates, on holiday, going to the bank*

Exercise 3 (Unit 2)

Names of tenses

The following table is a brief summary of the main tenses and their uses. For more detailed information, look in a good student grammar reference book.

PRESENT SIMPLE base form/base form + *-s*
- refers to general truths, permanent situations, regular habits, e.g. *The sun rises in the east. They live in Paris. We meet every week.*

PRESENT PROGRESSIVE *is/are* + present participle
- refers to things that are happening now or in the general present, e.g. *The phone's ringing.*
- refers to future arrangements, e.g. *We're interviewing someone this afternoon.*

PRESENT PERFECT SIMPLE *have/has* + past participle
PRESENT PERFECT PROGRESSIVE *have/has* + *been* + past participle
- refers to things which began in the past and are still continuing, e.g. *I've lived here all my life. Scientists have been studying the problem for several years.*
- refers to a recent past event, e.g. *I've just heard the news. It's been raining.*
- refers to a past event where the time is not important, e.g *I've had a tetanus injection.*

PAST SIMPLE base form + *-ed* (or irregular)
- refers to a completed past event or a series of events, e.g. *The accident happened at two a.m.*

PAST PROGRESSIVE *was/were* + present participle
- refers to something which was going on at a particular time in the past, e.g. *The economy was booming when the new government came to power.*

PAST PERFECT SIMPLE *had* + past participle
PAST PERFECT PROGRESSIVE *had* + *been* + present participle
- refers to an event which happened before another past event, e.g. *When we arrived, the concert had started. The washing machine had been leaking for ages before we called the plumber.*

FUTURE SIMPLE *will* + base form
- gives information about the future or makes a prediction, e.g. *The company will make a loss this year. I think the Democrats will win the election.*

FUTURE PROGRESSIVE *will be* + present participle
- refers to something that will be happening at a certain point in the future, e.g. *Don't phone at eight – I'll be watching the news.*

FUTURE PERFECT SIMPLE *will have* + past participle
FUTURE PERFECT PROGRESSIVE *will have been* + past participle
- refers to something that will be completed by a certain point in the future, e.g. *By November we'll have been married/working together for fourteen years.*

Name the tense in italics in each of the following sentences.

1 The cost of borrowing *has increased* over the last year.

2 The number of people out of work *had doubled* by 1989.

3 If management doesn't improve its offer, there *will be* a strike.

4 The price of fuel *fell* again in January.

5 More and more people *are taking* short breaks nowadays.

6 By the end of the year, there *will have been* two elections.

7 When winter *comes*, the situation will only get worse.

8 Sales of videos, camcorders and other luxury goods *were declining*.

9 The company *will* soon *be exporting* food.

10 Literacy rates *have been rising* for several years.

Exercise 4 (Unit 2)

Reporting tenses

When you are describing graphs or tables of statistics, it's important to establish the time frame and use an appropriate tense.

1 **Which of the tenses listed below is most likely to be used with these expressions?**

   1 Since last summer …

   2 During the period from June to December last year …

   3 Over the next few years, …

   4 For the time being, …

   5 By the year 2000, …

   6 Between 1958 and 1988 …

   7 For nearly twenty years now …

   8 In about 1900, …

   9 By the year 2050, …

Present	*Prices fall/are falling.*
Present perfect	*Prices have fallen/have been falling.*
Past	*Prices fell.*
Past perfect	*Prices had fallen.*
Future	*Prices will fall.*
Future perfect	*Prices will have fallen.*

2 **Complete the following sentences by putting the verbs in the correct tense.**

   1 This company (specialise) in microtechnology for over a decade.

   2 By the time the police called at the house, the suspect (leave).

   3 We are confident that during the coming months we (see) an increase in profits.

4 Between May and June each year, thousands of students (receive) their exam results.

5 Ten years have passed since the product first (become) popular.

6 The burglary took place while everyone (watch) television.

7 I'm not sure how many years we (know) each other.

8 During the last recession, a large number of companies (cease) trading

9 At the moment, we (do) everything in our power to find a solution to the crisis.

10 By the end of the year, I (teach) for 30 years.

Exercise 5 (Unit 3)

The passive

Look at these examples:

Active: *Armed soldiers broke the shop windows.*
Passive: *The shop windows were broken (by armed soldiers).*

1 **Complete these descriptions of the form and use of the passive.**

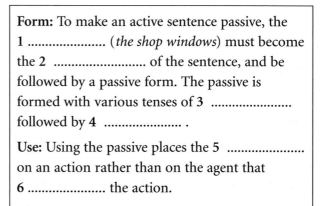

> **Form:** To make an active sentence passive, the 1 .... (*the shop windows*) must become the 2 .... of the sentence, and be followed by a passive form. The passive is formed with various tenses of 3 .... followed by 4 ....
>
> **Use:** Using the passive places the 5 .... on an action rather than on the agent that 6 .... the action.
>
> The most common type is a **short passive**, in which the agent is not expressed. In a **long passive**, the agent is expressed: *by armed soldiers.*

2 **Look back at the four descriptions of cities on pages 24–25 and underline all the examples of the passive.**

3 Complete the following texts by putting the verbs in brackets into an appropriate tense of the passive.

Aluminium cans – what a waste

In 1963, when aluminium **1** .... (first/use) for disposable beverage cans, one billion **2** .... (produce) in the USA – about five per person. By 1985, up to 66 billion cans **3** .... (sell) annually. Huge amounts of energy **4** .... (require) for aluminium production. Added to this, most aluminium comes from bauxite deposits in the tropics; huge areas of rainforest **5** .... (destroy) not only to make room for open bauxite mining but also for hydroelectric dams and reservoirs to power the mining operations.

Waste food

Waste food should ideally **6** .... (return) to farms and **7** .... (feed) to livestock, or **8** .... (use) to fertilise garden soil, but very few city dwellers are able to do this. Most of the food which **9** .... (eat) in cities **10** .... (package) in plastics and cardboard, further contributing to the waste problem.

▶ **LANGUAGE FACT**

The passive
- The short passive (without an expressed agent) is at least six times more common than the long passive in English.
- The short passive is most common in academic writing, which is concerned with generalisations rather than the individuals who carry out an action. It is also fairly common in news reporting, where the identity of the agent is often either not important or not known.

Exercise 6 (Unit 3)

Geographical positions

Read the following notes and answer the questions.

north/northern, etc.

The adjective *north*, etc. is generally used for fairly specific positions and *northern* for more general areas.
- *the **south** side of the house; the **north** face of the mountain*
- *the **northern** hemisphere; the **western** part of the island*

1 How do you make the comparative and superlative of *north*, etc?

2 What do the adjectives *northernmost/southernmost* mean? Complete this sentence:
Reykjavik is the .... capital city in the world.

in the north/to the north

3 Look at these examples, and say when you should use the preposition *in* + geographical position and when you should use *to*.
*Florida is **in** the south-east of the USA.*
*Cuba is **to** the south of Florida.*

Capital letters

4 Look at these examples and say when you should use capital letters at the beginning of geographical positions.
*He's gone to **North America**.*
*The **Southern** Alps are in New Zealand.*
*It's near the **northern** border of the country.*
*Some birds migrate **south** for the winter.*

5 Describe the position of the following places, according to this map of Australia.

1 Perth
2 Kakadu National Park
3 Great Barrier Reef
4 Tasmania
5 Great Sandy Desert and Gibson Desert
6 Canberra in relation to Sydney
7 South Australia in relation to Victoria
8 Cape York in relation to Australia

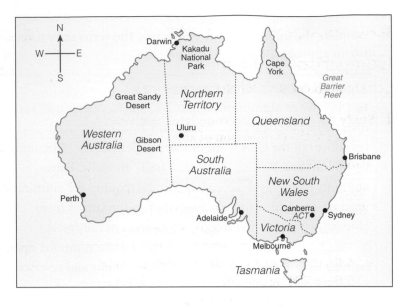

Exercise 7 (Unit 4)

Comparison 1: numerical and other comparative expressions

1 **Study the following information.**

half/twice/three times, etc. *as ... as*

nearly/just under about/approximately exactly more than/over	half twice three times, etc.	as	much/many X tall/expensive, etc.	as

three/four times, etc. / **50% + comparative**
With expressions like *three/four times*, etc. and with **percentages**, it's also possible to use a comparative:

> The computer system was **three times more expensive than** we'd expected.
> Prices are **25% cheaper** on the Internet **than** in the shops.

NB It's not possible to use a comparative after *half* or *twice*.

2 **Write sentences comparing the information in the following tables.**

1 This table shows the earnings of some of the richest football clubs in the world (2000).

	Turnover in £ million
Manchester United	110.9
Bayern Munich	83.5
Real Madrid	76.1
Chelsea	59.1
Barcelona	55.7
Lazzio	50
Liverpool	45.3
AS Roma	39.4
Leeds United	37
Celtic	33.4

2 This table shows how children aged seven to fifteen spend their money in the UK. The figures are percentages.

Children's expenditure by gender and type of purchase	Males	Females
Food and soft drinks	37	36
Leisure goods	29	17
Clothing and footwear	8	16
Household goods and services	5	8
Transport and fares	7	4

Comparison 2: forming comparatives and superlatives

1 Study the examples and complete the notes relating to the comparison of adjectives.

ADJECTIVES

long, longer, longest	grey, greyer, greyest
fine, finer, finest	flat, flatter, flattest
dry, drier, driest	neat, neater, neatest

- Adjectives of one syllable add -(e)r or -(e)st. If the adjective ends in a **1** .... followed by -y, this changes to -ier or -iest.
- If the adjective ends in a single consonant after a single **2** .... , the consonant is doubled.
- The following have irregular forms: good, better, best; bad, worse, worst; far, **3** ....
- The following determiners also have irregular forms: much/many, more, most; little, less, least.

secure, more secure, most secure
easy, easier, easiest
simple, simpler/more simple, simplest/most simple

- Most two-syllable adjectives take **4** ....
- Two-syllable adjectives ending in **5** .... add -ier and -iest.
- The following adjectives can take **6** .... :
  common   narrow   polite   simple
  likely   pleasant   quiet   stupid

interesting, more interesting, most interesting

- Adjectives of **7** .... take more and most.

ADVERBS

easily, more easily, most easily

- Most adverbs form comparatives and superlatives with **8** ....
- Adverbs with the same form as adjectives form comparatives and superlatives in the same way as adjectives, e.g. fast, faster, fastest; hard, harder, hardest; early, earlier, earliest.
- The following have irregular forms:
  well, **9** .... , ... ;
  badly, **10** .... , ...

2 Complete the following short texts by writing the appropriate form of the adjective or adverb and adding any other necessary words.

South America, the fourth (**1** *large*) continent in the world, stretches from Point Gallinas on the Caribbean coast to Cape Horn, (**2** *southerly*) point of Horn Island. Among its features are the Andes mountain range which, at over 7,000 kilometres, is (**3** *long*) the distance from London to Bombay, the world's (**4** *high*) city, La Paz in Bolivia, and one of the world's (**5** *important*) resources – the Amazonian rainforest. With an area of seven million square kilometres, this is twelve times (**6** *big*) than France. It is a major source of oxygen and is home to half of all known living species, including the anaconda, the world's (**7** *heavy*) snake, and the two-toed sloth, (**8** *slow*) animal. The continent experiences extremes of weather. Parts of Columbia are among (**9** *wet*) in the world, while the Atacama Desert in Chile, which has an average of only 0.5mm of rain a year, is (**10** *dry*) place on Earth. Spanish is (**11** *widely spoken*) language.

Railways have several advantages over road transport. Running on tracks, they use (**12** *little*) fuel than cars or lorries and allow heavy loads to be moved (**13** *efficiently*). Trains can also transport goods and passengers at (**14** *great*) average speeds and with (**15** *few*) hold-ups than road transport, making journeys (**16** *short*) and (**17** *stressful*). Rail networks are (**18** *commonly*) used in Japan and Europe than in the USA, and Russia has (**19** *high*) passenger railway usage of all. The (**20** *fast*) scheduled train service in the world is the French TGV's 254kph journey between Massy and St Pierre.

Exercise 9 (Unit 5)

Affixes

PREFIXES AND SUFFIXES

An *affix* is a group of letters which can be added to the beginning or end of a word to make a new word. Letters added to the beginning of a word, like *un-*, *in-* and *dis-*, are called *prefixes*. Letters added to the end of a word, like *-ness*, *-ful* and *-less*, are called *suffixes*. Affixes can be helpful in working out the meaning of words you don't know.

1 Below is a list of common affixes with example words; however, the meanings have been jumbled up. Match the affixes to their general meanings.

Affix	Example	Meaning
1 under-	*underweight/underused*	opposite/not
2 co-	*co-operate/co-worker*	too much
3 re-	*rebuild/rewrite/return*	against/opposite
4 mis-	*mislead/misinform*	outside/beyond
5 out-	*outlive/outpace*	with/together
6 in-/im-/il-/ir-	*imperfect/illiterate*	too little
7 over-	*overcooked/overflow*	wrongly
8 extra-	*extracurricular*	again/back
9 counter-	*counterproductive, counteract*	do better than
10 -proof	*waterproof/fireproof*	rather/somewhat
11 -ish	*childish/yellowish*	passive meaning (*X-ed* by another)
12 -y	*oily/rubbery*	make/become more
13 -en	*lengthen/harden*	like/having the quality of
14 -ee	*employee/interviewee*	protected from/not damaged by

THE SUFFIX *-proof*
e.g. *idiot-proof steps*

2 Complete the sentences below by adding *-proof* to suitable nouns from the list in the box to make adjectives.

A plus sign (+) means that *proof* is added without a hyphen.
A hyphen (-) means that *proof* is added after a hyphen.
If there is no hyphen or plus sign, the adjective is formed of two separate words.

> *bullet+ sound+ child+ fool+ shatter+ oven+ recession- earthquake*

1 To protect youngsters, most medicines are now sold in .... containers.

2 Transfer the mixture to a(n) .... dish and bake at 180°C for 45 minutes.

3 By law, all new buildings in the city must now be designed to be ....

4 The officer would have been killed if he hadn't been wearing a .... vest.

5 We have converted the garage into a .... recording studio.

6 Even economies based on high-tech industries may not be .... for ever.

7 No system can be entirely .... , but this one was certainly very easy to use.

8 Since the robbery, the bank has been fitted with new .... glass screens.

THE PREFIX *over-*
e.g. *work overload*

3 Find matching pairs of sentences.

1 We've got to make three people redundant.	a) It overran slightly.
2 Oh, no! Look at my bank statement.	b) It's rather overrated.
3 I'm sorry I lost my temper like that.	c) It was an overreaction.
4 The meeting was due to finish at twelve.	d) It's overdue.
5 You can't say we've had no success at all.	e) It was overweight.
6 They expected to sell their house for £1 million.	f) I overslept.
7 You must pay the electricity bill.	g) I'm overdrawn.
8 I'm sorry I'm late.	h) It was a serious overestimate.
9 I wouldn't stay at The Grand, if I were you.	i) That would be an overstatement.
10 I had to pay extra for my baggage.	j) The office is overstaffed.

Exercise 10 (Unit 6)

Cohesion: reference links

A text is cohesive if the sentences are well constructed and well linked together, and there are no unnecessary repetitions. One of the main ways of making a text cohesive is the use of *reference links*.

REFERENCE LINKS

- **Pronouns**, e.g. *he, she, it, they; himself, herself; this, that, these; what, who, where; one/any*

Many <u>people</u> wrote to complain.	<u>They</u> particularly objected to …
We receive about <u>twenty calls</u> a day.	<u>These</u> range from requests for …
The hospital receives <u>insufficient funding</u>.	<u>This</u> is a major problem.
He asked if I could lend him <u>a torch</u>.	Unfortunately, I didn't have <u>one</u>.

- **Auxiliary verbs**, e.g. *do/did; have/had; can/could; will/would*

We all <u>tell white lies</u> occasionally.	Life would be difficult if we <u>didn't</u>.
You need <u>to pay the fee now</u>.	If you <u>can't</u>, please let us know.
They asked me <u>to help</u>.	I said I <u>would</u>.

- *there/then, so/not, such*

<u>At the beginning of the 19th century</u> …	Things were very different <u>then</u>.
I expect <u>I'll see you at the meeting</u>.	If <u>not</u>, I'll call you over the weekend.
… you may experience <u>symptoms of nausea</u>.	<u>Such symptoms</u> are not uncommon.

- **Parallel expressions**

<u>his fellow mathematicians</u>	<u>his colleagues</u>
<u>feelings of anger and betrayal</u>	<u>strong emotions</u>

- **Articles**

<u>A</u> survey … (first reference)	<u>The</u> survey … (later reference)

- **Names/titles**

<u>Peter</u> Barclay (first reference)	<u>Mr Barclay</u> … (later reference)
<u>Professor John Lewis</u> of UCLA (first reference)	<u>Professor Lewis</u> (later reference)

1 Say what each of the reference links in bold in the following text refers to.

> Each year, some 270,000 UK workers take time off because of work-related stress, at a cost to **the nation** in sick pay, lost production and medical bills of about £7 billion. **These figures**, the most recent from the Institute of Management, would be **much higher** if the true toll of stress could be measured. **Its** effect on our personal lives is even **more profound**.

The IOM's survey confirmed **what stress experts have long suspected**: bosses suffer less from stress than **their** subordinates. Only nine per cent of junior managers looked forward to going to work, and only seven per cent felt **they** were in control of **their** jobs. **A similar situation** was found in a recent study of civil servants.

> **The control factor** is crucial. **It** has been demonstrated repeatedly that **those** who feel in control of **their** lives are usually able to control the ill-effects of stress. **That is** why 'empowerment' has become such a buzz word.

2 Underline the reference links in the following text, and say what they refer to.

> My research into workaholism shows that the workaholic whose physical and emotional health suffers from working long hours was someone who wanted to be unavailable emotionally. They would find a way of being so even if they weren't in paid employment, perhaps by taking up an obsessive hobby. But people who work long hours because they love what they are doing are physically and mentally uplifted by their work.
>
> For unwilling workaholics, forced to stay at their desks for fear of losing their jobs, long hours can be a killer. For those to whom work is a pleasure, being forced into unsought leisure time can adversely affect their health. Such people, I found, were the ones most likely to fall ill on holiday.

3 Fill in the missing reference links in the following advice about reducing stress.

- Enjoy what you are doing. If you 1 ...., write down why you 2 .... and see if you can make any changes to the things 3 .... block your enjoyment. If you 4 ...., take steps to do 5 .... If 6 ...., change your job!

- If you suffer from a lack of feeling in control, try to figure out how to overcome 7 .... One idea might be to suggest to your boss that 8 .... delegates more decision-making to you. 9 .... might be to join the management committee or become active in the union.

- While you may think that smoking, drinking coffee or comfort eating help you to deal with stress, 10 .... actually add to 11 .... So try to find other 12 .... of relaxing, like taking a walk, going for a swim, or reading a book.

Exercise 11 (Unit 7)

Talking about research

1 Read these sentences. The verbs in bold are used to discuss the results of research.

*Music constantly **emerges** in surveys as the most popular form of art.*
*A study **showed** … that certain pieces of music induce physical changes in the body.*
*That might **shed light** on why human beings alone attach so much importance to making music.*

2 Complete the following passages using each of the words below just once, making any changes necessary, and also using linking expressions from Exercise 4 on page 62 (*Yet, In fact, After all, What is more, However*).

> show/reveal/indicate   emerge   shed light on

A study of moral sensibility in four-year-olds, published in *The British Journal of Psychology*, 1 *shows/reveals/indicates* that, even at such an early age, girls have a better understanding of other people's feelings than boys, and that children with many close friends have a more finely tuned sense of morality than loners. The findings may help 2 *shed light on* the way in which pre-school children socialise. 3 *What is more*, they could provide teachers and parents with valuable help when trying to teach discipline to youngsters in their care.

Senior executives and directors commonly 4 *emerge* in opinion polls and surveys as 'fat cats', who award themselves huge pay rises each year. 5 *However*, research carried out for the Institute of Management has 6 *revealed / shown / indicated* that last year's pay rise of 5.7% was the lowest for four years. It is, 7 *In fact*, only fractionally higher than the national average for pay increases. The research also 8 *shows / indicates / reveals* that the average director is 47 years old, earns £109,000 a year and has been with the company for thirteen years.

Exercise 12 (Unit 8)

Cohesion: avoiding repetition

The following sentences contain unnecessary repetition. Replace the underlined sections with a suitable word or phrase chosen from the box below, and make any changes necessary. You can use any expression more than once.

> this   these   one   the former … the latter
> that   those   did so   respectively

1 Whereas only 34% of adults said they went to the cinema in 1987–88, more than half said that they [*did so*] went to the cinema in 1997–98.
2 Some museums introduced admission charges and [*these*] introducing admissions charges affected the number of visits made.
3 A higher proportion of people aged 35 and over said they attended classical music concerts than [*those*] people aged fifteen to 34.
4 We were shown a number of good videos in the Life and Culture course, but the [*one*] video I liked best was *Fawlty Towers*.
5 *Titanic* was the top box-office film of 1998 in the United Kingdom. [*This*] Titanic was followed by *The Full Monty* and *Saving Private Ryan*.
6 The two most popular cultural events after the cinema were plays and art galleries/exhibitions with attendances of 24% and 22% for plays and art galleries/exhibitions in that order. [*respectively*]
7 Excursions to Stratford-upon-Avon and Oxford have been arranged for this term. The excursion to Stratford-upon-Avon [*The former*] will be on the 16th of April and the excursion to Oxford [*the latter*] will be on the 2nd of July.
8 Approximately 25% of visitors made purchases in the museum shop. Of the 25% of visitors who made purchases in the museum shop [*those*], most spent less than £5.
9 In 1998, the number of visits made to the Tate Gallery rose to more than double the number of visits made [*that / than in*] in 1981.

Exercise 13 (Unit 8)

Conditionals

Conditional clauses are often used to introduce or develop arguments in academic writing, e.g. *If we continue to burn fossil fuels at current rates, our economies may be at risk from rising seas, more severe storms and more intense droughts.*

Conditional clauses can be categorised according to how probable the condition is.

1 Match descriptions A, B and C below with Types 1, 2 or 3.

A The condition is either impossible or unlikely to happen in the present or future. Type ... *2*
B The condition is always true, or is possible in the present or future. Type ... *1*
C The condition is impossible. Type ... *3*

Type 1: Real
If we don't offer good service, we'll go out of business.
When it rains, the roof leaks.
If you have any information, let me know.

If	+ present form + future form / *may/might/could* / imperative
If When	+ present form + present form/imperative

Type 2: Hypothetical
If we started using cleaner fuels, air quality would improve.
If I had any choice in the matter, I wouldn't take part.

If +	past simple or past continuous	*would/could/might* + infinitive

Type 3: Hypothetical (past)
If you had dealt with the situation earlier, it wouldn't have become so serious.

If +	past perfect simple or continuous	*would/could/might have* + past participle

MIXED CONDITIONALS

2 In the following examples, does the *if* clause refer to the past or the present? Does the main clause refer to the past or the present?

If you had dealt with the situation earlier, you wouldn't be facing a major problem now.
We would be rich now if you hadn't lost the lottery ticket.

PUNCTUATION

3 Look at these two examples and complete the rule about punctuation.

When the *if* clause comes first in a sentence, it is followed by ..*comma*..
When the main clause comes first, ..*no comma*..

CONDITIONAL LINKS

In addition to *if*, the following expressions can be used to introduce conditional clauses:

unless	*provided (that)*
as/so long as	*suppose/supposing (that)*
on condition (that)	

4 Rewrite the following as conditional sentences.

1 A hold-up on the motorway made me late for work. *If there hadn't been a hold-up on the motorway, I wouldn't be late*

2 We need to take immediate steps to prevent further redundancies.
Unless …

3 To avoid cancellation fees, reservations must be cancelled at least seven days in advance.
Provided that …

4 Our flight was delayed because of ice on the runway.

5 My lack of overseas experience makes it difficult for me to further my career.

6 The professor agreed to come, but insisted that we put him up in a five-star hotel.

7 Operations are having to be cancelled because of a shortage of medical supplies.

8 It's easy to get lost in the desert, so you should only go with an experienced guide.

9 A computer would enable me to get through my workload twice as fast.

10 The restaurant is very popular, so it's essential that you book in advance.

11 There was a poor harvest this year which is likely to cause winter food shortages.

12 Increased interest rates have made it difficult for people to buy their own homes.

Exercise 14 (Unit 9)

Derived adjectives

Complete the following sentences with adjectives ending in *-al* which are derived from the following words. Make any spelling changes necessary.

substance	finance	commerce	confidence
region	industry	liberate	environment

1 The unions are threatening to take *commercial* action unless their pay claim is met.

2 The government has given the company a *financial* aid package worth £2 million.

3 Of all the *regional* British accents, I think Scottish is my favourite.

4 There has been a *substancial* increase in confirmed cases of malaria in the area.

5 Tourism, the world's biggest industry, is responsible for much *environmental* damage.

6 This information is strictly *confidencial*, and I must ask you not to pass it on.

7 We need people who are licensed to drive vans and other *industrial* vehicles.

8 *Liberal* drug laws have made the Netherlands a gateway for the narcotics trade.

Exercise 15 (Unit 9)

Derived nouns

What are the nouns derived from the following words? They all appear in the texts in Unit 9 (*Water, water …*).

1 clear	6 emit	11 propose
2 complete	7 expand	12 provide
3 consume	8 extend	13 restore
4 despair	9 inhabit	14 diverse
5 destroy	10 oppose	15 sustainable

> ▶ **LANGUAGE FACT**
>
> By far the most common suffix used to form nouns in academic writing is *-ion*, which occurs more than twice as often as *-ity*, and many more times than *-ism* or *-ness*. The suffix *-ion* is used to form numerous common nouns and also to form many new words like *computerisation* and *politicisation*.

Exercise 16 (Unit 9)

Introducing sentences

1 Put the expressions below under one of the following headings, according to meaning.

Typically,	*Paradoxically,*	*As a general rule,*
Surprisingly,	*Inevitably,*	*By and large,*
Not surprisingly,	*In the normal course of events,*	
Predictably,		

Usually true	Expected outcome	Unusual/unexpected outcome

2 Choose one of the expressions above to complete the extracts.

It is thought that 1.3 billion people worldwide do not have safe drinking water.
1 *Not surprisingly* , the problem is much worse in rural areas than in towns. (Text 1)
2 *As a general rule* , 80 litres of water per person per day are enough for a reasonable quality of life. (Text 1)

LA has nine million cars, and 40 per cent of the population suffer from respiratory problems due to vehicle emissions. 3 *In the norm* , the city is now becoming the forum for some of the most progressive environmental thought in the USA. (Text 2)

The city is often seen as the essence of anti-nature. 4 *Paradox* , people often move to Los Angeles because of nature. (Text 2)

5 *Inevitably* , the concrete flood-control system had disastrous ecological consequences, destroying wetland areas which provided an important staging area for migratory birds. (Text 2)

Check your answers by referring to the texts in Unit 9 (pages 74 and 76–77).

Exercise 17 (Unit 10)

Expressing cause and result: *cause, result in, lead to; result from, as a result of*

1 Read the following text and look at the example sentences.

> The most violent tornado in recorded history struck in 1925, killing 689 people, injuring 1980 others, destroying four towns, severely damaging six others and leaving 11,000 people homeless across Missouri, Indiana and Illinois.

Cause		Result
• The tornado	caused/resulted in	the deaths of 689 people.
• The damage	led to	people losing their homes.

Result		Cause
• 689 people were killed	as a result of	the tornado.
• 689 deaths	resulted from	the tornado.

> **Grammar notes**
> - Look at these two ways of using the verb **cause**: *to cause a problem* (+ object); *to cause a problem to occur* (+ object + *to* + verb)
> - **result from**, **result in** and **lead to** are phrasal verbs, which are followed by an object or an object + *-ing*.
>   *The swelling resulted from an insect bite.*
>   *The illness led to him resigning.*
>   **Lead to** is used with results which happened after some time.
> - **as a result of** is used as a preposition before a noun or noun phrase:
>   *As a result of the drought, the harvest failed.*
>   *The harvest failed as a result of the drought.*

2 Make three sentences about the other results of the tornado, using *result in*, *result from* and *as a result of*.

3 Rewrite the following sentences using the expressions in brackets.

1 In New York in 1988 the temperature stayed above 32°C for 32 days, and the murder rate soared by 75 per cent.

   A heatwave in New York ... (result in)

2 When the Fohn wind blows in Geneva, traffic accidents rise by 50 per cent.

   There is ... (as a result of)

3 During the severe winter of 1962–63, economic activity in the UK dropped by about seven per cent.

   (result from)

4 It has been estimated that by 2030, sea levels will rise 18cm with global warming.

   (cause)

5 Following recent coastal flooding, insurance companies may increase premiums for homes and businesses.

   (lead to)

6 Floods worldwide cost about $16 billion a year in damage.

   (result from)

7 By 2030, warmer winters could melt the snow at many ski resorts around the world.

   (cause)

8 Changes in atmospheric pressure can make swollen joints more painful for arthritis sufferers.

   (as a result of)

Exercise 18 (Unit 11)

Articles

The **indefinite article** (*a/an*) is used with countable nouns:

- to mention a particular person or thing for the first time:
  There was *a fire* in *a local warehouse*.
- to refer to something general rather than particular:
  I'm looking for *a job*.
- to refer to one example of a general class:
  My sister is *an engineer*.

The **zero article** is used with uncountable nouns and plurals:

- to refer to an indefinite number or amount:
  Drink plenty of *water*.
  The investigation will take *months*.
- with proper names and place names, including countries, cities, streets and public buildings:
  Professor Jordan, Asia, Peru, Texas, Paris, Oxford Street, Heathrow Airport
- to refer to single mountains and lakes:
  Everest, Lake Como
- in certain phrases:
  have breakfast/lunch/dinner
  (See also *Special cases* on page 200.)

The **definite article** (*the*) is used with countable and uncountable nouns to refer to:

- something which has already been mentioned:
  There was a fire in a local warehouse. *The fire* is thought to have been started deliberately.
- a specific example of a general concept:
  The water in the well was polluted. (Compare: *Water* is essential for life.)
  The heat was unbearable. (Compare: *Heat* kills insect larvae.)
- things which are unique:
  the Sun, the Moon, the Earth, the Internet
- oceans, seas, rivers, mountain ranges:
  the Pacific, the Nile, the Himalayas
- something which is clear in the context:
  The director has resigned. *The library* is closing.
- superlatives:
  the longest river, the highest crime rate

SPECIAL CASES

	ZERO ARTICLE	DEFINITE ARTICLE
Transport	*travel by **sea/boat/train/air/car***, etc.	*We took **the train** to the airport.* *You can buy a ticket on **the bus**.*
Communications	*contact by **phone**; send by **post***	*He's on **the phone**.* ***The post** is late today.*
Times of day	*at **dawn/daybreak/midday/lunchtime/sunset/night***	*The telephone rang in the middle of **the night**.* *We met **in the morning/afternoon/evening**.*
Days, months, seasons	*on **Sunday**, in **September**, in **summer***	*on **the third Sunday** of the month* *in **the summer** of 2001*
Countries	*Jordan, Switzerland*	Plural countries and countries with a word like *republic* or *state* in their name take the definite article: ***the Philippines**, **the Czech Republic***
Institutions	With zero article the focus is on the general purpose of the institution: *He's **at school/college/university**.* (studying) *She's been taken **to hospital**.* (for treatment) *He spent a year **in prison**.* (as punishment)	With an article, the focus is on some other aspect of the institution: *He's a caretaker at **the university**.* ***The hospital** is opposite **the school**.* ***The prison** was built last century.*

Complete the following texts by adding *a/an*, *the* or leaving a blank (zero article).

---

1 .... Maldives is 2 .... archipelago of 1,190 small coral islands situated in
3 .... Indian Ocean south-west of 4 .... Sri Lanka. None of 5 ....
islands rises above 1.8m, making 6 .... country 7 .... lowest place on
Earth. As 8 .... result, 9 .... country is threatened by 10 .... rise in sea
level caused by 11 .... global warming, and 12 .... sea wall has been built
around 13 .... capital island, 14 .... Male.

---

15 .... world's most easy-going prison system is about to be reformed after
16 .... protests that convicts frequently leave 17 .... jail richer than when
they arrived. 18 .... Prisoners in Greenland are allowed to go out to
19 .... work in 20 .... local community, and 21 .... wages they earn
are paid into their bank accounts. 22 .... regime, which emphasises
23 .... rehabilitation above 24 .... punishment, is becoming increasingly
unpopular among 25 .... public, according to 26 .... John Meyer, director
general of 27 .... island's police force. 28 .... team of judges and
magistrates is working on 29 .... reform plans which will be presented by
30 .... end of 31 .... year.

32 .... Symptoms of jet lag are well known.
33 .... Tiredness, and with it 34 .... lack of
35 .... energy, 36 .... enthusiasm and
37 .... concentration, is commonplace. Jet lag
is much worse for people who live by
38 .... strict timetable – those, for instance,
who must have 39 .... breakfast at eight a.m. or
who always go to 40 .... bed at 41 ....
same time and need 42 .... precise amount of
sleep each night. 43 .... Westward journeys
induce less jetlag than 44 .... eastern journeys,
partly because 45 .... sleep is easier when
travelling with 46 .... sun. 47 ....
Experienced travellers always try to travel westward
so they have 48 .... advantage of 49 ....
alertness and 50 .... mental agility after
51 .... good night's sleep.

Exercise 19 (Unit 12)

Vocabulary: collocations

Complete the following sentences with one of the verbs in the box. Make any changes necessary. You may use any verb more than once.

make	do	draw	play	set
have	give	take	pay	

1 He didn't .... the slightest notice of my advice.

2 He .... a serious error of judgement.

3 Every applicant must .... a spelling test.

4 You need to .... this matter your full attention.

5 We have to .... a distinction between private and state education.

6 More research into the causes of truancy needs to be ....

7 I expect you to .... an example for the others.

8 Your state of mind .... an important part in your ability to listen effectively.

9 You won't .... any progress unless you study.

10 Stress .... a negative effect on learning.

11 Please .... careful attention to what I'm going to say.

12 Two hundred people .... part in the survey.

Exercise 20 (Unit 12)

The ... the ... (comparatives)

Look at this sentence from Listening Task 2.

The older you are, the more likely this is to happen.

This structure is a common way of showing how two things develop in relation to each other. Here are some more examples.

The harder I work, the less progress I seem to make!
The more experienced the salesperson, the more money they make.
The earlier you arrive, the better.

Notice that:

1 *the* can be followed by both **adjectives** (e.g. *earlier, more experienced*) and **adverbs** (e.g. *harder, more quickly*);

2 the normal rules of forming comparisons apply;

3 a short form can be used with sentences which end *the better*.

1 Complete the following examples.

  1 The more words you try to learn in one go, the .... (*likely*) you are to remember them.

  2 The .... (*motivated*) you are when you start learning a language, ... (*fast*) you'll progress.

  3 The .... you work, ... mistakes you'll make.

  4 .... (*thoroughly*) you revise, ... you'll feel.

  5 .... (*far*) you travel, ... everywhere seems to be.

  6 .... the dictionary, ... the information it will provide.

2 Now compare the following.

  1 Price/Quality
  2 Education/Opportunity
  3 Age/Wisdom

Common verbs in -ed and -ing clauses

According to the *Longman Corpus of Written and Spoken English*, only a small number of verbs are really common in *-ed* and *-ing* clauses in academic prose. These verbs are shown in the following boxes.

1 In each group, three of the verbs are the most common. Can you guess the top three in each case?

> **-ing clauses**
> *having, being, using, concerning, involving, containing*

> **-ed clauses**
> *made, based, used, taken, caused, given, concerned, obtained, produced*

2 Complete the following sentences with verbs chosen from the lists above.

1 A number of problems .... with health and safety issues remain to be solved.

2 It's a long and complicated rail journey .... several changes.

3 A new drug .... on ginseng is undergoing clinical trials at the moment.

4 A memo .... highly confidential information has been leaked to the newspapers.

5 Farmers are keen to promote fruit and vegetables .... in this country.

6 Drugs .... illegally are not subject to quality control.

7 He was the ideal candidate for the job, ... both well qualified and experienced.

8 A shortage of Atlantic cod .... by overfishing has led to massive price rises.

9 He managed to slip out of the country .... a false passport.

10 The measures .... by the government to reduce unemployment have failed.

Doubt

Look at the use of the verb *doubt* in the following sentence:
I doubt very much that any form of media we have today will survive that long.

Tick the correct uses of *doubt* in the following sentences, and correct any errors. Check your answers by referring to the notes below.

1 I doubt if I'll have time for lunch today.
2 He may be the best person for the job, but I doubt so.
3 Whenever I doubt the meaning of a word, I look it up in a dictionary.
4 I doubt whether she'll take the slightest notice of what I said.
5 The interviewing panel had doubt about her suitability for the job.
6 After yet another injury, his football career looks in doubts.
7 If you have any kind of doubt about what to do, don't hesitate to contact me.
8 People still doubt about the benefit of alternative medicine.

> **Grammar notes**
>
> - **to doubt *if/whether/that*** = to think something is unlikely, e.g. *I doubt if he'll come now.*
>
> - **to be in doubt about** and **to have (your/some) doubts about** = to feel unsure, e.g. *Call the Help Line if you are in any doubt about your insurance cover.*
> *We had some doubts about the wisdom of the new policy.*
>
> - **(to be/seem/look) in doubt** = to be uncertain, e.g. *A successful outcome looks in doubt now.*
>
> - **I doubt it** (short form) = think unlikely, e.g. *Do you think he'll get the job? I doubt it.*

Exercise 23 (Unit 14)

Topic vocabulary: the media

1 **Match the following words or phrases (1–10) to the correct meaning (a–j).**

1 (the) press	....	6 copy (*n*)	....
2 (the) media	....	7 journalist	....
3 to broadcast	....	8 correspondent	....
4 coverage	....	9 readership	....
5 edition	....	10 circulation	....

a) someone who writes or talks about a particular subject, especially a serious one, for a newspaper or news programme

b) the number of copies of a newspaper or magazine that are sold in a particular period

c) send out radio or television programmes so that people can hear them

d) all the organisations that are involved in providing information to the public, especially newspapers, television and radio

e) a single newspaper or magazine

f) newspapers and the people who write for them

g) the number of people or type of people who regularly read a particular newspaper or magazine

h) the way an event or subject is reported in the news, especially how much space or time is given to reporting it

i) someone who writes for a newspaper or magazine, or who appears on news programmes on television or radio

j) the version of a newspaper of magazine that is printed on a particular occasion

2 **Complete the following sentences with the correct word or phrase.**

1 There was an interesting letter in the Saturday .... of *The Times*.

2 And now for a report on bullying in schools from our education .... , Tim Low.

3 The magazine is aimed at a .... of mainly eighteen- to 30-year-olds

4 During his long career as a .... , he won many awards.

5 You haven't by any chance got a .... of yesterday's paper, have you?

6 The president's speech is due to be .... on Channel 8 tonight.

7 The resignation of the Foreign Minister received widespread media ....

8 There's going to be a debate in parliament on the subject of the freedom of ....

Exercise 24 (Unit 15)

-ing forms vs infinitives

> *-ing* forms
>
> A–E below show some of the main uses of *-ing* forms.
>
> A in **verb forms**, with auxiliary verbs, e.g. *It was raining when we set off.*
> B like **nouns**, e.g. *Swimming is prohibited.* (subject); *He likes swimming.* (object)
> C after certain **verbs**, e.g. *Do you remember meeting her? I hate queuing.*
> D after all **prepositions**, e.g. *He was fined for speeding; I look forward to meeting you.*
> E in **participle clauses**, e.g. *He left in a hurry, slamming the door.* (See page 105.)

1 **Match each sentence below with one of the uses above by labelling it A, B, C, D or E.**

1 .... Today there is a better than 95% chance of surviving a heart attack.

2 .... Understanding the biological effects of cosmic rays is a priority.

3 .... Lying in wait beyond the Earth's atmosphere, solar radiation poses additional problems.

4 .... Researchers are building artificial liver, bone and cartilage tissue right now.

5 .... Dennis Tito's plans involve spending a week on the Mir space station.

infinitives

A–E below show some of the main uses of the infinitive.

with *to*

A   to express purpose, e.g. *I'm here to see Mr Simon. To make a call, press 9.*

B   after certain verbs, e.g. *We can't afford to wait. He's decided to sell his house.*

C   after *too* and *enough*, e.g. *There isn't enough evidence to arrest him. It's too hot to handle.*

without *to*

D   after **modal auxiliary verbs**, e.g. *It must be time to go. They could arrive any minute.*

E   after *let* and *make*, e.g. *Don't let him bully you. He made us work overtime.*

2   **Match each sentence below with one of the uses above by labelling it A, B, C, D or E.**

1   .... NASA can be proud of the technology it has developed.

2   .... Cosmic rays possess too much energy for shielding to be effective.

3   .... To get answers to these questions, Daniel Goldin established the NSBRI.

4   .... When astronauts had few tasks, it made them feel stressed.

5   .... Monitoring devices will allow astronauts to take refuge from solar radiation.

-*ing* or infinitive?

3   **Complete the following sentences with suitable forms of verbs chosen from the box below.**

Motion sickness afflicts more than two-thirds of astronauts upon 1 .... orbit. Though everyone recovers after a while, body systems continue 2 .... 3 .... too much fluid, the body begins 4 .... it, including calcium, electrolytes and blood plasma. The production of blood cells decreases, 5 .... astronauts slightly anaemic. Spinal discs expand, and so does the astronaut, who may 6 .... five centimetres and 7 .... backache.

Russian cosmonauts returned from long flights unable to stand without 8 .... Americans back from months-long flights also paid the price, 9 .... losses in weight, muscle mass and bone density. NASA geared up 10 .... how – even if – humans would 11 .... a mission to Mars

Jeffrey Sutton has treated the head trauma, wounds, kidney stones and heart rhythm irregularities that one could 12 .... on the way to Mars. 13 .... with infection, Sutton plans a factory 14 .... drugs, even new ones.

The NSBRI team found that the diagnostic device they had developed can 15 .... as part of a standard test 16 .... patients at risk from heart rhythm irregularities.

survive	faint	sense	reach
see	use	identify	cope
suffer	make	render	excrete
suffer	change	gain	encounter

Exercise 25 (Unit 16)

Expressing probability

Use language from the following tables to discuss the probability of the events below.

Introducing a personal opinion | Introducing a more impersonal opinion

I think/don't think …	It seems/appears …
I believe …	There seems to be …
In my opinion/view …	They/people say …

Adjectives: *possible/probable/likely*

It is	quite	**possible**	
It is	quite/very/highly	**probable/likely**	that X will happen.
It is	rather/very/highly	**unlikely**	
X is	rather/very/highly	**likely/unlikely**	to happen.

Adverbs: *certainly/definitely/probably/possibly*

I will	most	**certainly/definitely**	do X.
X will	very	**possibly/probably**	happen.

Nouns: *possibility/chance/prospect; probability/likelihood*

There is a	remote/slight strong	**possibility/chance/prospect**	
There is a	strong/90%	**probability**	of X happening. that X will happen.
There	is (very) little isn't much	**possibility/chance/prospect** **likelihood**	
The	**possibility/chance prospect/likelihood**	of X happening	is remote/small/slight.

Questions

What is the	**possibility/chance** **prospect/likelihood**	of X happening? that X will happen?

Other expressions

- ***In all probability,*** *Leeds United will win the cup.* (very probable)
- ***There's every possibility*** *that the economy will improve before long.* (very probable)
- *It's **more than likely** that there'll be a general election next year.* (very probable)
- *There's **little or no chance** of finding any more survivors.* (very unlikely)

1 In your opinion, what is the likelihood of the following events happening in the next twenty years? Give reasons for your answers.

1 A woman will become president of the USA.
2 A cure for cancer will be found.
3 A British football team will win the World Cup.
4 Global warming will be reversed.
5 No one will read books any more.
6 Every home will be connected to the Internet.
7 Spanish will become the official language of the USA.
8 A non-polluting 'green' car will be developed.

2 Choose one or more of the following topics and make sentences about possible future events in your life.

e.g. *I think it's quite likely that I'll go to live in the USA.*
There's a remote possibility that I'll win a scholarship to Harvard.

1 The IELTS test   4 Your next holiday
2 Study plans   5 Your family
3 Career plans   6 Your home

British vs American vocabulary

Give the British equivalent of the following. There is a list of jumbled answers below.

1 auto(mobile)   9 railroad
2 back-up   10 subway
3 beltway   11 traffic circle
4 expressway   12 trailer
5 freeway   13 (public) transit
6 gasoline/gas   14 trunk
7 hood   15 underpass
8 license plate

petrol   underground (railway)
public transport   boot   caravan   railway
bonnet   number plate   car   subway
roundabout   motorway (in city)   tailback
motorway   ring road

Idioms with *face*, etc.

Complete the following sentences using words from the box below. Any word may be used more than once. Check the meaning of any idioms you are not familiar with in a good dictionary.

head   face   eye   eyes   nose
ear   tongue   mouth

1 It seems a good offer on the .... of it, but I need to look into it a bit more carefully.
2 I'm sorry I'm late, but the traffic was .... to tail all the way into town.
3 I doubt if she'll be able to help. She's up to her .... in work at the moment.
4 Setting up in business was difficult, but he managed to keep his .... above water.
5 I made the suggestion .... in cheek, but unfortunately they took me seriously.
6 I haven't had time to prepare for the interview, so I'll just have to play it by ....
7 It may be common practice, but it's still an offence in the .... of the law.
8 There was no formal announcement, but the news spread rapidly by word of ....
9 It's so annoying! His name is on the tip of my .... I'll think of it in a minute.
10 He's never seen .... to .... with his boss about policy.

► Writing practice bank

Task 1: Presenting and comparing data

GUIDED PRACTICE

Look at the following exam question and table.

> *The table below gives information on participation in various leisure activities. Write a report for a university lecturer describing the information shown below.*

Complete the model answer below by referring to the information in the table. Write NO MORE THAN THREE WORDS or A NUMBER in each space.

When you've finished, underline the linking expressions in the text.

SELECTED LEISURE ACTIVITIES Participation rates in the four weeks before the interview by age.			
Leisure activities	% of age group		
	16–19	25–29	60–69
Watching TV/video	99	99	99
Visiting/Entertaining friends or relations	98	98	95
Listening to tapes/CDs	98	93	65
Listening to the radio	95	94	83
Reading books	63	64	66
DIY	25	50	38
Gardening	15	35	61
Dressmaking/Needlework/Knitting	9	14	27

Source: *Social Trends*

The table 1 .... the percentages of people taking part in certain leisure activities. 2 .... the figures, the single 3 .... leisure activity in the UK is watching television and video, which has a 99% 4 .... across all sections of the population. Visiting friends and relations is almost 5 .... , with 95% or more of all age ranges socialising on a regular basis.

Listening to music is most popular with the two 6 .... groups, while the figure is approximately 7 .... lower for older people. On the other hand, gardening and needlework are more popular with 60–69-year-olds. For example, almost 8 .... older people enjoy gardening 9 .... 20–29-year-olds. Finally, it seems that DIY appeals most to people in their twenties.

From the information we can see that the figures for the most popular activities are fairly similar across the age groups. However, there are considerable 10 .... when we look at the more minority interests

Exercise 2 (Unit 8)

Task 1: Describing information from a table

Look at the following exam question and table.

> *The table below gives information about visits to museums and galleries in England in three separate years.*
>
> *Write a report for a university lecturer describing the information shown below.*

Visits to national museums and galleries in England

Millions

	1981	1991	1998
British Museum	2.6	5.1	5.6
National Gallery	2.7	4.3	4.8
Tate Gallery	0.9	1.9	2.2
Natural History Museum*	3.7	1.6	1.9
Science Museum*	3.8	1.3	1.6

*These museums introduced admission charges in the late 1980s.

Source: *Social Trends*

Complete these notes describing the table. Use NO MORE THAN THREE WORDS or A NUMBER in each space.

The British Museum, currently the most popular museum or gallery in Britain, 1 *5.6 mil* visitors in 1998, more than 2 *twice as many* as in 1981. By 3 *comparison*, the National Gallery and the Tate Gallery 4 *attracted 4.8* and 5 *2.2 mil* visitors respectively in 1998. 6 *Two museums/those* introduced admission charges in the late 1980s, and this had a(n) 7 *- effect* on their popularity. For example, in 1991 the number of visits made to the Science Museum fell to 8 *third tim lower* of the number ten years earlier. By 1998, despite 9 *gradual increase*, the number of visits still represented 10 *less than half* that in 1981.

Exercise 3 (Unit 8)

Task 1: Describing information from a table

Study the table below, including the heading and footnotes, and write your report. Read the advice at the bottom of the page before you begin.

You should spend about 20 minutes on this task.

The table below shows the number of visits to the UK by overseas residents between 1975 and 1998.

Write a report for a university lecturer describing the information shown below.

You should write at least 150 words.

Visits to the UK by overseas residents	1975	1987	1996	1997	1998
Number of visits (millions) of which	9.5	15.6	25.2	25.5	25.7
Total business	1.8	3.6	6.1	6.3	6.9
Total leisure[1]	7.7	12.0	19.1	19.2	18.9
Total by North American residents	1.9	3.4	3.7	4.1	4.6
Total by residents of Western Europe[2]	5.9	9.3	16.8	16.7	16.6
Total other residents	1.7	2.9	4.7	4.7	4.6

1 Holiday visits to friends and relatives and miscellaneous visits
2 EU and Western European countries

Source: *UK in figures 2000, National Statistics*

- Begin with an **introductory statement**, e.g. *The table/graph/bar chart shows ...*
- Don't try to describe every detail. Look for **significant features**: the greatest increase or decrease, the shortest time period, the overall trend, etc.
- Think about the clearest way to **express figures**, e.g. in percentages or expressions like *one in ten*, etc.
- Don't speculate about reasons for trends. **Stick to the facts.**
- End with a comment on **general trends**: *The figures for the period suggest that ...; From this evidence we can conclude that ...*, etc.

Exercise 4 (Unit 10)

Task 1: Describing a process

GUIDED PRACTICE

Read the following exam question, study the diagram and then complete the model answer below. If you need more help, choose from the words in the box at the bottom of the page, but remember to make any changes necessary.

> *The following diagram shows how greenhouse gases trap energy from the Sun. Write a report for a university lecturer describing the information shown below.*

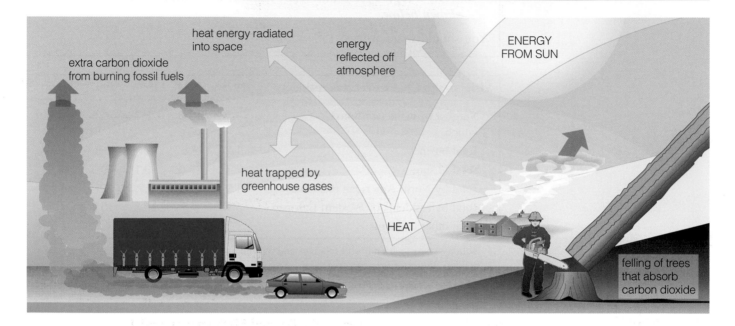

Energy from the Sun **1** .... the Earth as heat. Some of this heat energy is **2** .... radiated into space, while some of it is trapped by greenhouse gases in the atmosphere and reflected back to Earth. This is a natural process, but in recent **3** .... , human activities have **4** .... an increase in the **5** .... of greenhouse gases in the atmosphere which is now trapping too much heat.

One of the main greenhouse gases is carbon dioxide, and extra quantities of this **6** .... into the atmosphere **7** .... burning fossil fuels as a source of energy in power stations, factories and homes. Exhaust gases from cars and lorries **8** .... further emissions of carbon dioxide.

Plants serve to remove some of the carbon dioxide from the atmosphere by absorbing it through their leaves. However, as large areas of forest **9** .... in the Amazon and elsewhere, **10** .... carbon dioxide is removed in this way.

lead to	release	result in	subsequently	fell
reach	less	decades	amounts	as a result of

Exercise 5 (Unit 10)

Task 2: Presenting and justifying an opinion

You should spend about 40 minutes on this task.

Present a written argument to an educated reader with no specialist knowledge of the following topic.

Too much attention is given to headline-grabbing disasters like earthquakes and floods. Governments should concentrate their resources on educating people about the risks they face nearer to home, which can cost far more lives.

To what extent do you agree or disagree with this opinion?

You should use your own ideas, knowledge and experience to support your arguments with examples and relevant evidence.

You should write at least 250 words.

Exercise 6 (Unit 12)

Task 1: Interpreting statistics

Look at the graph on page 102 and complete the following model answer by writing NO MORE THAN THREE WORDS or A NUMBER in each space.

The graph shows the percentages of boys and girls achieving the highest grades in their school-leaving exams in 1993–94, by subject. Overall, pupils of both sexes 1 .... best in English and Mathematics, and 2 .... in Biology, Chemistry and Physics. Results for boys and girls were roughly 3 .... in Mathematics, Biology and Geography. In other subjects, 4 .... , there were some significant 5 .... Girls achieved by far their 6 .... in English, with a pass rate of 7 .... , which was 8 .... than the boys. The difference was even 9 .... in French, where 10 .... more girls achieved high grades. 11 .... , boys did better in Physics and in Craft, Design and Technology. The boys' pass 12 .... of 10% in Physics, although low in itself, was 13 .... 14 .... of the girls, and the 15 .... for Craft, Design and Technology (18.9%) was also significantly higher. In general, 16 .... that girls do better in arts subjects, while boys show more ability in science and technology.

Task 1: Presenting and comparing data

GUIDED PRACTICE

The results of a survey carried out by a motoring organisation in Britain are shown below. A hundred men and 100 women were asked the four questions listed on the left.

The letters A–E represent:

A Male driver under 25 years old   D Female driver more than 35 years old
B Female driver under 25 years old   E Older driver (55+)
C Middle-aged male driver

	 A	B	C	D	E
male % female %					
Who is the safest driver pictured?	2% / 3%	6% / 11%	53% / 16%	33% / 62%	6% ✓ / 8%
Who is the most dangerous driver?	71% ✓ / 67%	10% / 5%	5% / 6%	1% / 0%	13% / 22%
Who is most likely to drink and drive?	70% / 68%	0% / 3%	23% ✓ / 22%	0% / 0%	7% / 7%

Are speeding penalties too strict?   YES 14% / 19%   NO 67% / 81%

Source: *AA Members Magazine*

UNDERSTANDING THE DATA

1 Study the table and answer these key questions.

1 What are the correct answers to Questions 1–3? How do you know?
2 Which answers were given by men? How do you know?
3 Which driver did women think was safest?
4 Which driver did men think was safest?
5 Which question was correctly answered by both sexes?
6 Which driver was considered second most dangerous by both men and women?
7 Which driver was judged most likely to drink and drive?
8 Which group was most in favour of the present level of speeding penalties – men or women?

INTERPRETING THE DATA

2 Fill in the gaps with NO MORE THAN THREE WORDS or A NUMBER, based on your answers to the questions on page 193.

The results of a recent survey demonstrate that most people are
1 .... of the realities of gender driving habits and accident patterns.
Respondents of both sexes correctly 2 .... young males as the most
dangerous drivers. However, they were incorrect in judging older drivers as the
3 .... most dangerous, since this group is actually
4 .... on the road.

Interestingly, when asked about road safety, the respondents demonstrated a
bias towards 5 .... 6 .... of the men questioned felt
that middle-aged men would be the safest drivers on the road, while
7 .... of women thought middle-aged women were safer. Both
groups were 8 .... in thinking that young male drivers were the
most likely to drink and drive, 9 .... it is the middle-aged male
driver who is most likely to offend.

The survey also found that 10 .... of men felt that penalties for
inappropriate choice of speed were too strict, while 11 .... of
women felt that the penalties were 12 ....

Exercise 8 (Unit 20)

Task 1: Describing objects

GUIDED PRACTICE

Look at the diagrams on page 166 and complete the following description by
writing between ONE and THREE WORDS in each space.

All the cameras shown have the same basic structure, consisting of a body and a
lens. The Daguerrotype, 1 .... in 1839, was a large device
2 .... wood. It 3 .... three box-shaped sections with a
brass lens 4 .... , and was about 36cm 5 .... Towards
the 6 .... 19th century, the Kodak No. 1 was introduced. This
rectangular metal box was 7 .... and 8 .... in design,
measuring less than 9 .... of the Daguerrotype.

The first modern-looking camera was the Leica 1, which appeared in 1925. The
camera body was much 10 .... than 11 .... of the
Kodak, and it had a number of 12 .... along the top. Finally, in
2001, a credit-card sized digital camera became 13 .... Although
only 14 .... of the size of the original Daguerrotype, it provided a
15 .... of technical features, 16 .... Internet access.
Overall, the development of the camera has been one of decreasing 17
.... and increasing sophistication.

Task 1: Describing objects

EXAM TASK

In the following task you have to describe a number of types of bicycle.

> You should spend about 20 minutes on this task.
>
> *The diagrams below show a number of different types of bicycle.*
>
> *Write a report for a university lecturer describing the information.*
>
> You should write at least 150 words.

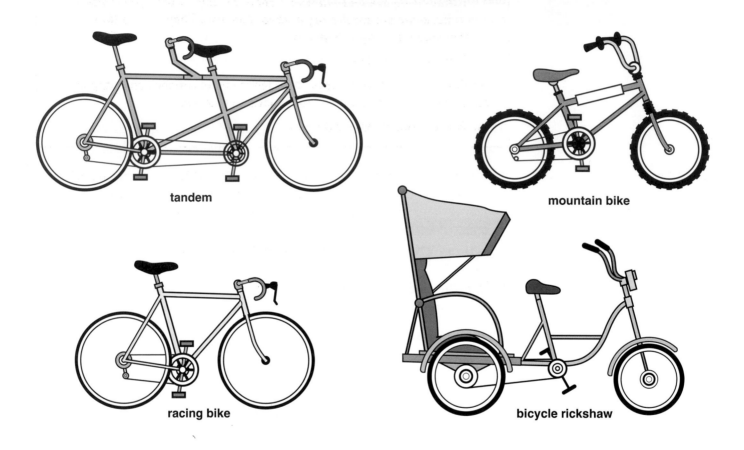

tandem

mountain bike

racing bike

bicycle rickshaw

Basic vocabulary: chain, frame, handlebar, gear, pedals, saddle, wheels

REMINDERS

- Begin by summarising the common features.
- Don't describe each type in detail – instead concentrate on the distinguishing features.
- End with a suitable concluding sentence.
- You are *not* expected to have technical knowledge or to use very specialist vocabulary. If you don't know the precise word, think of another way of saying it.

Task 2: Presenting and justifying an opinion

EXAM TASK

You should spend about 40 minutes on this task.

Present a written argument or case to an educated non-specialist audience on the following topic:

> *The use of CCTV (close circuit television) cameras in streets, stations, shops and other public places has increased rapidly in recent years.*
>
> *Although we are told that these cameras help in the fight against crime, some people are opposed to their use. They believe that everyone has a right to privacy.*
>
> *What are your views?*

You should use your own ideas, knowledge and experience and support your arguments with examples and relevant evidence.

You should write at least 250 words.

REMINDERS

- Underline key words or phrases in the question which need consideration.
- Think about any personal experience you can use to illustrate your views.
- Make notes and a paragraph plan to help you organise your argument logically.
- Consider both your own point of view on the subject *and* opposing arguments.
- End with a clear conclusion.

▶ Answer keys and additional material

Unit 1
Lead-in
1 (most energy) digging/heavy gardening 2 climbing stairs 3 light gardening
4 vacuuming/hoovering 5 cycling 6 walking

Unit 2
Lead-in
1 Healthy eating habits: a), c), d), e), h); Unhealthy eating habits: b), f), g), i), j).

Focus on writing 1
4

Sales of CDs, LPs, cassettes

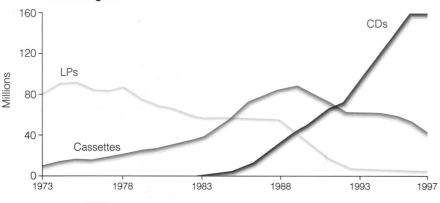

Unit 3
Lead-in
1 City facts
1 Tokyo (27.2 million) 2 Rome
(c. one million) 3 Bombay (annual
growth rate: 4.22%) 4 Mexico City
(2,255m above sea level) 5 London
(opened 1863) 6 Chicago (66.4 million
passengers per year)
2 City plans
A Hong Kong, China B Sydney,
Australia C Los Angeles, USA
D Amsterdam, Netherlands

Focus on speaking 1
2 1 year 2 15 3 second 4 twenty

Unit 4
Lead-in
2 World Quiz
1 B 2 B 3 C 4 C 5 A
6 1 Canada 2 Norway (according to
the UN's *Human Development Report*)
7 Japan (90.6%) 8 In this order: Japan,
Iceland, Canada 9 Italy (nine per
1,000)

Unit 6
Focus on vocabulary
3 Backpacker
adventurous, carefree, casual, free, fun,
fun loving, likes scenic beauty, loves fresh
air, naturalist, nature lover, needs to get
away from society, outdoor type, relaxed,
sociable

Unit 7
Focus on speaking 1
Survey 2000 Results
The percentages below represent
American and Canadian participants who
answered 'Like it very much' or 'Like it'.
oldies/classic rock 78.9%
classical music 74.4%
contemporary rock/pop 66.7%
rhythm and blues 61.3%
jazz 60.9%
modern folk music 56.7%
Caribbean music (e.g. reggae) 55.5%
your national music 55.3%
musicals (e.g. *Les Miserables,*) 54.1%
easy-listening music 53.7%

Latin music (e.g. mariachi, salsa) 46.3%
country and western music 32.2%
dance music 30.4%
opera 29%
heavy metal 19.1%
rap/hip hop 14.2%

Focus on speaking 2
Student A

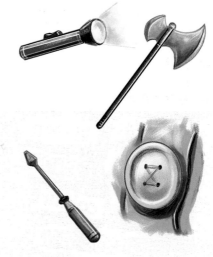

Unit 9

Lead-in

1	taking a bath	average 80 litres
	taking a shower	60 litres for 5 mins
2	washing dishes by hand (in a bowl)	average 5 litres
	using a dishwasher	average 35 litres
3	cooking per day	average 20 litres
	drinking	average 2 litres
4	washing the car	average 450 litres
	watering the garden	average 1,500 litres

Unit 10

Lead-in

2 Hazard characteristics in the following table are graded on a scale of 1 (largest or greatest) to 5 (smallest or least significant).

Overall Rank	Event	Length of event	Area affected	Loss of life	Economic loss	Social effect	Long-term impact
1	Drought	1	1	1	1	1	1
2	Tropical cyclone	2	2	2	2	2	1
3	Flood	2	2	1	1	1	2
4	Earthquake	5	1	2	1	1	2
5	Volcano	4	4	2	2	2	1
6	Tsunami	4	1	2	2	2	3
7	Bush fire	3	3	3	3	3	3
8	Landslide	2	2	4	4	4	5

Source: *Natural Hazards*

Focus on speaking

Probability of dying in any one year from various causes	
1 Smoking ten cigarettes a day	One in 200
2 Influenza	One in 5,000
3 Accident on road (driving in Europe)	One in 8,000
4 Playing field sports	One in 25,000
5 Accident at home	One in 26,000
6 Accident at work	One in 43,500
7 Floods (living in Bangladesh)	One in 50,000
8 Earthquake (living in California)	One in 2,000,000
9 = Hit by lightning	One in 10,000,000
9 = Wind storm (living in northern Europe)	One in 10,000,000

Unit 11

Lead-in
Memory Test: Part 1

Unit 12

Focus on listening 1

1 True   2 False   3 True   4 False
5 True   6 False

Give yourself two points for each correct answer. Most accomplished listeners will score ten or more. A score under six suggests you don't understand very much about the theory of listening. The chances are you are missing a lot of useful information.

Unit 13

Focus on reading 1

A mobile phone   B wristwatch
C book   D fax machine   E Internet

Unit 14

Focus on speaking 2

1	E-mail	89%
2	Hobbies/interests	84%
3	Work/school research	82%
4	Random surfing	81%
5	News/current affairs	66%
6	Music information	58%
7	Financial information	42%
8	Sports reports	42%
9	Movie information	42%
10	Shopping	41%

Unit 15

Lead-in

1 b) (*Sputnik*, USSR)
2 b) (Yuri Gagarin)
3 The first Moon landing (*Apollo 11*)
4 c)
5 Mars and Venus
6 a) (US space station)   c) (designed to carry people and equipment into space)   e) (Russian space station)
7 c) (Russian cosmonaut Valeri Polyakov on the Mir space station, 1994/5)
8 b)
9 True.

Unit 18
Lead-in
1 (*Total visitors in millions*)
  1 **France** (71)
  2 **Spain** (52)
  3 **USA** (47)
  4 China (37)
  5 Italy (36)
  6 UK (26)
  7 Mexico (20)
  8 Canada (19)
  9 Poland (18)
  10 Austria (17)

2 (*$ millions*)
  1 **Germany** (50.8)
  2 **USA** (48.7)
  3 **Japan** (37)
  4 UK (24.4)
  5 France (17.7)
  6 Italy (15.5)
  7 Austria (11.8)
  8 Netherlands (11.3)
  9 Canada (11)
  10 Russia (10.7)

3 (*Visitors per day*)
  1 **Disneyland** (Japan) (45,700)
  2 **Niagara Falls** (30,000)
  3 **British Museum** (15,400)
  4 Eiffel Tower (15,000)
  5 Grand Canyon (12,000)
  6 Great Pyramid (10,000)
  7 Tower of London (7,600)
  8 Empire State Building (7,000)
  9 CN Tower (5,000)
  10 Uluru (Ayers Rock) (900)

Focus on speaking 1
1 Adapted from results of a survey on
  fairer tourism carried out by VSO
  (Voluntary Service Overseas)
  1 b) (85%) **2** a) (80%)
  3 f) (79%) **4** e) (75%)
  5 d) (59%) **6** c) (52%)

Unit 19
Lead-in
1 **A** fear **B** contempt **C** anger
  D surprise **E** sadness **F** happiness
  G disgust

Unit 20
Focus on listening 2
1 1 A 2 A 3 C 4 Ronald Reagan
  5 India (produces 800 films a year –
  twice as many as the USA)

Unit 7
Focus on speaking 2
Student B

spanner   spade

Unit 11
Focus on speaking
Memory Test: Part 2

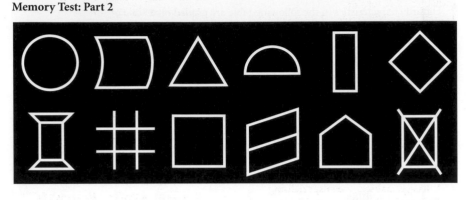

Key language bank

Exercise 1 (Unit 1)
1 *Long* and *strong* need spelling changes.
2 **1** soften **2** brighten **3** widen
4 strengthen **5** fasten **6** lessens
7 broadens **8** weakened

Exercise 2 (Unit 1)
1 **1** d **2** c **3** e **4** h **5** a **6** g
7 f **8** b
2 **1** c **2** f **3** b **4** a **5** g **6** h
7 d **8** e

Exercise 3 (Unit 2)
1 present perfect simple **2** past perfect
simple **3** future simple **4** past simple
5 present progressive **6** future perfect
simple **7** present simple
8 past progressive **9** future progressive
10 present perfect progressive

Exercise 4 (Unit 2)
1 **1** present perfect **2** past **3** future
4 present **5** past perfect **6** past
7 present perfect **8** past
9 future perfect
2 **1** has specialised / been specialising
2 had left **3** will see **4** receive
5 became **6** was watching
7 have known **8** ceased **9** are
doing **10** will have been teaching

Exercise 5 (Unit 3)
1 **1** object **2** subject **3** the verb *be*
4 the past participle **5** emphasis
6 performs/does
2 A is situated; is connected B was
founded; is situated C are devoted
D is linked; have been cut
3 **1** was first used **2** were produced
3 were (being) sold **4** are required
5 have been / are being destroyed
6 be returned **7** (be) fed **8** used
9 is eaten **10** is packaged

Exercise 6 (Unit 3)
1 further north, furthest north, etc., e.g.
*What's the furthest north you've
travelled?*
2 the furthest north, south, etc.;
northernmost
3 Use *in* to describe the position of a
place within a larger area. Use *to* to
describe the position of a place which
is outside another area.
4 Use capitals when the geographical
word is part of the name, but not at
the beginning of other nouns,
adjectives or adverbs.
5 (Example answers) **1** in the
(south-)west **2** in the north **3** to
the north-east **4** to the south(-east)

5 in the western part of the country
6 to the south-west **7** to the north-
west **8** the northernmost point

Exercise 8 (Unit 4)
1 **1** consonant **2** vowel **3** *further,
furthest* or *farther, farthest* **4** *more*
5 *-y* **6** *-er*
7 more than two syllables **8** *more*
and *most* **9** *better, best* **10** *worse,
worst*
2 **1** largest **2** the most southerly
3 longer than **4** highest
5 most important **6** bigger
7 heaviest **8** the slowest
9 the wettest **10** the driest
11 the most widely spoken **12** less
13 more efficiently **14** greater
15 fewer **16** shorter
17 less stressful **18** more commonly
19 the highest **20** fastest

Exercise 9 (Unit 5)
1 **1** too little **2** with/together
3 again/back **4** wrongly
5 do better than **6** opposite/not
7 too much **8** outside/beyond
9 against/opposite **10** protected
from/not damaged by
11 rather/somewhat **12** like/having
the quality of **13** make/become
more **14** passive meaning (*X-ed* by
another)
2 **1** childproof **2** ovenproof
3 earthquake proof **4** bulletproof
5 soundproof **6** recession-proof
7 foolproof **8** shatterproof
3 **1** j **2** g **3** c **4** a **5** i **6** h
7 d **8** f **9** b **10** e

Exercise 10 (Unit 6)
1 the nation = the UK; These figures = a
cost ... of about £7 billion; much
higher (than £7 billion); Its = stress;
more profound (than it already is)

what stress experts have long
suspected = bosses suffer less ...
(forward reference); their = the
bosses'; they = junior managers; their
= the junior managers'; A similar
situation (to that of the junior
managers)

The control factor = what is explained
in the next sentence; those = the
people; their = of those; That = what
is explained in the previous sentence
2 My research into workaholism shows
that the workaholic whose physical
and emotional health suffers from
working long hours was someone who
wanted to be unavailable emotionally.

They would find a way of being so
even if they weren't in paid
employment, perhaps by taking up an
obsessive hobby. But people who work
long hours because they love what
they are doing are physically and
mentally uplifted by their work.

For unwilling workaholics, forced to
stay at their desks for fear of losing
their jobs, long hours can be a killer.
For those to whom work is a pleasure,
being forced into unsought leisure
time can adversely affect their health.
Such people, I found, were the ones
most likely to fall ill on holiday.

3 **1** don't **2** don't **3** that/which
4 can **5** so **6** not / you can't
7 this (problem) **8** he/she
9 Another (idea)
10 they / such/these activities **11** it
12 ways / methods

Exercise 11 (Unit 7)
2 **1** shows/reveals/indicates
2 shed light on **3** What's more
4 emerge **5** However
6 revealed/shown/indicated
7 in fact **8** reveals/shows/indicates

Exercise 12 (Unit 8)
1 did so **2** this/that **3** those **4** one
5 This/That **6** respectively
7 The former; the latter **8** these/those
9 that

Exercise 13 (Unit 8)
1 A Type 2 B Type 1 C Type 3
2 The *if* clause refers to the past; the
main clause refers to the present.
3 a comma; it is not followed by a
comma
4 (Example answers)
1 If there hadn't been a hold-up ... I
wouldn't have been late for work.
2 Unless we take immediate steps, there
will be further redundancies.
3 Provided that you cancel a
reservation / reservations are
cancelled at least ... , there will be no
cancellation fee(s) / cancellation fees
will not be charged.
4 If there had not been ice on the
runway, our flight would not have
been delayed.
5 Unless I get more overseas
experience, it will be difficult for me
to further my career.
6 The professor agreed to come on
condition that we put him up in a
five-star hotel.

7 So/As long as there is a shortage of medical supplies, operations will have to be cancelled.
8 You run the risk of getting lost in the desert unless you go with an experienced guide.
9 If I had a computer, I could get through my workload twice as fast.
10 You won't get a table at the restaurant unless you book in advance.
11 If there hadn't been such a poor harvest this year, we wouldn't be facing the prospect of food shortages.
12 If interest rates hadn't increased, it would be easier for people to buy …

Exercise 14 (Unit 9)
1 industrial   2 financial   3 regional
4 substantial   5 environmental
6 confidential   7 commercial
8 Liberal

Exercise 15 (Unit 9)
1 clarity/clearance   2 completion
3 consumption/consumerism
4 desperation   5 destruction
6 emission   7 expansion   8 extension
9 inhabitant/habitat/habitation
10 opposition   11 proposal
12 provision   13 restoration
14 diversity/diversion/diversification
15 sustainability

Exercise 16 (Unit 9)
1 **Usually true**: Typically, As a general rule, By and large, In the normal course of events
Expected outcome: Inevitably, Not surprisingly, Predictably
Unusual/unexpected outcome: Paradoxically, Surprisingly
2 NB Any expression from the same group as the following is acceptable.
1 Not surprisingly   2 As a general rule   3 Surprisingly
4 Paradoxically   5 Inevitably

Exercise 17 (Unit 10)
2 (Example answers)
The tornado resulted in the destruction of four towns.
Severe damage to six other towns resulted from the tornado.
Eleven thousand people were made/ became homeless as a result of the tornado.

3 1 A heatwave in New York resulted in a 75 per cent increase in the murder rate.
2 There is a 50 per cent rise in traffic accidents in Geneva as a result of the Fohn wind.
3 The seven per cent drop in economic activity in the UK in 1962–63 resulted from the severe winter.
4 It has been estimated that global warming will cause sea levels to rise 18cm by 2030.
5 Recent coastal flooding may lead to an increase in insurance premiums.
6 Damage of about $16 billion a year results from worldwide flooding.
7 By 2030, warmer winters could cause snow to melt at many ski resorts around the world.
8 Arthritis sufferers' swollen joints can become more painful as a result of changes in atmospheric pressure.

Exercise 18 (Unit 11)
1 The   2 an   3 the   4 –   5 the
6 the   7 the   8 a   9 the   10 the
11 –   12 a   13 the   14 –   15 The
16 –   17 –   18 –   19 –   20 the
21 the   22 The   23 –   24 –   25 the
26 –   27 the   28 A   29 the   30 the
31 the   32 –   33 –   34 –   35 –
36 –   37 –   38 a   39 –   40 –
41 the   42 a   43 –   44 –   45 –
46 the   47 –   48 the   49 –   50 –
51 a

Exercise 19 (Unit 12)
1 take   2 made   3 take/do   4 give
5 draw/make   6 done   7 set   8 plays
9 make   10 has   11 pay   12 took

Exercise 20 (Unit 12)
1 (Example answers)
1 less likely   2 more motivated; the faster   3 more/faster; the more
4 the more thoroughly; the better / more confident   5 The further; the more similar   6 The bigger / The better; the more detailed / the better

Exercise 21 (Unit 13)
1 Three most common verbs in -ing clauses: *being, containing, using*
Three most common verbs in -ed clauses: *based, given, used*

2 1 concerned   2 involving   3 based
4 containing   5 produced
6 obtained/produced/used   7 being
8 caused   9 using   10 taken

Exercise 22 (Unit 13)
1 ✓   2 … but I doubt it.
3 Whenever I am in doubt about … / I'm not sure about …   4 ✓   5 … had (some) doubts about …
6 … looks in doubt.   7 If you are in any doubt about …   8 People still have (some/their) doubts about the effectiveness … / People still doubt if/ whether alternative medicine is effective.

Exercise 23 (Unit 14)
1 1 f   2 d   3 c   4 h   5 j   6 e
7 i   8 a   9 g   10 b
2 1 edition   2 correspondent
3 readership   4 journalist   5 copy
6 broadcast   7 coverage
8 the press

Exercise 24 (Unit 15)
1 1 D   2 B   3 E   4 A   5 C
2 1 D   2 C   3 A   4 E   5 B
3 1 reaching   2 to change / changing (no significant difference in meaning)
3 Sensing   4 to excrete / excreting (no significant difference in meaning)
5 rendering   6 gain   7 suffer
8 fainting   9 suffering   10 to see
11 survive   12 encounter
13 To cope   14 to make
15 be used   16 to identify

Exercise 26 (Unit 17)
1 car   2 tailback   3 ring road
4 motorway (in city)   5 motorway
6 petrol   7 bonnet   8 number plate
9 railway   10 underground (railway)
11 roundabout   12 caravan
13 public transport   14 boot
15 subway

Exercise 27 (Unit 19)
1 face   2 nose   3 eyes/ears   4 head
5 tongue   6 ear   7 eyes
8 mouth   9 tongue   10 eye; eye

Writing practice bank

Exercise 1 (Unit 6)

1 shows   2 According to
3 most popular   4 participation rate
5 as popular   6 younger (age)
7 30%/one-third   8 twice as many
9 as/compared with   10 differences/
variations

Exercise 2 (Unit 8)

Example answers

1 attracted 5.6 million   2 twice as many
3 comparison   4 attracted 4.8 (million)
5 2.2 million visitors   6 Two museums
7 negative/adverse effect   8 about a
third   9 a gradual increase
10 less than half

Exercise 4 (Unit 10)

1 reaches   2 subsequently/then
3 decades   4 led to   5 amounts
6 are released / have been released
7 as a result of
8 result in / have resulted in
9 are (being) felled / have been felled
10 less

Exercise 6 (Unit 12)

1 did   2 worst   3 comparable/
equivalent/equal/the same   4 however
5 differences   6 best results   7 61.5%
8 almost 50% / far/much higher
9 greater/more marked
10 (well) over 50%   11 Conversely / On
the other hand / By contrast   12 rate
13 almost double   14 that
15 figure/percentage/pass rate
16 it seems/appears / we can say

Exercise 7 (Unit 17)

1   1 E, A and C (because they are ticked)
2 The circled answers (because the
key indicates this)   3 D   4 C
5 Question 2
6 E   7 A   8 Women

2   1 unaware/not aware/ignorant
2 identified/chose/judged/named
3 second/next   4 the safest
5 their own sex/gender
6 More than half / Fifty-three per
cent / The majority   7 62% / more
than half / the majority
8 wrong/incorrect
9 since/because/when
10 one-third/33%   11 81% / the vast
majority / over three quarters
12 not strict enough / insufficiently
strict

Exercise 8 (Unit 20)

1 invented   2 made of   3 consisted of
4 at the front / in front   5 in length /
long   6 end of the   7 smaller
8 simpler   9 half the length
10 thinner   11 that / the body
12 controls/knobs   13 available/
popular   14 a fraction
15 (whole/wide) range/variety / a (large)
number   16 including / such as
17 size

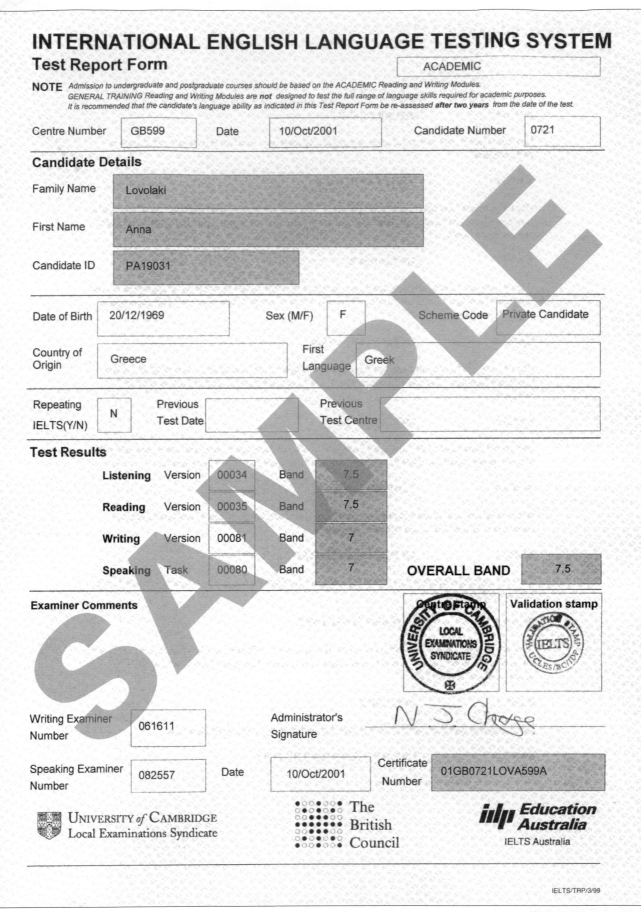

INTERNATIONAL ENGLISH LANGUAGE TESTING SYSTEM
Test Report Form

ACADEMIC

NOTE *Admission to undergraduate and postgraduate courses should be based on the ACADEMIC Reading and Writing Modules.*
*GENERAL TRAINING Reading and Writing Modules are **not** designed to test the full range of language skills required for academic purposes.*
*It is recommended that the candidate's language ability as indicated in this Test Report Form be re-assessed **after two years** from the date of the test.*

Centre Number	GB599	Date	10/Oct/2001	Candidate Number	0721

Candidate Details

Family Name	Lovolaki
First Name	Anna
Candidate ID	PA19031

Date of Birth	20/12/1969	Sex (M/F)	F	Scheme Code	Private Candidate
Country of Origin	Greece	First Language	Greek		

Repeating IELTS(Y/N)	N	Previous Test Date		Previous Test Centre	

Test Results

Listening	Version	00034	Band	7.5
Reading	Version	00035	Band	7.5
Writing	Version	00081	Band	7
Speaking	Task	00080	Band	7

OVERALL BAND 7.5

Examiner Comments

Centre Stamp

Validation stamp

Writing Examiner Number	061611	Administrator's Signature	N J Chase

Speaking Examiner Number	082557	Date	10/Oct/2001	Certificate Number	01GB0721LOVA599A

UNIVERSITY *of* CAMBRIDGE
Local Examinations Syndicate

The British Council

Education Australia
IELTS Australia

IELTS/TRP/3/99

Index of language

This index lists structural and vocabulary items covered in *Focus on IELTS*. Each entry gives the page number and type of coverage. It is followed by an index of items in the Error Hit Lists.

Key

KL – Key language
FR – Focus on reading
FS – Focus on speaking
FW – Focus on writing
FV – Focus on vocabulary
LI – Lead-in

A

affixes 192 KL
although 100 FW
articles 199 KL
avoiding repetition 195 KL

B

because/because of 53 FW
British vs American vocabulary 206 KL

C

expressing cause and result 198 KL
cohesion reference links 193 KL
cohesion avoiding repetition 195 KL
common verbs in *-ed/-ing* clauses 202 KL
expressing comparison 111 FS
comparatives 191 KL
comparing and contrasting 15 FS
conditionals 196 KL
contrasting 111 FS

D

derived adjectives 197 KL
derived nouns 197 KL
describing
   an event 64 FS
   leisure activities 51 FS
   objects 63 FW; 166 FS
   people 49 FS
   places 30 FS
despite 100 FW
expressing differences 111 FS
expressing disagreement 68 FW
doubt 202 KL

E

-ed clauses 202 KL
even though 100 FW

F

idioms with *face* 206 KL
describing function 131 FW
future perfect 187 KL
future perfect progressive 187 KL
future progressive 187 KL
future simple 187 KL

G

geographical positions 189 KL
grammatical terms 186 KL

H

however 100 FW

I

discussing implications 69 FW
-ing clauses 202 KL
-ing forms vs infinitives 203 KL
in spite of 100 FW
interpreting information from diagrams 17 FW
introducing sentences 197 KL

J

justifying an opinion 100 FW

L

lead to 198 KL
linking expressions 52 FV

M

the media (topic vocabulary) 203 KL

N

names of tenses 187 KL
nevertheless 100 FW
in the north 189 KL
north/northern 189 KL
northernmost 189 KL
numerical and other comparisons 190 KL

O

on the other hand 100 FW

P

participle clauses 105 FR
parts of speech 186 KL
passive 188 KL
past perfect 187 KL
past perfect progressive 187 KL
past progressive 187 KL
past simple 187 KL
prefix *over-* 193 KL
present perfect 187 KL
present perfect progressive 187 KL
present progressive 187 KL
present simple 187 KL
expressing probability 205 KL

Q

qualifiers 67 FW

R

expressing reasons 53 FW
reference links 193 KL
reporting tenses 188 KL
as a result of 198 KL; 53 FW
result from/in 198 KL

S

describing shape 166 FW
describing size 166 FW
so/such 53 FW
expressing stages in a process 84 FW

stress in long words 95 LI
describing structure 131, 166 FW
suffix *-en* 186 KL
suffix *-proof* 192 KL
summarising sentences 134 FW
superlatives 191 KL

T

talking about personal interests 9 FS
talking about research 195 KL
expressing tastes (in music, etc.) 56 FS
the … the comparatives 201 KL

W

whereas 100 FW
while 100 FW

ERROR HIT LIST

affect/effect 121
after/afterwards 87
after all/finally 121
compared with/compared to/in comparison 39
concentrate/listen/play 55
contain/consist/include 167
differ/vary 103
distinction/difference 103
do/play/go 23
economic/economical/financial 87
at/in the end 71
few/a few; little/a little 135
at first/firstly/first 87
game/match 55
a great deal of/a great many 167
half/a quarter 71
increase/decrease 23
in spite of/despite 135
journey/trip/travel 151
at last/lastly 87
level/standard 39
make/do 103
middle position adverbs 135
news/media/press 121
nevertheless 135
number/amount 39
old/elder/elderly 167
one in ten/nine out of ten 71
percentage/proportion 39
plural expressions with numbers 55
possibility/opportunity 151
reach/arrive 151
rise/raise/fall 23
surely/certainly 167
television/TV/radio 55
university 103
which 23
worth/value 71

Pearson Education Limited
Edinburgh Gate, Harlow
Essex CM20 2JE, England
and Associated Companies throughout the world

www.longman.com

© Sue O'Connell 2002

First published 2002

Fourth impression 2003

Set in 11/13pt Minion

Printed in Spain by Gráficas Estella

ISBN 0 582 44773 9

Author acknowledgements

Special thanks to John Walsh of the Bournemouth English Book Centre for
sound advice at the outset; to my students at the City of Bristol College, who
played a central role in the development of this material; and to my friend,
Clare McDowell, who willingly shared her wealth of experience on IELTS
matters.

I am extremely grateful to my editor at Pearson, Pietro Alongi, for his
enthusiasm, insight and honesty; to Catriona Watson-Brown who managed the
project with the greatest professionalism and good humour; and last but not
least, to Heather Jones, my publisher, without whose faith in the project and
support this book would not have come about.

Finally, heartfelt thanks to Peter for sharing this and so much more.

Publishing acknowledgments

The author and publisher wish to thank all the teachers and students whose
feedback helped us develop this course, in particular the following people:
Eleftheria Arapoglou, Vakalis Foundation, Thessaloniki, Greece; Stephanie Atkin,
The Netherlands; Patrick Brook, UK; Zosia Chlebik, UMIST, UK; Sue Goldrick,
UMIST, UK; Rita Khosla, The Central School of English, London, UK; Olya
Madylus, British Council Thessaloniki, Greece; Alice Matthews, Crawley College,
UK; Sally Parry, United International College, London, UK, Carmel Roche,
UMIST, UK; Lesley Sanderson, Stratigakis School, Thessaloniki, Greece;
Jane Thomas, City of Bristol College, UK; Konstantina Toli, Greece;
Judith Wilson, UK.

We would also like to thank the following for reporting on early drafts of the
material: Ben Russell, University College Dublin Language Centre; Morgan Terry.

We are grateful to the following for permission to reproduce copyright material:
Carel Press for charts adapted from 'Exams' and 'ITV's Average Week' published
in Fact File 1997, 'News Report 1' and 'News Report 2' published in Fact File
1999, 'Couch Potatoes', 'Keeping the Children Quiet?' and 'Top of the League'
published in Fact File 2001; Coburn and Spence for the table 'Probability of
dying in any one year from various causes'; Brian Dana Akers for an extract
adapted from 'Falling Forward: A Science-Fiction Writer Looks at the
Twenty-First Century' from his website www.briandanaakers.com; Gaia Books
Ltd for charts adapted from 'Mountains of Rubbish' and 'The World's 40
Largest Cities' by Herbert Girardet published in The Gaia Atlas of Cities;
Geographical Magazine for an extract adapted from 'The Ecology of Hollywood'
by Rory Spowers published in Geographical Magazine August 2000;
The Guardian Newspapers Ltd for extracts adapted from 'Working to a Frenzy'
by Victoria McKee published in The Guardian 1st October 1996 © The Guardian
1996, and 'Coming to a Screen Near You' by Merope Mills published in The
Guardian 18th September 2000 © The Guardian 2000; HarperCollins Publishers
Ltd for the cover of How to Gain an Extra Hour Every Day: New Time Strategies
that Work by Ray Josephs; The Mirror Group Newspapers Ltd for an extract
adapted from 'Why Ironing Shirts is Better than Pumping Iron' by Helen Reilly
published in The Sunday Mirror 4th September 1994; National Geographic Society
for extracts adapted from 'Surviving in Space' by Michael E. Long published in
National Geographic January 2001, and 'Tastes in Music' from their website

www.nationalgeographic.com (Survey 2000); New Scientist for an extract
adapted from 'Bones to Phones' by Margaret Wertheim published in
New Scientist 23rd October 1999 © RBI 1999; Pearson Education Inc. for the cover
of The Complete Idiot's Guide to Managing your Time by Jeff Davidson; Penguin
Books Ltd for extracts and tables adapted from Dorling Kindersley
World Desk Reference, Dorling Kindersley Illustrated Fact Finder 1999, and
The Social Psychology of Leisure by Michael Argyle © Michael Argyle 1996;
Scientific American for an extract adapted from 'Is Global Warming Harmful
to Health?' by Paul R. Epstein published in Scientific American August 2000;
The Telegraph Group Ltd for an extract adapted from 'Greenland Calls Time
on the Good Life in Prison' by Julian Coman published in The Telegraph
21st October 2001 © Telegraph Group Limited 2001; and The Times Newspapers
Ltd for extracts and charts adapted from 'Communication – Do You Make
Yourself Clear?' by John Nicholson published in The Sunday Times 7th June 1987
© John Nicholson/Times Newspapers Limited 1987, 'How To Put Yourself in the
Picture' and 'Use it or Lose it: Keeping The Brain Young' by Ian Robertson
published in The Times 10th January 1996 © Ian Robertson/Times Newspapers
Limited 1996, 'Ten Ways to Slow Down Your Life' by Anjana Ahuja published in
The Times 29th September 1999 © Times Newspapers Limited 1999, 'British
Drivers Are the Worst Off in Europe' by Arthur Leathley published in The Times
26th November 1999 © Times Newspapers Limited 1999, 'Why We Are Touched
by the Sound of Music' by Anjana Ahuja published in The Times 23rd February
2000 © Times Newspapers Limited 2000, 'Sleep Better Than Midnight Oil on Eve
of Exams' by Mark Henderson published in The Times 22nd November 2000
© Times Newspapers Limited 2000, and 'Jet Lag's Ill-Effects on Blair' by
Thomas Stuttaford published in The Times 18th October 2001 © Dr Thomas
Stuttaford/Times Newspapers Limited 2001; University of Cambridge Local
Examinations Syndicate for the Sample answer sheets and Test report form.

We are grateful to the following for permission to reproduce copyright
illustrations and photographs:
Natural Hazards, by Frampton, Chafey, Hardwick and McNaught, Hodder and
Stoughton (80); Andrew Wright from How to Improve Your Mind, CUP (98);
Mosedale from Essential Articles, Carel Press Ltd (99); Martin Honeysett from
British Airways High Life/Punch (133); Clive Goddard from Travel Matters, Carel
Press/Prospect (147); Matt from Telegraph Magazine (148); Sharon Constant
from The Face by Daniel McNeil, Penguin (155).

In some instances we have been unable to trace the owners of copyright material
and we would appreciate any information that would enable us to do so.

Designed by Linda Reed and Associates
Project managed by Clare Nielsen-Marsh and Catriona Watson-Brown
Freelance picture research by Michèle Faram

Illustrated by:
Kathy Baxendale, Colin Brown (Beehive Illustration), Paul Collicutt, Robin
Edmonds, Darren Hopes (Debut Art), Oxford Designers and Illustrators, Nigel
Paige, Katja Rosenberg (The Art Market), Tech Type, Shirley Walker, Geoff
Waterhouse (Just for Laffs).

The Publishers are grateful to the following for their permission to reproduce
copyright photographs:
Action Images for 15 top; Bryan & Cherry Alexander for 107 left; All Sport
for 160 C; Associated Press for 86; BBC/Bronwyn Kidd for 152; Corbis Images
for 8 bottom right, 8 top middle right, 14, 57, 66, 75 and 124;
Corbis Stock Market for 8 top middle left, 48 top right and 110 top right;
FPG International for 8 bottom left, 48 bottom left and 112; French Magazine
Mar/April 2002 for 160 A; Garden & Wildlife Matters Photo Library for 8 top
right; Ronald Grant Archive for 163 bottom; Robert Harding Picture Library
for 70 left and 144 right; Hulton Archive for 107 right, 128 and 163 top;
The Hutchison Library for 73 top; ICCE for 73 middle; Image Bank for 35
and 44; The Kobal Collection for 79; New Internationlist for 145 bottom;
PA Photos for 160 E and 160 G; The Photographers Library for 110 bottom left,
110 bottom right, 140, 144 left and 145 top right; Photonica for 48 top left;
Pictor International for 73 bottom and 76; Popperfoto for 15 bottom and
159 left; Rex Features for 70 right and 145 top left; Science Photo Library for 32,
90, 122 and 160 F; Stone for 8 top left, 27, 43, 64, 110 top left and 159 top;
UNICEF for
159 right.
160 B, 160 D and 162 have been supplied by the author.

Cover photograph © Stone